THE SAFE HAVEN IN NORTHERN IRAQ
International Responsibility for Iraqi Kurdistan

Helena Cook

First Edition

Human Rights Centre, University of Essex.
Kurdistan Human Rights Project, London.

FOREWORD

In March 1991, following the Gulf War a radical act of humanitarian intervention by Britain France and the United States, invoking Resolution 688 of the Security Council, established safe havens in Northern Iraq. The objective was to protect the Kurds and other inhabitants from the onslaught of Sadam Hussein's Republican Guards, an objective which has been achieved through the threat of the use of airpower from bases in Turkey and by agreement with Turkey. Four years on, this important report on the background to the safe haven policy and what has happened since, is intended to remind the international community of its continued responsibily for its own creation of Iraqi Kurdistan.

In the intervening years the Kurds have established for themselves a democratic administration which under pressure of the effects of international sanctions has suffered greatly leading to severe conflict between the major political factions. The territory has also endured an internal economic embargo by Iraq, aerial bombardment and invasion from Turkey and missile attacks from both Iraqi and Iranian forces. The most recent Turkish invasion in March 1995 in pursuit of the PKK has underlined the complete vulnerability of the people in supposedly internationally protected territory. (See addendum to the study).

The fate of the "safe areas" in eastern Bosnia , Srebenicia and Zepa, must serve as a reminder to the United Nations that failure to agree upon a clear policy in advance and to commit the resources to implement that policy forseeably results in agression. The study argues for a new Security Council Resolution on Iraqi Kurdistan . Its purpose would be to establish, more firmly than Resolution 688, a United Nations Protected Area within Iraq with international guarantees of its autonomy. The study proposes that international involvement should continue under UN jurisdiction until there is a negotiated settlement, in which the Kurds must have full and equal participation. Until that happens the international community as a whole must remain responsible to ensure the protection of the Kurds against Iraqi military threat as well as military incursions from other countries. The author also details a range of human rights policies addressed to both the United Nations and the Kurds themselves. It calls for international initatives to ensure the economic and social development of Iraqi Kurdistan, including the exemption of the area from the international sanctions regime now imposed on the whole of Iraq.

This report is a thorough and scholarly analysis of urgent and as yet unanswered questions- what is to be the future of the autonomy achieved in Iraqi Kurdistan? Should the Security Council vote to lift sanctions on Iraq, what human rights and democratic guarantees will it offer to the Kurds in the aftermath? The study is offered as a resource to those who must now address these issues. The debate that must occur should not just be among those few countries presently providing aerial protection for the enclave but the entire United Nations as well as Iraqi Kurds themselves.

This study was undertaken by Helena Cook, a Fellow of the Human Rights Centre, Univerity of Essex and formerly head of Amnesty International's legal division. The research, writing and publication of this report was made possible by the support of the Frankfurt based NGO, Medico International which has a major humanitarian involvement in Iraqi Kurdistan. It is published jointly with the London based NGO, the Kurdistan Human Rights Project, to the work of which charity, staff and students at Essex have contributed significantly in their personal capacities. The advise and assistance of member s of the Human Rights Centre and other experts in preparing this study is greatfully acknowledged as is the research assistance of Rebecca Juste.

Kevin Boyle
Director Human Rights Centre
Colchester
July 1995

The Human Rights Centre at the University of Essex is a multi disciplinary centre for research, publication and teaching on the theory and practice of international human rights.

Human Rights Centre, University of Essex, Colchester, CO4 3SQ, U.K.

The Kurdistan Human Rights Project is a British, independent, non-political project, founded in December 1992. It is committed to the protection of human rights of all persons within Kurdistan, irrespective of race, religion, sex, political persuasion or other belief or opinion. Its supporters include both Kurdish and non-Kurdish people. The KHRP is a registered charity.

Kurdistan Human Rights Project, Suite 236 Linen Hall, 162-168 Regent Street, London WIR 5TB

About the Author
Helena Cook is an international lawyer and a Fellow of the Human Rights Centre, University of Essex. From 1990 to 1994 she was the head of Amnesty International's Legal and Intergovernmental Organisations Office, and has since worked as a lecturer and consultant in International Law and Human Rights.

ISBN   1 900175 00 2

Published by the Human Rights Centre, University of Essex and the Kurdistan Human Rights Project, London.

This study was made possible by the financial support of medico international, Germany.

Copyright © 1995, Human Rights Centre, University of Essex and the Kurdistan Human Rights Project, London.

All rights reserved. No part of this publication may be reproduced, stored in a retrieval system or transmitted in any form or by any means, mechanical, photocoping, recording or otherwise without written permission of the publishers.

TABLE OF CONTENTS

INTRODUCTION		1
I.	**THE KURDS**	6
I.1	WHO ARE THE KURDS?	6
I.2	THE TREATY OF SEVRES	8
I.3	THE KURDS IN IRAQ	9
II.	**KURDISH RIGHTS IN THE INDEPENDENT STATE OF IRAQ**	15
II.1	THE BRITISH GOVERNMENT AS MANDATE AUTHORITY	15
II.2	THE LEAGUE IMPOSES CONDITIONS FOR MINORITY RIGHTS PROTECTION	18
II.3	LEGAL IMPLICATIONS OF IRAQ'S DECLARATION ON MINORITY RIGHTS	20
III.	**STEPS TOWARDS KURDISH AUTONOMY IN IRAQ**	23
III.1	CONSTITUTIONAL RECOGNITION	23
III.2	THE 1970 AUTONOMY AGREEMENT	24
III.3	THE AUTONOMY LAW OF 1974	27
III.4	RESTRICTIONS ON AUTONOMY	28
III.5	THE CURRENT STATUS OF AUTONOMY	30
III.6	FURTHER NEGOTIATIONS ON AUTONOMY	31
IV.	**THE ESTABLISHMENT OF THE SAFE HAVENS**	34
IV.1	THE BUILDING OF A CRISIS	34
IV.2	ADOPTION OF SECURITY COUNCIL RESOLUTION 688	36
IV.3	THE ESTABLISHMENT OF THE SAFE HAVENS	39
IV.4	THE REFUGEES AND DISPLACED RETURN HOME	42
IV.5	INTERNATIONAL SECURITY FOR IRAQI KURDISTAN	44
IV.5.1	OPERATION POISED HAMMER	45
IV.5.2	THE UN GUARDS CONTINGENT	46
IV.5.3	LIMITATIONS OF THE INTERNATIONAL SECURITY MEASURES	47
IV.6	IRAQ WITHDRAWS AND IMPOSES AN EMBARGO ON THE KURDS	50
IV.7	THE LEGAL BASIS FOR ESTABLISHING THE SAFE HAVENS	52
V.	**THE INTERNATIONAL HUMANITARIAN AID PROGRAMME**	56
V.1	HUMANITARIAN NEEDS OF THE IRAQI POPULATION	56
V.2	THE MEMORANDUM OF UNDERSTANDING	58
V.3	FOOD FOR OIL	60
V.4	THE OPERATION OF THE AID PROGRAMME	61
V.5	THE FUTURE OF THE AID PROGRAMME	64
VI.	**THE ESTABLISHMENT OF A DEMOCRATIC ADMINISTRATION IN IRAQI KURDISTAN**	69
VI.1	INTERNATIONAL STANDARDS	70
VI.2	THE DOMESTIC LEGAL BASIS FOR THE ELECTIONS	72

VI.3	THE ELECTORAL PROCESS	74
VI.4	THE OUT-COME OF THE ELECTIONS	78
VI.5	THE REACTION OF THE INTERNATIONAL COMMUNITY	78
VI.6	THE KURDISH ADMINISTRATION	80
VII.	**THE FUTURE OF THE SANCTIONS REGIME AGAINST IRAQ**	83
VII.1	THE MAIN POINTS OF RESOLUTION 687(1991)	84
VII.2	CONDITIONS FOR THE LIFTING OF SANCTIONS	85
VII.3	GROWING PRESSURE TO LIFT SANCTIONS	86
VII.4	THE IRAQI TROOP BUILD-UP IN OCTOBER 1994	88
VII.5	THE IMPACT ON MOVES TO LIFT SANCTIONS	89
VII.6	THE RELATIONSHIP OF RESOLUTION 688 TO THE SANCTIONS REGIME	90
VIII.	**GROSS VIOLATIONS OF HUMAN RIGHTS IN IRAQ**	93
VIII.1	IRAQ'S OBLIGATIONS UNDER INTERNATIONAL LAW	94
VIII.1.1	INTERNATIONAL HUMAN RIGHTS LAW	94
VIII.1.2	INTERNATIONAL HUMANITARIAN LAW	96
VIII.2	THE GENERAL HUMAN RIGHTS SITUATION IN IRAQ	99
VIII.3	HUMAN RIGHTS VIOLATIONS AGAINST THE KURDS	104
VIII.3.1	A HISTORY OF OPPRESSION	105
VIII.3.2	THE CONTEXT OF THE ANFAL CAMPAIGN	108
VIII.3.3	THE CONDUCT OF THE ANFAL CAMPAIGN	110
VIII.3.4	THE CRUSHING OF THE MARCH 1991 UPRISING	112
VIII.4	UN ACTION IN RESPECT OF HUMAN RIGHTS VIOLATIONS IN IRAQ	113
VIII.5	HUMAN RIGHTS MONITORS FOR IRAQ	116
IX.	**IRAQ'S OBLIGATIONS TO PROTECT THE RIGHTS OF MINORITIES**	118
IX.1	THE INTERNATIONAL PROTECTION OF MINORITY RIGHTS	118
IX.2	NON-DISCRIMINATION	118
IX.3	THE INTERNATIONAL COVENANT ON CIVIL AND POLITICAL RIGHTS	120
IX.4	THE UN DECLARATION ON THE RIGHTS OF PERSONS BELONGING TO NATIONAL OR ETHNIC, RELIGIOUS AND LINGUISTIC MINORITIES	121
IX.5	IMPLEMENTING MINORITY PROTECTION IN IRAQ	122
X.	**SELF-DETERMINATION AND AUTONOMY**	124
X.1	SELF-DETERMINATION	124
X.2	AUTONOMY	130
XI.	**THE RESPONSIBILITY OF THE INTERNATIONAL COMMUNITY IN IRAQI KURDISTAN**	136
XI.1	INTERNATIONAL RESPONSIBILITY FOR THE PROTECTION OF HUMAN RIGHTS	137
XI.1.1	THE UN CHARTER	137

XI.1.2	THE UN HUMAN RIGHTS SYSTEM	138
XI.1.3	THE SPECIAL NATURE OF INTERNATIONAL HUMAN RIGHTS OBLIGATIONS	140
XI.1.4	IS THERE A DUTY ON OTHER STATES TO ACT?	142
XI.2	INTERNATIONAL RESPONSIBILITY FOR MINORITY PROTECTION	143
XI.2.1	MINORITY PROTECTION BY THE LEAGUE OF NATIONS	144
XI.2.2	MINORITY PROTECTION AT THE UN	145
XI.2.3	MINORITY PROTECTION BY OTHER INTERGOVERNMENTAL ORGANIZATIONS	147
XI.3	PRINCIPLES OF INTERNATIONAL REFUGEE PROTECTION	149
XI.4	RESPONSIBILITY ASSUMED BY THE INTERNATIONAL COMMUNITY IN IRAQI KURDISTAN	152
XI.5	THE RESPONSIBILITY OF OCCUPYING FORCES	156
XII.	**FORMAL LEGAL MEASURES AGAINST IRAQ**	160
XII.1	A CASE OF GENOCIDE?	160
XII.2	FORMAL MEASURES UNDER OTHER HUMAN RIGHTS TREATIES	162
XII.3	ESTABLISHING INTERNATIONAL CRIMINAL JURISDICTION	164
XII.3.1	VIOLATIONS OF THE LAWS AND CUSTOMS OF WAR	165
XII.3.2	CRIMES AGAINST HUMANITY	166
XII.3.3	CRIMINAL PROSECUTIONS BY OTHER STATES	168
XIII.	**CONCLUSION**	
	A UN PLAN OF ACTION FOR IRAQI KURDISTAN	170
XIII.1	A NEGOTIATED SETTLEMENT	172
XIII.2	INTERNATIONAL PROTECTION	172
XIII.3	RESPECT FOR HUMAN RIGHTS	173

INTRODUCTION

"It is the state that the international community should principally entrust with the protection of individuals. However, the issue of international action must be raised when states prove unworthy of this task, when they violate the fundamental principles laid down in the Charter of the United Nations and when - far from being the protectors of individuals - they become tormentors...In these circumstances the international community must take over from the states that fail to fulfil their obligations".

The UN Secretary-General (1993)

"This new effort, despite its scale and scope, is not intended as a permanent solution to the plight of the Iraqi Kurds...it is an interim solution designed to meet an immediate, penetrating humanitarian need. Our long-term objective remains the same: for Iraqi Kurds and, indeed, for all Iraqi refugees, wherever they are, to return home and to live in peace, free from repression, free to live their lives".

US President Bush (1991)

"We went into northern Iraq in order to persuade the Kurds to come down from the mountains - to save lives. We don't want the operation to end in a way that will merely re-create the same problem".

UK Foreign Secretary (1991)

This report examines the situation of Iraqi Kurdistan four years after the international community took unprecedented steps to establish an internationally-protected area for the Kurds inside Iraqi territory. It reviews the historical context of the struggle for Kurdish autonomy in Iraq, the events that led to the setting up of safe havens for the Kurds, the subsequent emergence of Iraqi Kurdistan as a self-governing area and the current scope of international protection and involvement there. In the context of Iraq's shocking human rights record and its history of brutal repression of the Kurds, it examines the nature of the international community's responsibility in Iraqi Kurdistan and outlines the further steps that are urgently needed in order to meet that responsibility and avert a second human tragedy for the Kurds. The report takes account of events up to and including the beginning of March 1995.

The international community went to extraordinary lengths in 1991 to protect the Kurds from the Iraqi Government's violent suppression of the internal rebellion that took hold in the wake of the Gulf War. The terrified flight of almost two million Kurds to the borders of Iraq to escape the military onslaught led to the adoption of Resolution 688 (1991) by the UN Security Council. This

Resolution determined that the consequences of internal repression in Iraq amounted to a threat to international peace and security. It demanded that the repression be brought to an end and insisted that Iraq allow international organizations access to provide humanitarian assistance throughout the country. Thousands of foreign military troops then entered Iraq to set up safe havens and to hold Iraqi forces back in order that the refugees and the displaced could return to their homes. A massive UN aid programme was also launched in the country, with special security provided by a UN Guards Contingent.

A few months after the safe havens had been set up the Iraqi Government withdrew its military forces and its civilian administration from most of Iraqi Kurdistan. Shielded by the continuing international protection of the area, the Kurds held democratic elections in the region in 1992 and established the legislative and administrative structures of self-government. Four years on, Iraqi Kurdistan functions as a de facto autonomous area and new elections are planned for 1995. International protection, though scaled down, continues and Iraq still keeps its distance, despite its attempts to weaken and destabilize the area. International aid has allowed for some economic and social rehabilitation and has cushioned the Kurds from the worst effects of the "double embargo" resulting from international sanctions and an internal economic embargo imposed by Iraq.

The setting up of the safe havens in Iraq in 1991 was hailed as a break-through for human rights protection; the international community had torn aside the cloak of state sovereignty in order to protect an oppressed people from the brutality of their own government. Although conceived as a crisis measure to induce the return of the refugees to Iraq and to deliver humanitarian assistance, this intervention has had much wider implications. It has effectively conferred a special protected status on the area which has been maintained ever since and which has enabled Iraqi Kurdistan to function as a de facto autonomous region.

Yet what are the future prospects for Iraqi Kurdistan? The extraordinary measures taken in 1991 were an emergency response and had no long-term political goals or objectives. The Kurdish administration is generally accepted as the de facto authority (except by Iraq) but it has no recognized international legal status, no independent claim on international aid and assistance and no basis on which to participate in international decision-making on the future of the Kurdish people. External military protection is limited to policing a no-fly zone that covers only part of Iraqi Kurdistan and is effectively dependent on wavering Turkish authorization. The UN's humanitarian aid programme limps along, but with its security component greatly reduced and with no formal agreement with Iraq in place since the Government refused to renew it two years ago. Kurdish reconstruction and development are impeded by rapidly dwindling international funding and the constraints of the double embargo. The Kurdish administration is fragile and internal conflict among Kurdish political groups is destabilizing the area and forfeiting international support. Political and commercial pressure is building to lift the sanctions imposed after Iraq's invasion of Kuwait and to normalize relations with the country.

Far from diminishing, the risk to the Kurds and their need for special protection is greater than ever before. Indeed, the international community bears a large part of the responsibility for that increased vulnerability. Effectively protected by the international community, the Kurds were emboldened to defy the Iraqi Government by setting up their own democratic administration that Iraq has denounced as illegal and clearly has no intention of recognizing. The Government has made it clear that it is determined to prevent effective autonomy for the Kurds at all costs. Inevitably, if and when it has the chance, it will crack down mercilessly to ensure that this experiment in real autonomy will never be repeated. It is a government already widely renowned for its brutality and contempt for the rule of law. Systematic and flagrant violations of the most basic human rights are its hallmark. The violent history of genocidal repression of the Kurds and the gross violations which are still continuing elsewhere in Iraq, particularly in the south, are indicative of the fate that awaits Iraqi Kurdistan if the international community turns its back again. After 1991 there can be no doubt as to the potential of the human tragedy waiting to happen and the enormous political and financial resources that will be required to deal with it.

In today's world, it is said, governments can no longer violate the human rights of their people on this scale with impunity. Since the adoption of the 1948 Universal Declaration of Human Rights an extensive body of international norms and standards has been developed which oblige governments to respect a whole range of rights and freedoms. International supervisory bodies have been established to monitor the human rights record of governments and to hold them to account when they breach their obligations. The international system for human rights protection has also reinforced the responsibility of the international community to step in to protect human rights when a state refuses to do so. It legitimates strong condemnation, close scrutiny and investigation and other increasingly intrusive measures to confront such governments and to protect their victims.

The concept of international responsibility to protect human rights when individual governments fail to do so has been further deepened and broadened in the post Cold War world. A more sophisticated awareness of what this responsibility entails has led to the development of new measures which further erode the outdated protectionism of state sovereignty and the principle of non-interference in international affairs. New-style comprehensive peace-keeping and peace-building operations; on-site human rights monitoring; the development of new standards and mechanisms to protect the rights of minorities; and the setting up of international criminal tribunals to bring perpetrators of gross violations to justice are all examples of the ways in which international responsibility for human rights protection is being progressively extended.

Now, however, the situation in Iraqi Kurdistan forces the international community to confront the true meaning of its human rights responsibilities. The action taken in 1991 stretched the existing parameters of politically acceptable intervention virtually to the limit. The UN and its member governments have still not faced up to the real challenge and test of human rights protection. Durable long-term protection means tackling the root causes of a crisis and taking concrete measures aimed at bringing about political and institutional reforms that guarantee and entrench respect for human rights within a society. Emergency responses, however bold and far-reaching, cannot be more than temporary first aid if they are not underpinned by wider objectives. Without a commitment to such objectives, a crisis response offers only a brief respite from an endless cycle of violence and repression. It also creates a dangerous illusion of security which, at best, raises expectations that will not be met and, at worst, encourages social and political change that invites even greater repression when emergency protection is withdrawn.

The international protection of the Kurds in Iraq cannot continue in its present form indefinitely. Security Council Resolution 688, while still relevant and important, does not provide a sufficient political or legal basis for the steps that now need to be taken. International sanctions alone cannot secure durable or well-founded political solutions and meanwhile serve to intensify the suffering and climate of insecurity in Iraqi Kurdistan. The international community has to adopt a comprehensive plan of action under UN auspices that both secures for the Kurds adequate protection for as long as it proves necessary and that is aimed at reaching a political settlement in Iraq to guarantee a form of Kurdish autonomy.

The UN cannot, however, merely rely on the good faith of the Iraqi Government to enter into any such negotiations. That Government has repeatedly made plain its contempt for international law and for the UN. Instead the UN should formalize the de facto special status of Iraqi Kurdistan that has been maintained for four years and designate the area a territory under UN jurisdiction until a satisfactory political settlement is reached and there is confidence that it will be fully honoured. The area should be adequately protected by the UN itself. The Kurdish democratic administration should be recognized as the governing authority under UN auspices and negotiations towards a settlement must involve the Kurds as full and equal parties. A settlement must also allow for the participation of other interested countries, particularly those in the region, in the interests of global and regional stability and to ensure that any settlement is secure against external destabilization. As long as the Iraqi Government persists in flouting its international obligations and continues to violate human rights, the implementation of the settlement must be placed under international supervision backed by international guarantees.

Of course this will not be an easy task. Misgivings expressed by many countries about the legitimacy of the actions taken in 1991 indicate a strong reluctance in many quarters to take international responsibility for human rights protection to the next logical stage - to look beyond an immediate crisis to the long-term implications and to match rhetoric with action. Yet this is the nettle that must be grasped if international cooperation to promote and encourage respect for human rights, one of the founding principles of the UN Charter, is to have meaning in today's world.

In this respect Iraqi Kurdistan represents a major challenge for the international community. A challenge to secure human rights for the Kurds themselves and a challenge to contemporary notions of sovereignty as well as to concepts of state and inter-state responsibility for human rights. Does the international community have the political will to take seriously its global responsibilities to protect human rights or are its pronouncements just empty rhetoric to salve the consciences of governments and to silence public outrage at political impotence? Are states prepared to move beyond emergency crisis measures and bring about the political and institutional changes in a country necessary to entrench respect for and the observance of human rights in the future? Or does state sovereignty still serve as a shield to protect the most brutal violators of human rights at the cost of the safety and even the lives of countless numbers of their own citizens? It remains to be seen whether the next steps taken in respect of Iraqi Kurdistan can provide constructive answers to these tough questions.

I. THE KURDS

1.1 WHO ARE THE KURDS?

The Kurds have retained a strong sense of ethnic and cultural identity for over two thousand years although they do not share a single language or religion. They are believed to be principally descendants of Indo-European origin settling amongst indigenous mountain tribes some 4,000 years ago. By the 7th century the ethnic term 'Kurd' was applied to an amalgam of Iranicized tribes, some autochthonous, some semitic and some Armenian communities. The term 'Kurdistan' first appeared in the 12th century when the Turkish Seljuk prince Saandjar created a province with that name. Tribal bonds of kinship and territory have always been very important within Kurdish society and are still influential, at least in the mountainous heartland of Kurdistan, although less so among the inhabitants of the plains and foot-hills.[1]

The Kurds do not have a single common language but speak a number of different dialects, some of which are not easily learnt or understood by fellow Kurds. In the north and northwest, the main dialect is Kurmanji (which has two written forms using cyrillic and Latin characters). The other main dialect, spoken mainly in the south, is Sorani (or Kurdi). Sub-dialects include Kirmanshahi, Leki, Gurani and Zaza.

The majority of Kurds are Sunni Muslims and adhere to the Shafi'i school. There are a number of other different religious affiliations among the Kurds, however and they include Jews; Christians; Alevis, who follow an unorthodox form of Shi'ism; adherents to the "established" faith of Iran - Ithna'asheri Shi'i Islam; the Ahl al Haqq (People of Truth), a small sect found in the south and south-east of Kurdistan; and Yazidis.

Since the break-up of the Ottoman Empire the majority of the Kurds have been split between Iran, Iraq and Turkey with a smaller number living in Syria. Kurdish communities are also found in Transcaucasian states of the former Soviet Union. Most inhabit the area known as 'Kurdistan', although this is a

---

[1] For further information on the origins, history, politics and characteristics of the Kurds see generally Chaliand People Without a Country (1980) and The Kurdish Tragedy (1994); van Bruinessen Agha, Shaikh and State (1992); McDowall The Kurds - A Nation Denied (1992); and Kreyenbroek and Sperl (eds.) The Kurds - A Contemporary Overview (1992).

geographical term and has never designated a Kurdish state. 'Kurdistan' - the land of the Kurds - spreads across the mountainous region where the borders of Iran, Iraq and Turkey meet. Claims as to the exact dimensions of Kurdistan vary but its backbone is the Taurus and Zagros mountain chains, and it stretches down to the Mesopotamian plain in the south and, in the north and north-east, up to the steppes and plateaus of what was Armenian Anatolia. The area is also inhabited by smaller minority communities, including Christians, Turkomans, Assyrians and Armenians.

The area is agriculturally rich and many Kurds are engaged in livestock farming and agricultural production. Tobacco is the main cash crop, as well as cotton and grain in some areas. Other products, such as fruit and vegetables, are mainly for domestic consumption. Once richly forested, the area has suffered from widespread deforestation which has devastated timber production and caused environmental damage. Parts of Kurdistan have important oil resources and disputes over its exploitation and revenues from oil have been one of the major causes of conflict between the Kurds and the ruling governments in the region. Other minerals found in the area include chrome, copper, iron, coal and lignite. There has been little effort made towards industrial development in the Kurdish areas, however - economic under-development is a convenient method for the governments in the region of keeping the Kurds under control.

There are no official population figures, not least because it has suited the countries inhabited by the Kurds to manipulate and down-play the size of their Kurdish communities. Estimated figures indicate that the largest number of Kurds are to be found in Turkey but that it is in Iraq where they constitute the highest proportion of the overall population. There are believed to be some 12 million Kurds in Turkey (20 per cent of the population); 4 million in Iraq (25 per cent of the population); 7 million in Iran (15 per cent of the population); and almost 1 million in Syria (9 per cent of the population).

The Kurdish people have long been recognized internationally as having a distinct identity with a common heritage and aspirations to political and territorial independence. Constituting some 25 million people, it has been observed that the Kurds "may be the largest geographically separate community in the world not to have achieved either statehood or some form of recognized territorial autonomy; they are certainly the largest among the many "nations" disappointed by the post-World War I territorial realignments in Europe and the Middle East".[2] Notwithstanding their strong sense of common identity and

---

[2] Hannum Autonomy, Sovereignty, and Self-Determination: The Accommodation of Conflicting Rights, (1990) at p. 199.

their relative geographical cohesion, however, there have always been deep divisions between the Kurds, among tribes, local rulers and political parties, and often marked differences as to the nature of the political status they seek and how to pursue it. These divisions have, of course, been greatly exacerbated by the fact that the Kurdish people are split among different countries and have had different historical and political experiences.

The Kurds do, however, have in common a history of harsh repression by the governments of the countries they inhabit and the consistent denial not only of their political aims and of any attempts to secure independence or autonomy, but also of their basic human rights. The scale of repression has undoubtably fuelled demands for Kurdish autonomy while, at the same time, making it virtually impossible to pursue negotiated solutions in the context of widespread killing, torture, disappearance, arbitrary arrest and detention, the suppression of peaceful political activity and persistent violations of the rights of free speech, assembly and association.

1.2 THE TREATY OF SEVRE

Historically, the Kurds enjoyed a considerable degree of semi-autonomy under the various regional powers seeking to exercise territorial authority over the lands inhabited by Kurdish tribes. However, the first, and so far the only, opportunity for the Kurds to establish an independent state came with the collapse of the Ottoman Empire and the end of the first World War in 1918.

In the after-math of the first World War there was a new preoccupation with the situation of minority groups - albeit driven primarily by strategic political considerations rather than concern for individual and group protection, well-being and development. In his Fourteen Point Program for World Peace President Wilson included the statement that the non-Turkish minorities of the Ottoman Empire should be "assured of an absolute unmolested opportunity of autonomous development". Although the Kurds themselves were far from unified in their demands, the Allies clearly recognized the Kurds as a distinct population with legitimate aspirations towards independence.

The Treaty of Sevres, signed by the Allied Powers and the Constantinople Government in 1920, actually envisaged an independent Kurdish state. Article 62 of the Treaty provided that a Commission appointed by the French, Italians and British would, within six months of the treaty entering into force, draft a scheme of local autonomy for the Kurdish areas lying East of the Euphrates, south of Armenia and north of Syria and Mesopotamia - with safeguards for other minorities within these areas. Article 64 further provided:

> If, after one year has elapsed since the implementation of the present treaty, the Kurdish population of the areas designated in Article 62 calls on the Council of the League of Nations and demonstrates that a majority of the population in these areas wishes to become independent of Turkey, and if the Council then estimates that the population in question is capable of such independence and recommends that it be granted, then Turkey agrees, as of now, to comply with this recommendation and to renounce all rights and titles to the area.... If and when the said renunciation is made, no objection shall be raised by the main Allied powers should the Kurds living in that part of Kurdistan at present included in the vilayet of Mosul seek to become citizens of the newly independent Kurdish state.

This last sentence referred to the fact that Mosul was then occupied by the British, who also controlled the 'vilayets', or provinces, of Basra and Baghdad. The British did, in fact, carry out a referendum in Mosul in 1921 but based the franchise on property ownership. They then turned the extremely poor poll into a pretext for annexation. In any event, the question of any voluntary adhesion by the inhabitants of Mosul to an independent Kurdish state was rendered moot by the collapse of the Treaty of Sevres.

This Treaty was never destined to be implemented. Mustafa Kemal (Ataturk) repudiated it and waged a war of national independence. Kurdish leaders petitioned the League of Nations and the British for recognition of Kurdish autonomy during negotiations on the 1923 Treaty of Lausanne. However, this instrument completely ignored the claims of the Kurds to any form of independent status and recognized only the protection of rights of religious minorities. Turkish sovereignty was re-established over part of the territory which had been the subject of the Treaty of Sevres and the remaining Kurdish areas were split between Iran and Iraq. Thereafter the Kurds were left to pursue their political and social destiny within the borders of the various states within which they were incorporated.

1.3 THE KURDS IN IRAQ

The state of Iraq emerged from the Ottoman provinces of Mesopotamia occupied by the British. In 1920 the British were appointed by the League of Nations as the mandate authority over the territory. The British were only too well aware of the absolute opposition of the Kurdish inhabitants of the territory to be brought under Arab control. Initial plans to secure some form of Kurdish autonomy were, however, shelved by the British in the interests of consolidating the new state of Iraq and bolstering the extremely fragile authority of the Emir Faisal, whom they had installed as King.

From the earliest days of the Iraqi state Kurdish claims to autonomy were perceived as deeply threatening and any attempts by the Kurds to secure political, economic or social development viewed with the greatest suspicion. While the Iraqi Kurds have, in fact, secured much greater advances towards autonomy than any of their brethren elsewhere, these gains have been mostly cosmetic and formalistic and have never resulted in a genuine functioning autonomy. The Kurds in Iraq have also endured some of the worst repression by a government whose clear intention is to keep them weak and submissive and firmly under central government control.

Over the years Iraqi Kurds have continued their struggle for recognition, for autonomy and for protection of their basic rights and freedoms. They have frequently resorted to armed conflict and have made political and military gains whenever the central Government has been internally weak or preoccupied with external threats. As soon as the Government has regained strength, concessions have been withdrawn and repression has resumed in full force. This consistent pattern was finally broken by international intervention in 1991 which has enabled the Kurds to develop the most far-reaching autonomous status that they have ever enjoyed in Iraq, founded on democratic elections.

Even before Iraq achieved independence, the League of Nations was concerned about the Kurds and insisted that their rights be fully protected in the new state of Iraq. A Declaration by Iraq in 1932 protecting the rights of its minorities was made a condition of its acceptance as a member of the League. The obligations set out in the Declaration were expressed to be international obligations overriding all future domestic laws and practices and subject to the political and judicial supervision of the League (see Section II).

Kurdish opposition to Arab rule continued in the early years of Iraqi independence, breaking out in open rebellion which the British assisted in crushing on several occasions. By this time the legendary Kurdish leader, Mullah Mustafa Barzani, was developing a political power base and leading an armed revolt against the Government. In 1943 the British finally began to exert pressure on the Iraqis to reach some kind of accommodation with the Kurds, which resulted in an amnesty and a temporary cessation of the conflict. In 1944

Barzani headed a delegation to negotiate a settlement but this foundered and the withdrawal of the British from any intermediary role further increased the impossibility of reaching a peaceful solution. Armed conflict broke out again in 1945 and Barzani sought refuge first in Iran and later in the USSR, where he spent the next 11 years in exile.

In 1958 the Hashemite monarchy was overthrown in a coup led by General Qasim. Barzani returned to Iraq and sought a new accommodation for the Kurds while building up his political base, the Kurdish Democratic Party (KDP), which was finally legalized shortly afterwards. There seemed fresh hopes for Kurdish autonomy when the new Provisional Constitution was adopted, recognizing the Arabs and the Kurds as two distinct component groups within the Iraqi state and guaranteeing their respective national rights. Kurds occupied some senior political positions and Kurdish publications and activities increased. There were internal political divisions among the Kurds, however, and increasing tension between Barzani and Qasim. Armed conflict resumed and by 1962 the Kurdish pesh merga (armed guerilla forces) had made significant gains, holding the north of the country from Zakho to the Iranian border. Qasim was then killed in a coup which brought the Ba'ath Party to power for the first time in February 1963.

The Ba'ath Party initially made some overtures to the Kurds and vaguely promised to recognize Kurdish national rights on the basis of "decentralization". Their underlying strategy, however, was to crush the rebellious Kurds by military assault coupled with a policy of "arabization", expelling Kurds from their homes and encouraging the settlement of Arabs, particularly in the strategic oil-rich area of Kirkuk. The impossibility of defeating the Kurds militarily brought the war to a stalemate, broken only by the fall of the Ba'ath Party in November 1963.

The new leader, General Aref, negotiated a cease-fire with Barzani with vague promises of autonomy but this only served as a breathing space to allow both sides to re-group their forces before the war resumed in 1965. Iranian military and political support for the Iraqi Kurds assisted them in repelling Iraqi military attacks and Barzani's forces secured a mountainous stronghold in the northern border areas that was maintained for ten years. General Aref's death opened the way for a further cease-fire and peace agreement in 1966, recognizing national rights for the Kurds leaving them with a semi-autonomy in practice that lasted three years, until the Ba'ath Party took power once more in 1968 and armed conflict resumed.

At first the Ba'ath Party again made overtures of settlement and in 1970 an Autonomy Agreement was signed, establishing a political framework for self-government in Iraqi Kurdistan. Tensions quickly mounted, however, notably over Baghdad's refusal to include Kirkuk as part of the Autonomous Area and following assassination attempts against Barzani. Negotiations led nowhere and in 1974 Saddam Hussein forced an Autonomy Law on the Kurds which was seen as a significant weakening of the commitments in the 1970 Agreement and a cover for continuing central government control. Full-scale hostilities broke out again almost immediately and the Government made significant military gains. The virtual collapse of the Kurdish resistance was secured when Iran withdrew its support for the Kurds and signed the Algiers Agreement with Iraq in 1975.

The 1974/5 conflict was one of the most bitter and destructive in Kurdish history, resulting in a heavy loss of life, massive internal displacement of Kurdish communities and the devastation of land and infrastructure. Saddam Hussein stepped up the repression of the Kurds and cleared a cordon sanitaire in the border areas, resettling thousands in new collective towns. It was at this time that the Kurdish political opposition, so far dominated by Barzani and the KDP, splintered in earnest and the Patriotic Union of Kurdistan (PUK), led by Jalal Talabani, emerged. The political scene was thereafter marked not only by the ebb and flow of relations with the central government but also by the often stormy relationship between these two major Kurdish political groups and the various alliances they have pursued inside and outside Iraq.

Although Saddam Hussein pushed ahead in the 1980s in setting up the puppet structures of Kurdish 'autonomy' as envisaged in the 1974 Autonomy Law, the main Kurdish political leaders and groups did not participate. This period was anyway dominated by the Iran-Iraq war in which both countries supported Kurdish opposition forces in the other's territory. The links between Iran and the Iraqi Kurds only served to harden Baghdad's attitude still further towards the Kurdish population who were seen as active collaborators in Iranian attempts to secure a military victory against Iraq. With the Iraqi military fully occupied in the war, however, it was not until the cease-fire in 1988 that Saddam Hussein was able to turn his full attention once more to the Kurds. This time he determined to crush them once and for all in the context of the so-called "Anfal campaign". These well-planned military assaults, using chemical and conventional weapons, have been condemned as acts amounting to genocide. It is believed that between 50,000 and 100,000 people died in the course of the campaign, which also effectively destroyed the Kurdish rural economy and infrastructure.

The latest major onslaught against the Kurds followed just three years later, in March 1991. This time it was in retaliation for an extraordinary internal uprising that followed on the heels of Iraq's heavy defeat after its 1990 invasion of Kuwait. The internal rebellion started in the south of the country and spread quickly to the north, affecting almost the entire area of Iraqi Kurdistan which fell to Kurdish opposition forces. Iraq responded with characteristic ruthlessness and unleashed a military offensive that prompted almost two million Kurds to flee towards and across the borders into Iraq and Turkey. The dimensions of this human flood in desperate and freezing conditions finally resulted in the setting up of the safe havens in Iraqi Kurdistan by the direct intervention of thousands of foreign troops. The international protection of the area, which has been maintained in some form ever since, has given the Iraqi Kurds the opportunity to establish a genuine democratic regional government for the first time in their history.

The emergence of a de facto autonomous area in Iraqi Kurdistan has been watched with growing apprehension and alarm by Turkey, Iran and Syria. All these countries share the greatest suspicion of any move towards Kurdish autonomy for fear that this will unleash political forces beyond their control within their own Kurdish minority populations. The three countries have been holding regular consultation meetings to assess the regional implications of the situation in Iraqi Kurdistan. In 1992 they criticised the objective of a federal union supported by the newly-elected government in Iraqi Kurdistan and warned that "We believe that acts and efforts that may divide Iraq will have negative and dangerous consequences for regional peace and security".[3] At their sixth meeting in August 1994 they denounced groups in some Western countries who were encouraging separatism and indicated that they viewed northern Iraq as a source of instability. The then Turkish Foreign Minister stated that "We are particularly concerned by the possibility of northern Iraq turning into an independent Kurdish state and by the interference of certain Western countries in the issue. It is out of the question for us to allow such a development to take place".[4]

---

[3] Christian Science Monitor November 27-December 3 1992, quoted in Keen The Kurds in Iraq - How Safe Is Their Haven Now? (Save The Children, 1993) at p.17 (hereinafter cited as "Keen").

[4] Kurdish Affairs, Vol 1, No.2 (1994) at p.10.

The historical record demonstrates beyond any doubt that the Kurds will never be able to live in peace and security, much less to enjoy political rights, if they are abandoned and left alone to pursue their claims with the Iraqi Government. Any future political settlement and guarantees of their rights must be fully protected and secured at the international level. Equally it is clear that any settlement for Iraqi Kurdistan cannot be pursued in a vacuum. It has profound implications for the Kurdish populations elsewhere and for the countries which they inhabit. It is imperative that steps towards a settlement take into account the complexity of the regional context and the need for the other countries affected to abide fully by their international obligations.

II. KURDISH RIGHTS IN THE INDEPENDENT STATE OF IRAQ

Iraq was essentially a creation of the British Government which occupied large parts of the territory after the first World War. As mandate authority, the British had a special responsibility for the whole population of the territory until Iraq's emergence as a newly independent state. Although the British and the League of Nations recognized the Kurds as a distinct group with legitimate claims to autonomy, very little was actually done to secure such status. The British did nothing to ensure legislative or institutional protection for Kurdish autonomy. Instead, they played a far greater role in repressing the Kurds and were largely responsible for the incorporation of southern Kurdistan into the state of Iraq without adequate guarantees of Kurdish political rights. The British thereby contributed in no small part to the situation the Kurds find themselves in today.

Iraq's membership of the League of Nations was, however, conditioned on its acceptance of international obligations to protect the civil and political rights of the Kurds and their rights as a minority group. Although this proved insufficient to guarantee and protect their rights, it did constitute early recognition of the role and responsibility of the international community for the protection of the Kurds and other minority groups.

II.1 THE BRITISH GOVERNMENT AS MANDATE AUTHORITY

The League of Nations recognized the British Government as the mandate authority over Iraq in 1920, the same year that the ill-fated Treaty of Sevres was signed. The mandate system was set up by the Principal Allied and Associated Powers in conjunction with the League under Article 22 of the League's Covenant. According to the International Court of Justice, "The Mandate was created, in the interest of the inhabitants of the territory, and of humanity in general, as an international institution with an international object - a sacred trust of civilization".[5] The countries which administered territories under this "sacred trust", were responsible for fulfilling the aims of the mandate system, including ensuring the well-being and development of the peoples in the territory and securing guarantees for performance of international obligations.

---

[5] International Status of South West Africa , ICJ Reports 1950, 128 at 132.

The British were acutely aware of the aspirations to independence of the Kurds under their authority and the fact that they were fiercely resistant to enforced amalgamation into a new Arab state of Iraq. The British had had their own difficulties in Sulaimaniya with an armed rebellion led by the Kurdish nationalist leader, Sheikh Mahmud of the Barzinja tribe, who was also vehemently opposed to Turkish or Arab control. Having quelled the uprising by force, the British initially sentenced Sheikh Mahmud to death, but then sent him off to India to prison and exile.

Initially, British policy appeared to be to keep the Kurdish area separate and autonomous. At the time of the Paris Peace Conference, for example, the British envisaged "autonomous Kurdish states under Kurdish chiefs who will be advised by British political officers".[6] The Treaty of Sevres had envisaged the possibility of voluntary union of the inhabitants of the Mosul province to an independent Kurdistan. At the 1921 Cairo Conference, at which a future Arab state of Iraq was discussed, a memorandum from the British Government's Middle East Department stated "We are strongly of the opinion that purely Kurdish areas should not be included in the Arab state of Mesopotamia, but that the principles of Kurdish unity and nationality should be promoted as far as possible by H.M.G." Winston Churchill, then heading the Colonial Office, predicted that an Arab leader in Iraq "would ignore Kurdish sentiment and oppress the Kurdish minority" and it was decided to keep Kurdistan under separate administration headed by a British High Commissioner.[7]

The High Commissioner in Iraq, Sir Percy Cox, had long been convinced, however, of the desirability of incorporating the Kurdish areas into an eventual Arab state. He was supported by the new Arab King of Iraq, Emir Faisal, brought in by the British and anxious to consolidate his fragile support and authority. Cox continued to press the need for incorporation and, fuelled by fears of renewed Turkish claims on the area, Churchill capitulated in October 1921 and agreed that the Kurdish areas should be included in Iraq and should participate in the National Assembly, although still on condition of local autonomy. Progress towards the emergence of Iraq as an independent state was reflected the following year when Anglo-Iraqi relations were put on a treaty basis by the Treaty of Alliance of 1922. Yet it still appeared that the British might honour their commitment to Kurdish autonomy when they issued a Joint Declaration with the Iraqi Government communicated to the League of

---

[6] Korn "The Men Who Put the Kurds Into Iraq: Percy Cox and Arnold T. Wilson" Kurdish Affairs, Vol. 1 No. 2 (September 1994).

[7] Ibid.

Nations in December 1922 recognising the right of the Kurds to form a government within the borders of Iraq.

The League of Nations reinforced Kurdish claims to autonomy and their need for special protection in 1924. In the context of settling the border between Turkey and Iraq, the League of Nations set up an international commission of inquiry which went to Mosul in 1925. It found that five-eighths of the population of the disputed territory was Kurdish. It indicated that this pointed towards an independent state on the basis of ethnicity alone, although it noted that those living north of the Greater Zab were more closely connected with the Kurds of Turkey and those living south had more in common with the Persian Kurds. The Commission finally recommended that the disputed territory of Mosul remain within Iraq. It did, however, express great concern about the stability of Iraq and considered that guidance and protection in the form of a League mandate ought to be maintained for a substantial period of time to enable the consolidation and development of the state. Its recommendation to leave Mosul within Iraq appeared to be predicated on the continuation of the mandate system, since it noted that Turkish sovereignty over Mosul would be preferable to granting it to a new state of Iraq not yet ready for independence.

The League accepted the Commission's recommendation against partition of the area and decided in favour of attaching Mosul to Iraq. However, this was on condition that it remained under League mandate for 25 years and that due consideration was given to conferring responsibility for local administration, the justice system and education on Kurdish officials and having Kurdish as the official language. The British, as the mandate authority, were invited to report to the League on the administration of Mosul, the promulgation of a form of autonomy and recognition of the rights of the Kurds. The 1922 Alliance Treaty was accordingly amended to secure the British mandate for 25 years or until Iraq's admission as a member of the League, whichever was sooner.

The only concrete step towards British fulfilment of the obligations set out in the League's resolution was a 1926 Local Languages Law, allowing Kurds in Arbil and Sulaimaniya to have primary education and to print books in their own language. However, when various Kurdish cultural societies were formed in 1926 and 1927, which took an increasingly political stance, they were dismantled by police operations conducted by the British.

At this time the whole of Iraqi Kurdistan was still refusing to accept an Arab administration and the British were repeatedly involved in measures to suppress opposition and unrest. In fact, Baghdad's authority over Iraqi Kurdistan was still not secured at the time of Iraqi independence. The British had initially brought back Sheikh Mahmud to Sulaimaniya in 1922 hoping that he would repel any Turkish aggressive moves on the area. Sheikh Mahmud, however, not only declared himself King of Kurdistan and formed an embryonic administration but attempted to play off Turkey and Britain against each other. The British called for his surrender and launched an offensive in 1923 to prevent him joining forces with the Turks, following which he was forced to flee. His attempts to regain power led to RAF bombing raids. A year later, further unrest in Mosul after legislative elections in 1924 was put down with more bombing raids and led to a resumption of British occupation in Sulaimaniya.

Although the situation was clearly far from stable, and notwithstanding the League's recommendation that Mosul remain under mandate authority for 25 years, the British moved ahead rapidly towards the emergence of Iraq as an independent state. In 1930 another Anglo-Iraq Treaty of Alliance was signed, aimed at ending the British mandate and regulating future British relations with Iraq. The Treaty made no mention of the Kurds, still less did it do anything to secure Kurdish autonomy or basic rights. Leaders in Sulaimaniya sent petitions to the League, recalling its 1925 decision, but these were ignored. Unrest flared again; in September 1930 troops fired directly into crowds protesting in Sulaimaniya, killing dozens of people. Many suspected Kurdish nationalists were arrested and Shaikh Mahmud, who was again leading protests, was severely defeated and forced to surrender to the Baghdad Government. He was placed under house arrest and kept there for more than 20 years until his death in 1956.[8]

II.2 THE LEAGUE IMPOSES CONDITIONS FOR MINORITY RIGHTS PROTECTION

The Permanent Mandates Commission of the League had undertaken an extensive inquiry before it recommended termination of the British mandate. The Council of the League agreed in principle to termination, subject, however, to Iraq entering into certain undertakings before the Council. Those undertakings were set out in a Declaration approved by the Council in its Resolution of 19 May 1932 and signed and ratified by Iraq and deposited with the Secretary-General. They were effectively a condition precedent to Iraq joining the international community as a member of the League of Nations.

---

[8] Chaliand The Kurdish Tragedy (1994) at pp. 53-54.

The 1932 Declaration dealt primarily with the protection of minority rights in Iraq. It secured for minorities not only physical protection and respect for all civil and political rights but also specifically covered at least the more traditional minority rights - language, culture and religion. It was premised on two important interlocking principles - equality and non-discrimination on the one hand and special measures to ensure the preservation of the group's identity and distinct characteristics on the other. Although it did not explicitly guarantee self-government for the Kurds, it could possibly be interpreted as contemplating some form of autonomy within the terms of its provisions.

Chapter I of the Declaration guaranteed to all Iraqis equal protection of all civil and political rights, without discrimination as to race, religion or language. It ensured "full and complete protection of life and liberty"; freedom of religion; equality before the law; and the prohibition of restrictions on the use of any language in private intercourse, commerce, religion, the press and all other publications and at any public meetings. It also provided for an electoral system that guaranteed "equitable representation" to minorities in Iraq. It did not spell out exactly what this would entail, but since it presumably meant something other than one person one vote, it could perhaps be interpreted as contemplating some form of political autonomy for minorities.

In addition racial, religious and linguistic minorities in Iraq were to enjoy the same treatment and security in law and in fact as other Iraqi nationals. They were to be permitted to set up and to use their own language and religion in charitable, religious and social institutions as well as in schools and educational establishments. In areas with substantial minority populations, provision would be made for primary education in minority languages (alongside obligatory teaching in Arabic, the official language) and for an equitable share of public funds for educational, religious or charitable purposes. The Declaration further specified that Kurdish was guaranteed as the official language - with Arabic - in the "liwas" of Mosul, Arbil, Kirkuk and Sulaimaniya. In these areas, as far as possible, public officials were to be selected from the local population.

Article 1 of the Declaration guaranteed that its provisions "are recognized as the fundamental laws of Iraq, and no law, regulation or official action shall conflict or interfere with these stipulations, nor shall any law, regulation or official action now or in the future prevail over them". Article 10 furthermore stipulated that the minority protection provisions of the Declaration "are declared to constitute obligations of international concern and will be placed under the guarantee of the League of Nations. No modification will be made in them without the assent of a majority of the Council of the League of Nations".

Chapter II of the Declaration contained a number of other more generic guarantees, including a uniform system of justice to secure the full exercise and protection of rights of all nationals and foreigners alike and the safeguard that all rights of any nature acquired by individuals, associations or juridical persons before termination of the British mandate would be respected. Unlike the minority rights provisions, these additional guarantees were not expressed to override all present and future laws and official action but they were to constitute obligations of international concern that could not be modified without a majority vote of the League.

Any breach or anticipated breach of the minority rights provisions of the Declaration could be submitted to the Council of the League by any Council member and the Council was authorized to take any measures or give such directions as it saw fit. A dispute of law or fact arising out the Declaration could also be submitted to the Permanent Court of International Justice. Following the adoption of the Declaration, the independent state of Iraq was declared a member of the League of Nations on 3 October 1932.

II.3 LEGAL IMPLICATIONS OF IRAQ'S DECLARATION ON MINORITY RIGHTS

The current legal status of the obligations set out in Iraq's Declaration and, in particular, the extent to which they might be held legally enforceable today is unclear. The Declaration formed part of a whole system for minority protection established by the League comprising a series of other declarations and treaties for the protection of certain minorities in particular countries. All were drafted in very similar terms. When the League was dissolved this minority protection system ceased to function. It was not taken over directly by the United Nations (UN) when that was set up in 1945, since the philosophy behind rights protection by that time was the establishment of a universal system of human rights applicable equally to all member states. The emphasis was on the protection of a much wider set of individual rights, rather than a focus on the rights of particular groups, such as minorities.

A study by the UN secretariat in 1950 examined the validity of the League's minority protection system and reviewed each instrument adopted as part of that system on a case-by-case basis.[9] In the case of the unilateral Declarations,

---

[9] Study of the Legal Validity of the Undertakings Concerning Minorities, UN Doc. E/CN.4/367.

such as that of Iraq, it concluded that these were suspended pending a decision by the UN to take over the powers and functions of the League. General Assembly Resolution 24 (I) of 1946 left it to the discretion of the Assembly to decide either not to assume any function or power of the former League or to determine which UN body should exercise that function. The General Assembly has never taken a formal decision to assign to any existing UN body the political supervision of the minority instruments which was formerly exercised by the Council of the League. The secretariat study concluded that, reviewing the situation overall, "between 1939 and 1947 circumstances as a whole changed to such an extent that, generally speaking, the system should be considered as having ceased to exist". It found that "the whole minorities protection regime was an integral part of the system established to regulate the outcome of the first World War" and that this system was overthrown by the Second World War and the emerging new philosophy of the "general and universal protection of human rights and fundamental freedoms".[10]

Clearly the "system" of minority rights protection set up by the League is no longer in force since the UN decided not to maintain or set up comparable structures to continue to supervise the implementation of the old minority treaties and Declarations. The question remains, however, whether the substantive terms of Iraq's Declaration might still be enforceable by recourse to the International Court of Justice. The political and judicial elements of the supervisory system for the minority instruments were separate - recourse to the Permanent Court to resolve a dispute was not tied to and did not require the prior exhaustion of the procedure for raising breaches in the Council. Thus, judicial recourse cannot be said to have been abrogated by the fact that the UN did not designate any UN body to take over the Council's supervisory functions.

Article 37 of the Statute of the International Court of Justice states that when "a treaty or convention in force" provides for reference of a matter to a tribunal instituted by the League of Nations or the Permanent Court of Justice the matter may be referred to the International Court of Justice.[11] Although Iraq has not recognized the compulsory jurisdiction of the International Court under

---

[10] Ibid.

[11] A case in which the status of one of these minority treaties may be considered is currently pending before the International Court of Justice. Bosnia and Herzogovina has sought to rely on the 1919 Minorities Treaty between the Allied and Associated Powers and the Kingdom of the Serbs, Croats and Slovenes in its Application to the International Court of Justice alleging violations by Yugoslavia (Serbia and Montenegro) of the Convention on the Prevention and Punishment of the Crime of Genocide. The Court has not yet ruled on the merits in that case. In its second order of 13 September 1993 concerning provisional measures, the Court did not consider whether the Treaty was still in force since it found that it was, in any event, irrelevant to the request for provisional measures as any obligations would be limited to the present territory of Yugoslavia and no claim had been made concerning the treatment of minorities in that territory. The Genocide Convention Case, ICJ Reports 1993, 325 at 339-340.

Article 36(2) of the Court's Statute, under the terms of the Declaration it clearly did accept the Permanent Court's jurisdiction in the event of a dispute concerning the Declaration. The secretariat's 1950 study, the conclusions of which are not, in any event, legally binding, found only that the terms of the minority Declarations were "suspended". It also considered that the minority undertakings had not been implicitly abrogated by the UN Charter since the Charter did not address minority rights expressly and those concepts are different from the concepts of individual human rights protection addressed in the Charter.

If a case could be made out that the Declaration remains enforceable, a complaint alleging breaches by Iraq of its obligations under the Declaration could probably only be submitted to the International Court by a state that was formerly a member of the Council of the League of Nations. Alternatively an advisory opinion on the question of the status of the Declaration, the scope of rights guaranteed by it and Iraq's compliance with its terms could be requested by a competent UN body, such as the Security Council, the General Assembly or the Economic and Social Council.

An advisory opinion confirming the provisions of the Declaration still to be valid and enforceable or a court judgment against Iraq for breach of its terms would carry significant political weight. Its practical effects today might be more limited, however, and in many respects the subsequent development of minority rights in international human rights law goes much further than the Iraqi Declaration. The real significance of the Declaration is that it demonstrates international recognition of and the assumption of international responsibility for the protection of basic rights of the Kurds as a condition to the ending of the British mandate and the acceptance of Iraq into the League of Nations.[12]

---

[12] In a separate opinion appended to the second Order made by the International Court in the Genocide Convention case, Judge Lauterpacht (essentially supporting the Court's order and reasoning) did not address the current legal status of the 1919 Treaty, but did state that, in his view, only a state which had been a member of the Council of League of Nations would have the right to bring proceedings pursuant to that Treaty, Ibid. at p. 415.

III. STEPS TOWARDS KURDISH AUTONOMY IN IRAQ

On paper, the Kurds in Iraq have secured much greater political gains towards autonomy than in other countries with significant Kurdish populations. In practice, however, these achievements have been minimal and mainly cosmetic. Progress towards any form of autonomous status has been slow and painful. Political concessions have been hard won, often through armed conflict. A pattern of repression and violence against the Kurds has been repeated over and over again and has undermined political negotiations and eroded all confidence in the Government's commitment to Kurdish self-government. The Iraqi Government has always ensured that it retains overall political control and the major stumbling blocks have never been resolved. Principal among these is the lack of any agreement on the extent of the Kurdish autonomous area, and particularly whether it includes the oil-rich area of Kirkuk which is seen as a fundamental issue by both sides. The only real experience of a functioning autonomy in Iraqi Kurdistan is that which the Kurds have established themselves, free from government interference, over the past four years since the safe havens were set up and international protection held the Government at bay.

III.1 CONSTITUTIONAL RECOGNITION

The first important political and legal step in relation to the recognition of the special status of the Kurds in Iraq came in 1958. The Provisional Constitution adopted on 7 July 1958 recognized the Kurds as a distinct national group for the first time. Under its terms Kurds and Arabs were accepted as associates in the state of Iraq and their respective national rights were guaranteed. In a further symbolic gesture, the arms of the new republic, which had just over thrown the monarchy in a coup, were made up of an Arab sword crossed with a Kurdish dagger.[13]

Constitutional recognition of the Kurds was again affirmed in the Provisional Constitution of 16 July 1970, adopted after the Ba'ath Party gained power in Iraq for the second time. This 1970 Constitution, as subsequently amended, remains in force in Iraq today and is, therefore, of current relevance to the

---

[13] Chaliand The Kurdish Tragedy (1994) at p.56

discussions of Kurdish rights and autonomy.[14] The Constitution enshrines recognition of the "Kurdish people" as one of the main national groups in Iraq with distinct rights. Its Article 5(b) stipulates that "The Iraqi people consists of two main ethnic groups, namely Arabs and Kurds" and it recognizes "the ethnic rights of the Kurdish people, as well as the legitimate rights of all other minorities, within the framework of Iraqi unity".[15]

The Constitution also guarantees the official status of the Kurdish language in Article 7(b) and provides that all citizens are to be equal before the law without any discrimination on account of sex, race, language, social origin or religion.

In 1974 the Constitution was further amplified to secure constitutional protection for Kurdish autonomy. Article 8 provides that "The region in which the majority of the population are Kurds shall enjoy autonomy in accordance with the provisions of the law". This coincided with the promulgation of the 1974 Autonomy Law, discussed below.

III.2 THE 1970 AUTONOMY AGREEMENT

The 1970 Autonomy Agreement was adopted as part of the initial overtures to the Kurds by the Ba'ath Party when it took power in 1968. The new political leaders were anxious to secure some kind of accommodation with the Kurds. The Ba'ath Party's attempts to defeat the Kurds militarily in their first brief period in power in 1968 had been unsuccessful and military confrontation loomed again when the Kurdish leader, Barzani, attacked Kirkuk's oil installations in 1969. Military attacks on the Kurds did not cease, but Saddam Hussein decided to push through an Autonomy Agreement with the Kurds, signed on March 11 1970.

On paper, at least, the Autonomy Agreement, recognizing Kurdish national rights and the economic and cultural development of Kurdish areas within a unified Iraq, was relatively far-reaching. Most importantly it recognized a distinct Kurdish ethnic identity and secured Kurdish participation in central government as well as local administrative control in the Kurdish areas. It provided for economic development and assistance to Kurdish areas and recognized freedom of political expression and association as well as cultural

---

[14] The government has announced that the Constitution is under revision and a revised version will in due course be submitted to a referendum. It is not known whether any amendments are proposed to the references to the Kurds and to Kurdish autonomy in any new version of the Constitution.

[15] Cited in The International Commission of Jurists Iraq and the Rule of Law, (1994) at p. 142.

and linguistic freedom, secured through educational establishments and public dissemination of information and literature. It committed the Government to implementation within four years.

The Autonomy Agreement guaranteed the participation of the Kurds in the central government. It provided that one of the Vice-Presidents of the Republic was to be a Kurd (although this was to be a powerless symbolic post) and that Kurds could participate in the legislature in proportion to their general ratio in the population. The legitimacy of Kurdish ethnic identity was recognized.

A degree of self-government in areas with a majority Kurdish population was to be ensured by the decentralisation of local administration under Kurdish, or at least Kurdish-speaking, officials. In these areas the principal officials - the Governor, district officer and chiefs of police and security - would be Kurds. An official census was to be the basis for unifying Kurdish administrative areas and governorates in order to "deepen and broaden the Kurdish people's process of exercising their national rights as a measure of ensuring self-rule", albeit with natural resources in the area remaining the prerogative of the Republic.

The Kurdish areas were also to benefit from economic assistance and development. The Agrarian Reform Law would be speeded up to ensure fair distribution of land. An economic and development plan would be undertaken with due regard for Kurdish under-development and relief and assistance would be given to the needy and unemployed. Arabs and Kurds would be repatriated to their villages, although villages might still be requisitioned by the central government "for public utility purposes" with compensation for those to be re-settled.

Linguistic and cultural rights were to be protected. In areas with a majority Kurdish population Kurdish would be official language, together with Arabic, and this provision was also be secured in the Constitution. Kurdish would be taught in all schools and educational institutions, including the Military and Police College. Measures would be taken to redress educational disadvantages, such as building more schools and providing scholarships for Kurdish students.

There would be wide dissemination of Kurdish scientific, literary and political literature "expressive of the national and nationalist ambitions of the Kurdish people" and Kurdish writers would be assisted in forming a federation, having their work published and developing their artistic and scientific talents. A Kurdish publishing and printing house would be set up, as well as a directorate general of Kurdish culture, a weekly paper and monthly magazine, and a TV station broadcasting exclusively in Kurdish. In addition, Kurds could set up their own student, youth, womens' and teachers' organizations affiliated to their Iraqi counterparts.

Finally, there would be a general amnesty for all civilian and military personnel who took part in hostilities in the Kurdish areas and pensions for those who had lost family members in the fighting.

A number of provisions of the Autonomy Agreement were implemented. Senior Kurdish officials were appointed, including senior KDP members as governors of Dohuk and Arbil and Kurdish police chiefs in Arbil, Dohuk and Sulaimaniya.[16] Some progress was made in agrarian reform, the opening of Kurdish schools, rebuilding of houses, construction of roads, factories, hospitals and other public facilities and the founding of a Kurdish Academy for the development of the Kurdish language.

At the political level, however, progress towards self-government on the basis of the Autonomy Agreement quickly foundered. There was deep disagreement over the delimitation of the Kurdish areas. The Iraqi Government refused to consider the inclusion of Kirkuk which was considered essential by the Kurds. Demands by the Kurds for greater political and military authority and the manner of their participation in government could not be resolved. The Kurds accused the Government of pursuing its policy of arabization, in order to disrupt the demographic balance before the census was held that would determine the precise boundaries of the Autonomous Area. In fact the census was never held and remained a bone of contention. There was also no confidence between the two sides. The Government feared the growing political strength of the Kurds and their relations with Iran. The Kurdish candidate for Vice-President, the KDP secretary, was rejected by the Government and no agreement could be reached on an alternative. Attempts were made on Barzani's life and renewed clashes broke out between Government and Kurdish forces. Negotiations continued during 1973 and 1974 to resolve the deadlock but the situation was fast approaching full-scale armed conflict once more. In an attempt to force the issue, the Government pushed ahead with its Autonomy Law that has never been accepted by the Kurds.

Although the implementation of a satisfactory form of autonomy was undermined by continuing political divisions and conflict, the 1970 Autonomy Agreement

---

[16] Minority Rights Group The Kurds (1989) at p. 21.

is still seen as providing some basic political framework for the establishment of self-rule in Iraqi Kurdistan. It was relied on by some Kurdish political figures as the foundation for the holding of democratic elections in the region in May 1992 (see section VI below). It does, therefore, provide a starting point and a framework for what effective autonomy really means.

III.3 THE AUTONOMY LAW OF 1974

The Law for Autonomy in the Area of Kurdistan (Act No. 33 of 1974) was not negotiated with the Kurds; it was unilaterally promulgated and the Kurds were given fourteen days to accept it. The Autonomy Law purported to establish Kurdistan effectively as a self-governing region with considerable authority over key aspects of social and economic affairs. It also spelt out in more detail the administrative and legislative structures for the administration of the Area which was to be defined in accordance with the 1970 Agreement and the 1957 census records, as no new census had been held. However, the terms of the 1974 Law were much weaker than the Kurds had been pressing for and they did not consider that it met the commitments of the Autonomy Agreement. It also envisaged a high degree of continuing Government control. It has never been accepted by the Kurdish political leaders as a legitimate basis for autonomy, although it remains in force and the Government has attempted to implement its terms and to set up the structures that it provided for. Its promulgation coincided with the resumption of hostilities that resulted in the devastating war of 1974/5.

Under the terms of the Autonomy Law the Autonomous Area was to be an integral administrative unit with juridical personality and autonomy within the Republic of Iraq, with Arbil as its metropolitan centre. Kurdish was to be an official language and the language of education, together with Arabic which was also to be taught. The Autonomous Area was to have its own budget with financial resources derived from local taxation and other charges and profits as well as appropriations from the central budget. The governing structures it established were an elected legislature - the Legislative Council - and an appointed administrative body - the Executive Council. Executive Council members hold ministerial rank and report directly to the Council of Ministers. The Iraqi Government has stated that "this is a clear indication of the legal importance attached to these autonomous institutions".[17]

The Legislative Council can adopt decisions relating to the development of the

---

[17] UN Doc. CERD/C/132/Add.2 (1985).

area and the promotion of its local social, cultural and economic aspects; the development of culture and national characteristics and traditions; and the functioning of local departments, institutions and administrative bodies. It has the task of ratifying plans and programs of the Executive Council on economic and social matters, and on development, education and health. It also maintains financial oversight and control.

The areas of administration under the control of the Executive Council are as follows: education and higher education; works and housing; agriculture and agrarian reform; internal affairs; transport and communications; culture and youth; municipalities and Summer Resorts; social affairs (including health and labour); economic and financial affairs (including trade and industry); and state property. The Executive Council has a much more restricted responsibility for matters relating to the administration of justice, security and public order and the appointment of officials for the Autonomous Area who are to be Kurds or well-versed in the Kurdish language.

III.4 RESTRICTIONS ON AUTONOMY

The 1974 Autonomy Law imposes significant limitations on Kurdish self-government. Some of these limitations are those which might naturally be expected to be exercised by a central government to ensure that a local or regional self-governing area operates in accordance with the law and within the authority of its devolved powers. For example, all other state powers in respect of the Area, other than those specified in the Law, rests with the central authorities. These central authorities are authorized to give "general guidance" to the local administration and a Minister of State of the central government has a general coordinating role in respect of the Autonomous Area. He is authorized to attend all meetings of the autonomous bodies. The Minister of Justice can contest the validity of any decisions by the Autonomous authorities within 30 days and contested decisions are suspended pending a ruling by a special committee of the Iraqi Court of Cassation which can declare them null and void.

These limitations may not appear very exceptional or restrictive as drafted. In practice, however, in the Iraqi context, where the central Government exercises such ruthless and authoritarian control, they can operate seriously to undermine self-government. In a system where the courts are not independent and there can be no effective challenge to executive authority concentrated in the hands of the President, the extent of Kurdish autonomy rests on the will of Saddam Hussein.

Other restrictions in the Autonomy Law are even more intrusive and undermine the whole notion of a self-governing area presided over by locally-elected officials. For example, subsequent amendments to the Law have imposed significant restrictions on those who may stand for election to the Legislative Council, which has also been reduced in size from 80 to 50 members. Candidates must be Iraqi citizens born of Iraqi parents and, by a law introduced in 1986, must "believe in the leading role of the Arab Baa'th Socialist Party and in the principles and aims of the glorious revolution of 17-30 July 1968 and should have played a notable role in the implementation of those principles and aims". A further restriction was introduced in 1989, requiring that candidates should not have been convicted of "conspiring against the revolution of 17-30 July 1968 or against the regime, nor should they have been convicted of attempting to overthrow the regime or of maintaining contacts with a foreign body".[18] The list of candidates has to be approved by the central Government. These stipulations ensure that the only candidates for the Legislative Council are those sympathetic to the Iraqi Government and not necessarily the free choice of the Kurdish people.

Furthermore, considerable control remains with the President of Iraq by virtue of his role in selecting and appointing one of the Legislative Council members to preside over the formation of the Executive Council. This appointed member in turn selects the Council's Chairman and members. The President also retains the right to dismiss the Chairman of the Executive Council at any time which would result in the Council's dissolution. The appointment of some local officials requires a Republican ordinance or the approval of the President. Also the central authorities exercise a special degree of control and oversight in respect of local police and security personnel and operations.

The Autonomy Law also provides for the full protection of the rights of Arabs and other minorities in the Area. It secures their representation on all autonomous bodies in proportion to their ratio of the population of the Area and provides for their participation in the local civil service. While it is certainly laudable in principle to ensure the participation of other minorities within a self-governing area, there is considerable scope here for manipulation by the Iraqi Government by means of its policy of arabization, which has the effect of increasing the ratio of Arabs within the population and, therefore, also within the autonomous structures.

---

[18] The International Commission of Jurists Iraq and the Rule of Law (1994) at pp. 144-145.

III.5 THE CURRENT STATUS OF AUTONOMY

The Iraqi Government has persisted in its attempts to implement the 1974 Autonomy Law. Elections for the Legislative Council were held in 1980, 1986 and apparently most recently in 1989, although these elections have not respected the three-year term provided for in the Law. By the time of the democratic Kurdish elections in 1992, following the Government's withdrawal from the area, the Legislative Council did not have a quorum and appeared to be non-functional legally and in practice.

Iraq continues to hold out the Autonomy Law and the institutions and structures it established as evidence of its commitment to Kurdish autonomy and the protection of the rights of the Kurds, including their cultural and linguistic development. Iraq's periodic reports to the UN committees which supervise implementation of the international human rights treaties to which Iraq is a party regularly contain a section detailing the legislation governing Kurdish autonomy. However, the Government never provides any information about how these arrangements function in practice nor does it admit to any problems in respect of the Kurdish minority. Accusations against Iraq and allegations of human rights violations against the Kurds are dismissed out of hand as attempts to interfere in Iraq's internal affairs and to inflame public opinion against it. In one such report to a UN treaty-monitoring committee the Iraqi Government stated:

> Iraq holds the view that the Kurdish problem has been solved in a legal and democratic manner that is unprecedented in any other country with a Kurdish ethnic minority. The political aspect of the problem is merely a result of foreign interference aimed at prejudicing Iraq's territorial integrity...[19]

More recently, in 1991, the Iraqi representative appearing before one of these committees denied that the Kurds "had ever been treated as a separate people in a negative, discriminatory sense".[20] That same year another UN committee was told:

> ...when disturbances occurred, causing deaths in the north of the country, the Iraqi authorities could not shirk their responsibility or cease to guarantee security throughout the national territory. Moreover the Government had to see to it that the northern region of the country benefitted from all the public services, whether economic, cultural or

---

[19] UN Doc. CERD/C/132/Add.2 (1985) at p. 7.

[20] UN Doc. CERD/C/SR 920 (1991) at para. 3.

other, that were available in the other regions. There could, therefore, be no question of State officials - judges, doctors, university teaching staff, etc. leaving that region.[21]

Yet it was in 1991 that the Iraqi Government ruthlessly crushed the internal uprising in the north with excessive and illegal force, precipitating the flight of almost two million people, and then withdrew from the northern area completely, imposing an economic embargo on it.

The Government also admitted to the same UN Committee in 1991 that so far the experiment of autonomy for the Kurds had not come to much, in part due to "outside factors". It informed the committee that the Autonomy Law was "certainly not exhaustive" and could be improved. It stated that the Law was being revised and its provisions would be strengthened "to ensure the enjoyment of their rights by the Kurds in conformity with the Constitution and Iraqi law".[22] On 8 January 1992 Deputy Prime Minister Tariq Aziz even stated unequivocally to the Special Rapporteur on Iraq that "Iraq would be the first to recognize Kurdish independence".[23] Such an assertion rings hollow in light of the Iraqi Government's treatment of the Kurds and its responses to the concerns of the international community.

III.6 FURTHER NEGOTIATIONS ON AUTONOMY

Negotiations between the Kurds and the Iraqi Government on a new autonomy agreement were resumed in mid-April 1991 in the wake of the establishment of the safe havens. In the circumstances then prevailing it was hardly surprising that many Kurds were deeply sceptical and fearful of seeking any new political arrangements with the Government and the decision to resume autonomy talks was highly divisive within the Kurdish opposition alliance. Uncertain as to how long the international protection in northern Iraq might continue, the Kurdish leadership appealed that any settlement be bolstered by international guarantees.

The UK was one country which also explicitly recognized the necessity of international guarantees to achieve a satisfactory agreement. The UK Foreign Secretary stated in June 1991 that the conclusion of the negotiations on autonomy, as well as an expanded UN presence, would be necessary before the

---

[21] UN Doc. CCPR/C/SR 1107 at para. 19.

[22] Ibid. para. 30.

[23] UN Doc. E/CN.4/1992/31 at para. 108.

coalition forces withdrew.[24] Later, in October, the British Government said it was still awaiting the outcome of the on-going talks and that "we have made it clear that we are willing to consider what the international community might be able to do to underpin such an agreement".[25] It even suggested that sanctions might be used to secure Iraqi compliance with an agreement.[26] However, there were no serious attempts at direct international involvement in the negotiations nor any suggestions of international guarantees, to which Saddam Hussein made clear his absolute opposition throughout.

On 24 April the PUK leader, Jalal Talabani, announced an agreement had been reached in principle, although it had not been signed by Masoud Barzani, leader of the KDP. It affirmed the principle of democracy, freedom of the press and recognition that the Kurds could return to villages destroyed in 1987-88. However, the Iraqi Government was not prepared to accept the proposed geographical extent of the autonomous area to include Kirkuk, demands for free elections, the drafting of a new Constitution or any international guarantees.

In mid-May at a meeting between Saddam Hussein and a Kurdish delegation headed by Barzani some further progress appeared to be made on issues such as an amnesty for Kurdish guerillas; the return of Kurds to their homes; the repeal of emergency laws restricting Kurds; the opening of a university in Sulaimaniya; the economic development of Kurdistan; and Kurdish participation in the army and other state institutions. Saddam Hussein remained adamant, however, in his refusal to countenance other key Kurdish demands.

Far from getting any international assistance, the negotiating strength of the Kurds was progressively undercut during the first half of 1991 by indications that a withdrawal of the coalition forces was imminent. It appeared that Saddam Hussein was merely stalling on any agreement until the foreign troops left. Kurdish leaders were still divided over the desirability of continuing negotiations at all or the extent to which a reduced set of demands might be acceptable if it was the most that could be achieved while the leverage of the foreign troop presence remained.

In June, following assurances that there was no firm schedule for the coalition withdrawal, further proposals were made by Saddam Hussein, including joint

---

[24] Keen at p. 92.

[25] Third Report of the Foreign Affairs Committee 1990-91, quoted in Keen at p.21.

[26] Freedman and Boren "'Safe Havens' for Kurds in post-war Iraq" in Rodley (ed.) To Loose the Bands of Wickedness (1992) at p.66 (hereinafter cited as "Freedman and Boren").

control of Kirkuk pending discussions about its future. According to a KDP spokesman, the agreement proposed would enable Kurds to return from abroad; families of killed or injured pesh merga would receive pensions; Kurdistan would benefit from Iraqi oil revenues and an urgent reconstruction program would be undertaken; elections in Kurdistan would be held within three months; and the leader of the Executive Council would hold a senior government post in Iraq. Free elections in Iraq, under a multi-party system with separate legislative, executive and parliamentary functions would be held within six months to a year and freedom of the press would be guaranteed.[27] The promises to hold multi-party elections in the whole of Iraq were viewed with particular suspicion, especially coupled with demands that the Kurds support the Ba'ath Party, hand over all heavy weapons, suspend the Kurdistan Front's broad-casting services and sever any foreign links. While Barzani still supported reaching an agreement, Talabani rejected it. In the following months negotiations wavered on, interrupted by periodic armed clashes, but broke down decisively in January 1992.

The Iraqi Government appears to be persisting in looking for opportunities to exploit internal divisions among the Kurdish political parties with offers of resuming negotiations. When internal conflict again erupted in Iraqi Kurdistan in early 1995, Baghdad radio reported that "the leadership is open-minded to accommodate and react to any serious national initiative". There can be little confidence, however, that further bilateral negotiations without any international support, input or guarantees can achieve a genuine and acceptable settlement between the Kurds and the Iraqi Government. The Kurds were, after all, probably in their strongest position to negotiate in 1991 the wake of the Gulf War, the adoption of Security Council Resolution 688 and with a heavy coalition military and a growing UN presence in northern Iraq. Yet it proved impossible to secure a satisfactory agreement, much less to have any confidence that the Iraqi Government by itself would fully implement it.

Had the international community intervened more constructively in 1991 to create the conditions for a negotiated settlement to be pursued under UN auspices and secured by international guarantees some further progress might have been possible. Instead, by limiting international intervention strictly to immediate physical protection and humanitarian relief, a valuable opportunity was lost leaving the Kurds in the uncertain and highly vulnerable position they find themselves in today.

---

[27] Ibid. at p.68 and footnotes accompanying text.

IV. THE ESTABLISHMENT OF THE SAFE HAVENS

The Kurds' struggle for protection of their rights and their efforts to secure an acceptable form of autonomy attracted little international interest or concern over the years. Shifting alliances with and support for the Iraqi Kurds at various times by other powers were dictated by wider political and strategic interests in the region rather than genuine concern for the situation of the Kurdish people. Even the shocking revelations of the chemical weapons attack on the town of Halabja in Iraqi Kurdistan in 1988, which left at least 5,000 dead, elicited no concerted international response or action. The crisis which finally forced the international community to confront the situation of the Iraqi Kurds head-on and which provoked the extraordinary measures for their international protection came only after the 1991 Gulf War and in response to a human tragedy of unimagined proportions.

IV.1 THE BUILDING OF A CRISIS

Iraq's bitter defeat following its invasion of Kuwait in August 1990 sparked off an extraordinary internal rebellion which began in the cities in the south of the country in March 1991. It spread like wild-fire among disaffected army units and civilians in an outpouring of hatred and frustration at the government. News of the rapidly spreading rebellion reached the northern Kurdish areas quickly. Demonstrations and armed clashes first broke out in Ranya, a township near Sulaimaniya, and rapidly spread to other areas. Thousands of Iraqi troops surrendered and many joined the uprising. By 19 March virtually all of Iraqi Kurdistan, including Sulaimaniya, Arbil, Dohuk and even Kirkuk, was under Kurdish control.

The uprising was integrally linked to the Gulf War. Human rights rhetoric and condemnations of Iraqi brutality had been prominent ever since Iraq's invasion of Kuwait; although the main focus was on violations related to the invasion, the history of internal repression and gross human rights violations committed by the Iraqi Government against its own people were very much in the spotlight. Suddenly it seemed that the world had woken up to the true nature of the Iraqi regime and was not prepared to stand by any longer. It has been noted that "it could not be ignored that the internal strife was in some respects a consequence of international military action, placing responsibility of a political and humanitarian character on the coalition to prevent massive attacks by Iraqi forces against non-combatants belonging to particular ethnic and religious communities".[28]

Although the coalition of governments that had led the military attack on Iraq vehemently denied that they had encouraged any internal rebellion, there were clearly expectations in and outside Iraq that the uprising would be encouraged and even supported from outside the country to force the surrender of the Iraqi Government itself and the ouster of Saddam Hussein. The now infamous remarks of President Bush on 15 February 1991 were reported in Iraq via the Voice of America:

> ...there's another way for the bloodshed to stop, and that is for the Iraqi military to take matters into their own hands to force Saddam Hussein, the dictator, to step aside.[29]

The Voice of Free Iraq radio, thought to be backed by the CIA, was also understood by some as encouraging rebellion.[30] At the very least, the defeat of Iraq and the widespread condemnation of Saddam Hussein gave the forces of opposition in Iraq, including the Kurds, new courage and resolve at a time when the Government had made itself an international pariah.

In fact, the uprising could not be sustained. It never took hold in Baghdad and the awaited outside support never materialised.[31] Instead Saddam Hussein found himself with a free hand to crush the internal rebellion. He proceeded to do so with characteristic ruthlessness and brutality, using heavy artillery, helicopter gunships and other weaponry.

The scale of this counter-offensive, fuelled undoubtably by the recent horrific experiences of many Kurds during the Anfal campaign, provoked a massive and rapid exodus of some 1.8 million refugees and displaced persons. The Iraqi crack-down began on 28 March; by mid-April there were over 450,000 refugees in Turkey and along the Turkish border and an influx of 1,400,000 refugees into Iran. The majority fled within a period of only 48 hours. According to the United Nations High Commissioner for Refugees, "[this] mass exodus

---

[28] Schachter "United Nations Law in the Gulf Conflict" 85 AJIL 452 (1991) at 469.

[29] Remarks made by Bush to the American Academy for the Advancement of Science reproduced, together with other statements by USA officials during the uprising, in Middle East Watch Endless Torment - the 1991 Uprising in Iraq and Its Aftermath (1992) at p.38 et seq.

[30] Keen at pp. 4-6.

[31] See Faleh 'Abd al-Jabbar "Why the Intifada Failed" in Hazleton (ed.) Iraq Since the Gulf War - Prospects for Democracy (1994).

35

represented the highest rate of influx in the 40 years of UNHCR's history".[32]

The situation of the refugees was desperate. Many had left in inadequate clothing without any possessions and were both terrified and utterly destitute. Appalling weather conditions, extreme cold, starvation and disease intensified the human tragedy; there were reports of up to 1,000 deaths per day in some camps.[33] Furthermore, the Western media in the area (who had been covering the Gulf war) were able to publish immediate live coverage and dramatic pictures of the desperate plight of the refugees, thereby generating a public outcry that demanded an exceptional response.

The urgency of the situation was exacerbated by two major factors. First the sheer scale and speed of the exodus; neither Turkey nor Iran was in a position to cope financially or logistically with the needs of close to two million refugees arriving within a matter of days. Secondly, Turkey was determined to prevent the influx of large numbers of Iraqi Kurds into its territory for fear that this would inflame unrest and instability among its own Kurdish population. It attempted to close its borders to the fleeing Iraqi Kurds and made it very clear that it was not prepared to accept the influx, still less to offer asylum. Although it was impossible to seal its borders completely, Turkey blocked attempts to provide refuge, assistance and aid to the refugees, leaving thousands stranded and exposed on the mountain sides in appalling conditions without any physical or legal protection. Such were the dimensions of the tragedy that finally prompted the international community to act.[34]

IV.2 ADOPTION OF SECURITY COUNCIL RESOLUTION 688

Iran, Turkey and France called for a meeting of the Security Council on 5 April to discuss the adoption of a resolution condemning the repression by the Iraqi Government of its own citizens. The resolution was submitted by Belgium and France and co-sponsored by the UK and the USA. Resolution 688 (1991) was eventually adopted by 10 votes - Cuba, Yemen and Zimbabwe voted against it while China and India abstained. Iraq lodged a formal protest against the resolution.

---

[32] UNHCR Report on Northern Iraq - April 1991 - May 1992 at para. 1.7 (hereinafter cited as the "UNHCR Report").

[33] According to official US figures, 13,000 Kurds died before reaching the safe havens. Keesing's Record of World Events, Vol 37 (1991) 38 at 308.

[34] Detailed accounts of the setting up of the safe havens can be found in Keen and in Freedman and Boren as well as in the Lawyers Committee for Human Rights Asylum Under Attack: A Report on the Protection of Iraqi Refugees and Displaced Persons One Year After the Humanitarian Emergency In Iraq (1992) (hereinafter cited as the "LCHR Report").

An opportunity was lost to tie this response to the latest atrocities directly into the package of conditions imposed on Iraqi following the Gulf War. Only two days before Resolution 688 was adopted, the Security Council had adopted Resolution 687 laying down the terms of the cease-fire with Iraq. This lengthy resolution, imposing stringent conditions on Iraq which included intrusive and extensive measures for on-going monitoring of its weapons capability, said not a word about human rights inside the country.

Resolution 688 dealt exclusively with Iraqi repression of its citizens and the urgent need for humanitarian assistance. The Resolution was not expressed to be adopted under Chapter VII of the UN Charter but it recalled in the preamble the Council's responsibilities for the maintenance of international peace and security and uses strong mandatory language.[35] Most importantly, it determined that the consequences of internal repression in Iraq, including in "Kurdish populated areas", amounted to a threat to international peace and security in the region. This finding established the necessary basis for the Security Council to take up the issue of internal repression and human rights violations inside Iraq.

The Resolution was strongly worded. Its first three operative paragraphs stated that the Security Council:

> 1. Condemns the repression of the Iraqi civilian population in many parts of Iraq, including most recently in Kurdish populated areas, the consequences of which threaten international peace and security in the region;
>
> 2. Demands that Iraq, as a contribution to removing the threat to international peace and security in the region, immediately end this repression and expresses the hope in the same context that an open dialogue will take place to ensure that the human and political rights of all Iraqi citizens are respected;
>
> 3. Insists that Iraq allow immediate access by international humanitarian organizations to all those in need of assistance in all parts of Iraq and to make available all necessary facilities for their operations.

The resolution also called for action by the UN. It requested the UN Secretary-

---

[35] Chapter VII of the UN Charter deals with "action with respect to threats to the peace, breaches of the peace and acts of aggression" and the provisions of resolutions adopted under it are mandatory and must be observed by all states. Enforcement measures, whether or not these involve armed force, must be taken under Chapter VII. Chapter VI deals with the pacific settlement of disputes and envisages non-coercive action by the Security Council in the form of recommendations.

General to pursue his humanitarian efforts in Iraq and to report on the plight of the Iraqis, in particular the Kurdish population. It further requested the Secretary-General to take action, using "all the resources at his disposal", to address urgently the critical needs of the refugees and displaced persons. It appealed to all other member states and humanitarian organizations to contribute to these relief efforts. Finally it stated that the Security Council would remain seized of the matter, thus retaining on its agenda the question of internal repression in Iraq and the provision of humanitarian assistance there.

Resolution 688 identified the threat to international peace and security to be the internal acts of repression by the Iraqi Government which had the consequence of generating a massive outflow of refugees towards and across international borders. It would appear from this that the threat must exist as long as internal repression continues, whether or not the transborder consequences have actually occurred. This gives Resolution 688 a continuing relevance today. As long as repression in Iraq is still going on, with a significant risk of a renewed exodus, a threat to international peace and security must remain and that threat ought to be addressed by the Security Council.

During the debate on the resolution a number of states on the Security Council raised concerns that the issues it addressed did not fall within the Council's competence and that the action amounted to interference in Iraq's domestic affairs. Article 2(7) of the UN Charter prohibits intervention in matters which are essentially within a state's domestic jurisdiction. However, it has long been accepted by the UN's human rights bodies that a state's human rights record is a matter of international concern and that international action in response to violations is legitimate. Although this position was not strongly defended in the Council debate, the finding of the threat to international peace and security established beyond doubt that this repression was within the Council's competence and could not be dismissed as falling within the internal affairs of Iraq nor immune from UN action. The resolution does refer to Charter Article 2(7) in the preamble of the resolution but it not clear what this was intended to signify; it could, for example, be taken as recalling that Article 2(7) cannot prejudice the application of any Chapter VII enforcement measures.[36]

---

[16] The Security Council has, on a few rare occasions, addressed human rights issues in certain contexts but generally such matters are understood to be within the competence of the General Assembly. There is no question, however, that the Security Council has authority to act if it is determined that there is a threat to international peace and security; indeed the UN Charter gives the Security Council the "primary responsibility" for the maintenance of international peace and security. For further discussion of the Council's debate on Resolution 688 see Alston "The Security Council and Human Rights: Lessons to be Learned from the Iraq-Kuwait Crisis and its Aftermath", 13 Aust.YBIL 107.

IV.3 THE ESTABLISHMENT OF THE SAFE HAVEN

The vast human exodus, the magnitude of the need for protection and relief, the inaccessibility of the mountainous areas where many had sought refuge and, in particular, Turkey's insistence that it would not formally grant the refugees any status in its territory created a seemingly insoluble legal and practical problem of unprecedented proportions.

Turkey is a signatory to the 1951 Convention Relating to the Status of Refugees but maintains the geographical restriction and does not recognize non-European asylum seekers as refugees. Turkey was unable to seal its borders completely and could not prevent the influx into its territory of thousands of refugees. Even so, Turkey would not permit these refugees to be processed or granted asylum and it obstructed the Office of the UN High Commissioner for Refugees (UNHCR) in the exercise of its protection functions.[37] Many more Kurds were left stranded in Iraq in desperate conditions; according to Turkish officials, at the height of the crisis there were 450,000 Iraqi Kurds inside Turkey and a further 250,000 camped on the Iraqi side of the border.

Iran was much more accommodating and did not prevent entry by the refugees that fled across its border but its resources were stretched to breaking point by the influx. Arranging international assistance in Iran was complicated by the bad state of relations between Iran and the Western countries and the fact that UNHCR had no formal relationship with the Iranian Government. The initial situation was chaotic and many of the refugees returned to Iraq before there was an opportunity for formal processing and registration. Although Iran stressed its willingness to grant asylum, conditions were difficult. There were reports of economic exploitation in some camps and of subtle intimidation to persuade the refugees either to return to Iraq or to move to camps deeper inside Iran. This forced the refugees "to make the unenviable choice between the extreme isolation of otherwise well-provisioned but heavily guarded and closed-off camps deep inside Iran, and the uncertain political situation that prevailed in northern Iraq".[38]

The international community was unprepared and ill-equipped to provide at such short notice the sheer volume of relief and assistance necessary. A large outflow of Kurdish refugees had, in fact, been predicted months before but the

---

[37] LCHR Report at pp. 30-42.

[38] Ibid. at p. 52.

numbers had been vastly underestimated and the preparations wholly inadequate. The task was made infinitely more difficult by the fact that so many of the Kurds were stranded in winter conditions in inaccessible mountainous areas which were almost impossible to reach by road. A huge relief operation - Operation Provide Comfort - was launched and from 7 April airlifts of supplies were dropped on both sides of the Turkish border. However, the relief operation was poorly organized and coordinated and airdrops were neither an adequate nor safe method of delivery of relief supplies.

It seemed imperative in all these circumstances to persuade the Kurds to return to Iraq where the necessary aid and assistance could be properly organized. Yet it was abundantly clear that those who had fled would not voluntarily return to Iraq of their own accord, no matter how terrible were the conditions of the make-shift camps and no matter how desperate their physical needs.

At an EC Summit meeting on 8 April the British Prime Minister, taking up a proposal made a week earlier by the Turkish President, called for the creation of UN-protected Kurdish enclaves in northern Iraq. Initially he suggested an area roughly equivalent to the whole Kurdish autonomous area, but this was later scaled down to a smaller area stretching from Zahko to Amadiya, reaching almost to Dohuk.[39] This proposal was finally taken up by the USA which announced on 16 April that a Combined Task Force of American, French and British troops would set up temporary encampments in northern Iraq where relief supplies could be distributed.

The plan was to establish six "zones of protection" or safe havens inside Iraq, protected by ground and air troops with supplies transported in from relief centres in Turkey. This called for a significant coalition military presence on Iraqi territory which amounted to almost 20,000 troops, the bulk of them from the USA, at the height of these operations. Iraq denounced the plan as "a serious, unjustifiable and unfounded attack on the sovereignty and territorial integrity of Iraq"[40] but the coalition governments made it clear that it would be imposed over Iraqi objections and that Iraq should not attempt to disrupt it. The USA reiterated its earlier prohibition of any Iraqi fixed- or rotary-wing aircraft flying north of the 36th parallel, thereby establishing a "no-fly" zone covering roughly half of the Kurdish autonomous area. Subsequently, when Iraqi military and paramilitary activity in the designated area threatened to undermine

---

[39] McDowall The Kurds - A Nation Denied (Minority Rights Group 1992) at p. 118.

[40] Letter to the UN Secretary-General, UN Doc. S/22513.

the operation, Iraq was given a 48-hour deadline to withdraw from the security zone with the threat of forcible expulsion if necessary.[41]

The establishment of the safe havens placed a significant area of northern Iraq under effective foreign military control. The protected area was progressively extended, as it had to be if the Kurds were to be persuaded to return to their homes. Coalition troops, encountering no resistance as Iraqi forces were pushed back, extended the zone north of the 36th parallel to some 40 kilometres east from Zakho to Sirsensk, including all territory within 30 kilometres of this line. To the south the zone extended to a ridge line north of the city of Dohuk.[42]

The coalition governments asserted that they were motivated only by humanitarian concerns and were acting in a manner "consistent" with Resolution 688 and in close cooperation with the UN. A military operation was said to be necessary in order to act with the required speed, but it was stressed that this was a temporary measure until the UN could take over the relief operation, the administration of the camps and the provision of security. US President Bush was at pains to stress the limited aims of the operation:

> The approach is quite simple: if we cannot get adequate food, medicine, clothing and shelter to the Kurds living in the mountains along the Turkish-Iraq border, we must encourage the Kurds to move to areas in northern Iraq where the geography facilitates, rather than frustrates, such a large-scale relief effort.
>
> Consistent with United Nations Security Council Resolution 688 and working closely with the United Nations and other international organizations and with our European partners, I have directed the US military to begin immediately to establish several encampments in northern Iraq where relief supplies for these refugees will be made available in large quantities and distributed in an orderly manner...adequate security will be provided at these temporary sites by US, British and French air and ground forces, again consistent with United Nations Security Council Resolution 688...I want to underscore that all we are doing is motivated by humanitarian concerns....[43]

The UN Secretary-General was more reticent about the plan which seemed to him to go beyond the scope of Resolution 688. He refused a request for the

---

[41] Freedman and Boren at p. 58.

[42] Ibid. at p. 59.

[43] News Conference, 16 April 1991, USIA, 18 April 1991, quoted in Freedman and Boren at p. 54.

coalition troops to be given official status as a UN peace-keeping force and there was initially confusion about what the UN's role in the operation would be.[44] The UN was anyway operating on a somewhat different but parallel track. UN officials had already been carrying out needs assessment missions of the situation in the whole country in the after-math of the Gulf War but their estimates had to be radically revised to take account of the urgent needs which had arisen in the north. The UN negotiated an agreement with the Iraqi Government in the form of a Memorandum of Understanding signed on 18 April. This established the basis for the UN to undertake a huge humanitarian operation. There was still uncertainty, however, as to whether the UN would take over responsibility for the camps set up and provisioned by coalition troops. UNHCR officials finally arrived in Zakho at the end of April and gradually the UN assumed responsibility for the camps in the safe havens as well as extending the relief operation throughout much of Iraqi Kurdistan.

IV.4 THE REFUGEES AND DISPLACED RETURN HOME

As soon as the safe havens plan was under way, strenuous efforts were made to encourage the refugees and displaced to return. The refugees began to return at the end of April. By May 250,000 had returned from Turkey and Iran and by the end of September, 90% of the Iraqi Kurds had returned, "marking the fastest rate of return in UNHCR's experience".[45]

Many factors facilitated the return - the extreme physical hardship; the intransigence of Turkey in not granting asylum; the resumption of negotiations on autonomy between the Kurdish leaders and the Iraqi Government; and the deliberate provisioning of most relief supplies inside Iraq. However, by far the most immediate and persuasive factor was the direct encouragement to return, particularly by military personnel, the assurances of safety and the highly visible presence in Iraq of the foreign troops and UN personnel. UNHCR clearly stated in its report that the "purpose of the coalition's intervention was to deliver assistance to the Kurds...and to <u>induce a perception of security for their repatriation</u>" (emphasis added).[46] "Blue routes" of return were mapped out for those who could walk, with relief and medical supplies provided along the way. A heavily armed soldier rode with the trucks taking other refugees back. Commmunity leaders were sometimes taken on ahead to verify for their

---

[44] Freedman and Boren at pp. 59-61.

[45] UNHCR Report at para. 1.11.

[46] Ibid. at para.1.8.

communities the absence of Iraqi forces and the foreign military and UN presence in the area. Leaflets and loudspeakers were used to encourage people to return. UNHCR was even somewhat wary of the enthusiastic efforts of the military and one official told the Lawyers Committee for Human Rights, "The US military was very goal-oriented. Each day they would say, 'Today, so many people will return".[47]

The fact that the return was conditioned on a secure environment protected from Iraqi military activity was further evidenced by the significant slowing down of the rate of the return and renewed mass flight whenever there were fresh attacks by Iraqi forces in the Kurdish areas. In October and December 1991, for example, 200,000 people were displaced in Sulaimaniya and Arbil governorates and a further 40,000 in the Arbil area in March 1992 following Iraqi attacks.[48] The refugees also refused to go to government-controlled areas of the collective towns and established cities that fell outside the security zone, despite attempts to target supplies in certain areas to persuade people to return there. UNHCR admitted that:

> The presence of military forces, in what are referred to as "government-controlled areas", has been one of the most important factors influencing the reintegration of returnees and displaced persons in the country. The primary effect of this state of affairs was that between 30 per cent and 60 per cent of the population refused, at one time or another, to return to their places of origin; in government-controlled collective towns or, as in the case of Kirkuk and Khanaquin, to cities. As of mid-March 1992, it was estimated that between 400,000 -500,000 persons in northern Iraq were internally displaced.[49]

This, then, was no ordinary voluntary repatriation of refugees. In a typical voluntary repatriation refugees essentially agree to return to their own country and to live under the authority of their own government. In this case most of the refugees agreed - and were expressly encouraged - to return to Iraqi territory but only on condition that they were offered continued international protection from their own government. Indeed, to have forced them to return to live under Iraqi authority would have amounted to a gross violation of the fundamental principle of <u>non-refoulement</u>. This principle of customary international law, which also forms part of the 1951 Refugee Convention, absolutely prohibits the

---

[47] LCHR report at p. 38.

[48] UNHCR Report at para 1.14.

[49] Ibid. at paras. 1.8 and 1.13.

return of refugees to any country where they may fear persecution and is the cornerstone of the international system for the protection of refugees.

It was also clear that neither the UN nor the coalition governments believed that it was safe to remove international protection for the Iraqi Kurds once the bulk of them had returned home. It was recognized that longer-term measures of security would have to be provided if a renewed exodus was to be avoided. The UK Foreign Secretary stated on 17 June "We went into northern Iraq in order to persuade the Kurds to come down from the mountains - to save lives. We don't want the operation to end in a way that will merely re-create the same problem".[50] The USA was particularly anxious not to commit its ground troops inside Iraq for a long period, but even it was persuaded that the coalition forces could only be withdrawn when alternative international security arrangements were in place. However imperfect these might be, they have been maintained to this day.

IV.5 INTERNATIONAL SECURITY FOR IRAQI KURDISTAN

Initially there was recognition that the emergency intervention had to be followed by a political settlement. The Kurds, who had resumed negotiations on autonomy with the Iraqi Government after the establishment of the safe havens, were calling for an agreement to be backed by international guarantees. The UK Government considered that the coalition forces must be replaced by UN forces and that a satisfactory autonomy agreement had to be concluded between the Kurds and Saddam Hussein, backed by the maintenance of UN sanctions until it was clear that the Government was respecting the agreement and with the threat of retaliatory measures against further repression. It was reported UK officials even proposed that these conditions should be given international status and registered with the UN.[51] The EU states also declared that "it would be appropriate for the international community to give its support to [a satisfactory autonomy] agreement on the basis of Resolution 688 of the Security Council".[52] In the event, the Kurds were left to pursue their negotiations alone and these eventually broke down altogether by 1992.

Continued security, however, remained a high priority. The difficulty was to determine how it should be arranged. Iraq made clear that it was adamantly

---

[50] Freedman and Boren at p. 71.

[51] Ibid.

[52] European Council Declaration on the Situation in Iraq, Luxembourg, 28-29 June 1991.

opposed to any UN military force that might replace the coalition troops. Eventually a two-pronged protection plan was put in place consisting of a coalition rapid reaction force on stand-by in Turkey and the deployment of a UN Guards Contingent to provide security for the humanitarian aid program. This paved the way finally for the withdrawal of most of the coalition forces from Iraqi territory in mid-July 1991.

These special security arrangements, which have been scaled down but essentially maintained to this day, are of great significance for the Kurds and have undoubtably had an important deterrent effect on Iraqi military activity. In the wider context of international sanctions and the other package of conditions imposed on Iraq by the Security Council, the security measures have maintained the special status of Iraqi Kurdistan and have been a major factor in its emergence as a de facto autonomous area. In practice, however, there are severe limitations to the protection provided and it has been insufficient to prevent conflict and attacks arising from various sources which have intensified the general instability and climate of fear and uncertainty in the area.

IV.5.1 OPERATION POISED HAMMER

The coalition governments first decided to position a 5,000 strong rapid reaction force in Turkey backed by air support. However, that force was first halved in size and then withdrawn completely in September 1991, leaving only a Combined Task Force (involving the USA, the UK, France and Turkey) to undertake air patrols. The Task Force polices the no-fly zone, which remains in force, and undertakes daily patrol flights north of the 36th parallel. It operates from Incirlik air base in Turkey. The coalition military presence was not undertaken directly pursuant to a Security Council resolution and is not a security operation under UN auspices. It is under the control of the countries that contribute to it and its use of the Incirlik airbase is subject to approval every six months by the Turkish Parliament. In December 1992, as a concession to Turkish public opinion at the time, a further clause was added which has given the Turkish Cabinet the right to revoke the agreement at any time. Turkey has military observers on all the coalition flights and has been in a position to give consent and impose conditions on specific military actions under the agreement.[53]

In addition a small coalition military presence - the Military Coordination Centre (MCC) - was left inside Iraq based in Zakho and still remains there. It

---

[53] During the confrontation between the allies and Iraq in January 1993, for example, Turkey made it clear that allied planes should only strike in immediate self-defence, Keen at p. 16.

consists of a number of military officers who keep an eye on Iraqi military activity and provide a certain coordination and intelligence function. Their activities are largely confined to the security zone.

IV.5.2 THE UN GUARDS CONTINGENT

In the face of the Iraqi Government's adamant refusal to agree to a UN military presence to take over when the coalition forces withdrew, the UN Guards Contingent was devised as a compromise security measure to operate inside Iraq. These lightly armed security guards were deployed with Iraqi agreement in the form of an annex to the earlier Memorandum of Understanding, signed on May 25 1991. Initially provision was made for 500 guards but this was reduced to 300 in 1992 when the third Memorandum of Understanding was signed. In practice the actual numbers deployed have fluctuated wildly over the past four years. The Guards were intended to take the place of the coalition ground forces but clearly a few hundred security guards could not fill the vacuum left by a coalition troop strength that had topped 20,000 at the height of the operation.

Whereas the coalition forces went in to secure the safe havens and to protect those returning, the mandate of the Guards Contingent is much more limited. They provide a visible UN security presence but they do not provide direct protection to the Kurdish people. Their primary task is to guard UN personnel and property and to provide security for the operation of the humanitarian aid programme. They are to ensure a safe passage for relief trucks, maintain a communications network and gather information on security incidents. For the most part they are armed security guards, rather than professional trained military or police personnel; in fact the first members of the Contingent were seconded security guards from UN headquarters in New York. They carry only light side-arms supplied by the Iraqis. Under the original agreement Guards were supposed to deployed anywhere in Iraq in connection with the humanitarian programme but their deployment has not been permitted in certain strategic areas, such as the south of the country.

In June 1991 the UN Secretary-General suggested that this "innovative" move would serve another function as a monitoring operation. He described the Guards as "a contingent of veritable 'humanitarian witnesses' whose task will be to ensure the smooth conduct of operations and the security of field personnel who are to carry them out and, as necessary, to prepare reports on any incidents affecting beneficiaries of United Nations programmes".[54] This was echoed by the Secretary-General's Executive Delegate heading the humanitarian programme when he said that, while the Guards would not intervene in law enforcement issues that do not involve UN resources, "any security or safety related incident will be reported on rapidly and communicated through United Nations channels".[55] The Guards Contingent was also held out as a solution by various UN officials in response to Amnesty International's call in July 1991 for a full-scale human rights monitoring operation in the northern area to protect the Kurds when the coalition forces withdrew. However, the Guards have had no explicit mandate, no human rights experience or training and none of the necessary language skills to monitor human rights. Their functions have never been integrated with the UN Special Rapporteur on Iraq (despite his repeated plea for monitors which has been endorsed by the Commission and the General Assembly) and their reports to the UN are confidential and can serve no purpose in exposing or addressing violations.

Deployment of the guards was slow to be implemented and their numbers have varied widely. The first 10 Guards went into Iraq on 19 May, before the agreement with Iraq on their deployment was signed. Only 60 were in place by June 1991. In anticipation of the withdrawal of coalition troops that July, the Guards Contingent was strengthened with further funding and manpower but they only reached full strength in October that year. By December 1991 their numbers had again fallen to 356 and at the beginning of September 1992 only 77 remained in the northern area and these had dropped to a derisory 30 a month later. By February 1993 they were back up to a total of 260 in the whole of Iraq, although the maximum agreed deployment was reduced to 300 in the third Memorandum of Understanding signed in October 1992. The latest UN Inter-Agency report in October 1994 indicated that their numbers have again fallen considerably to only 148 and UN officials anticipated that it would drop further. Their numbers have fluctuated both according to the level of funding available to the humanitarian programme and the state of relations with the Iraqi Government and its willingness to grant the required visas.

IV.5.3 LIMITATIONS OF THE INTERNATIONAL SECURITY MEASURES[56]

The coalition military presence in the area is not mandated by the UN Security Council but is an initiative dependent on the countries that contribute to it. The

---

[54] Statement by the Secretary-General of 12 June 1991, SG/SM/4574.

[55] Office of the Executive Delegate of the Secretary-General for a United Nations Inter-Agency Humanitarian Programme for Iraq, Kuwait and the Iraq/Turkey and Iraq/Iran border areas, Updated Appeal, 12 June 1991.

[56] For a more detailed analysis of the limits of international protection in Iraqi Kurdistan see Keen, Chapter 2.

required periodic renewal of Turkish authorization for the use of its air base adds to its uncertainty and renders the protection hostage to Turkish domestic politics and a largely hostile public opinion as well as to the state of Turkish relations with its Western allies, with other regional powers and, of course, with Iraq.

The coalition protection only extends to a small part of Iraqi Kurdistan. The MCC is confined essentially to the original safe haven security zone while the no fly zone only operates north of the 36th parallel. Even in these areas this type of military presence has limited capacity for protection. A no-fly zone alone would be no match for a determined onslaught by the Iraqi military on the ground, as is clearly demonstrated by the situation in the south of the country, where large-scale military attacks and massive human rights violations have continued despite the no-fly zone in force south of the 32nd parallel since 1992.

The capacity of the UN Guards Contingent for effective protection is equally limited. Their deployment is based on agreement with Iraq which has refused since March 1993 to renew the Memorandum of Understanding. Although Iraq has continued to grant the necessary visas and otherwise to permit deployment of the Guards, this 'cooperation' could be withdrawn at any time. The Guards' mandate is limited to protection only in relation to the UN aid programme and they are ill-equipped and untrained for a wider protection function. There appears to be uncertainty as to when they may use the light weapons they carry and they have been unable to defend themselves or others, such as non-governmental personnel, from terrorist attacks. On the contrary it has been observed that "in many ways, the guards have proved a useful and easily identifiable target for Baghdad-inspired terrorism".[57] Some non-governmental organizations have been concerned that the presence of the Guards has made their own personnel more vulnerable to attack and have preferred to use their own locally-recruited security guards.

The security situation in the north of Iraq has been highly precarious over the past four years. There have been numerous instances of attacks against UN personnel, the international aid agencies and journalists. Some individuals have been victims of targeted assassinations or killed or injured in bomb attacks against offices and vehicles. A 1994 UN Inter-Agency Report recorded 100 security incidents between January 1992 and July 1994. There has also been a number of other serious incidents aimed more generally at the local population. In January 1993, for example, a car bomb exploded in the centre of Arbil, killing

---

[57] Keen at p. 18.

11 and injuring 128 as well as destroying shops. More recently in February 1995 in Zakho, the hub of the security zone and the base of the MCC, a huge car bomb exploded causing the death of between 54 and 80 people and injuring dozens more. The PUK, suspected of involvement in this attack in a KDP stronghold, blamed the Iraqi Government.[58]

It has not been possible to identify those responsible for such attacks in all cases and certainly in-fighting between Kurdish political groups has greatly added to the general climate of insecurity. The Special Rapporteur on Iraq has, however, noted evidence of Iraqi Government involvement in a number of attacks. After the recent killing of a journalist and her Kurdish bodyguard in April 1994, for example, two people were arrested and confessed to acting on behalf of the Iraqi intelligence services in carrying out the killing and other terrorist attacks in the north. They said they had been offered payment and their families had been held hostage.[59] Wherever responsibility lies, the fact remains that the international security measures have not been capable of preventing these incidents.

International security measures have also not been capable of securing the area against more overt Iraqi military activity. In July 1991 renewed clashes between Iraqi troops and Kurdish pesh merga resulted in displacements of between 40,000 - 100,000 people. Others were forcibly removed from their homes in Kirkuk in a continuation of the "arabization" programme. Fighting worsened as negotiations on autonomy broke down and another mass exodus seemed imminent. A cease-fire was agreed in October but was violated almost immediately when the Iraqis began shelling the towns of Kifri, Kalar and Maydan. There have been periodic reports of threatening Iraqi troop build-ups on the internal demarcation line. Villages and agricultural property near this border have been shelled by Iraqi troops. Iraqi military attacks in Arbil and Kirkuk and on a number of collective villages in the spring of 1992 caused tens of thousands to flee their homes. Kirkuk, still under Iraqi Government control, is particularly vulnerable and the repression that continues there has caused further displacements as people have fled. Renewed attacks by the Iraqi military have again been reported inside the security zone in March 1995.

It is not only Iraq which has violated security. Bombing raids and border attacks have been carried out periodically by both Iranian and Turkish forces in Iraqi

---

[58] "Car Bomb kills 70 amid feuding by Iraq Kurd factions" The Times, 28 February 1995.

[59] UN Doc. A/47/651 at paras. 78-79.

Kurdistan since 1991. These have been directed against suspected bases of Turkish and Iranian Kurdish separatists but have also killed and injured civilians, impeded resettlement and generally have a highly destabilizing effect. In August 1991 the Turkish Government set up a three-mile buffer zone inside Iraq, taking advantage of the security vacuum in the north. The Turkish Prime Minister said:

> There is no authority in north Iraq. We can't stay disinterested. We are establishing a three-mile zone. Turkish military aircraft will attack anyone who comes into the area...Turkey is going to declare the zone to all the world.[60]

As its attacks escalated, with the reported use of napalm bombs and the targeting of civilian areas, the KDP leader protested that "these are centres of civilian population and do not contain armed groups". At least three of the villages attacked on that occasion were in the coalition security zone. No steps have been taken to prevent such attacks or to protect the population. Turkish and Iranian military activity inside Iraq has continued to be reported. In November 1994, for example, Iraq accused Iran of firing Scud missiles into a camp used by Mujahideen Khalq guerrillas, calling this "an aggression against Iraq" and adding that "Iraq reserves its full right of legitimate defence in the face of unjust Iranian aggression".[61] In fact, although Iraq has protested these periodic attacks and incursions into its territory by Turkey and Iran, the international protection of the area prevents it from taking any measures to repel these attacks and no steps have been taken by the coalition governments to protect the inhabitants.

Finally, internal conflicts between Kurdish groups have also claimed lives, undermined security and stability and impeded the humanitarian program. The UN reported that during the May 1994 clashes both sides had given assurances that UN and NGOs would not be targeted. However, the primary concern of the UN was the protection of its personnel and the aid program; no measures were taken to protect the local population from the cross-fire and other effects of the conflict.

IV.6 IRAQ WITHDRAWS AND IMPOSES AN EMBARGO ON THE KURDS

As the refugees and displaced returned home in 1991 and began to rebuild their lives, negotiations were continuing between Kurdish leaders and Saddam

---

[60] Freedman and Boren at pp. 77-78.

[61] "Iran attacks guerrillas inside Iraq", Reuters report, 6 November 1994.

Hussein in an attempt to forge a new autonomy agreement. The Kurds were particularly anxious to secure the terms of an agreement, backed by international guarantees, before the coalition forces withdrew. The Government was equally anxious to delay an agreement until foreign troops were removed from the area. In July the Government proclaimed a series of amnesties to encourage normalization of the situation, although previous experience of such amnesties had left the Kurds highly suspicious of such moves. Any confidence that the Government was genuinely willing to reach a new accommodation with the Kurds was further eroded by renewed clashes between Iraqi forces and Kurdish pesh merga. These continued between April and October 1991, despite the clear warnings to Iraq to cease military aggression in the area and not to disrupt the return of the refugees and displaced. They provoked renewed displacements as people fled from the fighting.

Then, in an abrupt change of tactics, Iraq began to withdraw its forces on 20 October from the three northern governorates of Arbil, Dohuk and Sulaimaniya, although not from Kirkuk or Mosul. A few days later it also withdrew its entire civil administration from the area, effectively halting all public services. Civil servants were ordered to relocate under threat of losing their salaries and pensions; those who did not comply lost their livelihood. The Kurdish opposition alliance, the Iraqi Kurdistan Front, stepped into the administrative vacuum and exercised governmental authority until new administrative and legislative structures were set up following the holding of democratic elections in 1992 (see Section VI below).

At the same time Iraq imposed a severe punitive economic embargo on the area which has been maintained and progressively tightened ever since. This has had a particularly harsh impact in a region already devastated by years of conflict where economic and social needs are acute. The embargo was imposed just as winter was setting in and extended to medical supplies, foodstuffs, gasoline and heating oil. Government food rations were cut to only 10% of the amount given to other citizens. In May 1993 the Government withdrew from circulation the 25 dinar bank note. Elsewhere in the country Iraqis could exchange the obsolete notes but those in the Kurdish area, sealed off from the rest of the country, could not and consequently lost about a half of their wealth in Iraqi currency. This was followed in August 1993 by the cutting off of the electricity supply to Dohuk, affecting water and health facilities particularly badly.[62] The embargo has been enforced through armed check-points on every route along the border separating the area under Kurdish control from the rest of the country. No humanitarian

---

[62] UN Doc. A/48/600 at paras. 72-76.

exceptions have been permitted. This has left the Iraqi Kurds suffering under a "double embargo" of the combined effects of UN sanctions, applicable to Iraq as a whole, and the internal embargo and has deepened their dependency on humanitarian aid.[63]

IV.7 THE LEGAL BASIS FOR ESTABLISHING THE SAFE HAVENS

While the moral necessity of the international action to establish the safe havens and to secure the return of the refugees and displaced has not been in question, there are serious questions about the legal basis for it. The questions arise primarily in connection with the coalition's military intervention. The UN humanitarian aid programme, including the deployment of the UN Guards, was negotiated with and agreed to by Iraq in the Memorandum of Understanding and its supplementary annex. These actions were also probably consistent with the authority given to the Secretary-General under the terms of Resolution 688 to pursue his humanitarian efforts using all the resources at his disposal.

Military intervention by states in the territory or affairs of another state is generally prohibited. Article 2(4) of the UN Charter prohibits the threat or use of force by UN member states against the territorial integrity or political independence of another state. Article 51 preserves the right of individual or collective self-defence by states but only if an armed attack occurs against a member state and only until the Security Council takes measures to maintain peace and security. It is a matter of some dispute as to whether general international law permits humanitarian intervention - that is forcible intervention by states in the territory of another state for humanitarian purposes. Desirable though it may be for such a concept to be developed in carefully defined circumstances, it is fairly widely acknowledged that at the present time the Charter provisions limiting the use of force, relevant international rulings and decisions and the evidence of state practice probably militate against a recognized right of unilateral humanitarian intervention. Some international lawyers do consider, however, that such intervention may be legitimate, even if there are few, if any, "pure" examples of the exercise of it by states.[64]

Any right or duty of humanitarian intervention is certainly not yet clearly established as a principle of international law, although there may be some basis

[63] In September 1992 when the Turkish Kurdish Workers Party (PKK) imposed a de facto embargo on the Turkish border the Iraqi Kurds suffered what they termed a "triple embargo".

[64] See Rodley "Collective intervention to protect human rights" in Rodley (ed.) To Loose the Bands of Wickedness (1992). In his examination of the question he summarises the arguments for and against these two positions and refers to some of the other major contributions to this much-debated subject.

for arguing that such a concept is beginning to emerge and gain wider acceptance. Although international action in Iraqi Kurdistan may be one of the very few examples of a more "pure" form of humanitarian intervention (although wider strategic interests certainly underpinned it), it has not generally been accepted as providing a sufficient precedent for nor an example of a generally accepted norm of international law.[65] In any event, the coalition governments did not seek to rely on any general right or duty to intervene, but linked their action to Security Council Resolution 688.

The US was at pains to stress that the safe haven operation was carried out purely for humanitarian reasons and was "consistent" with Security Council Resolution 688. It was to be undertaken in close cooperation with the UN which was expected to take over the whole operation, including security provision, as soon as possible.

It is, of course, open to the Security Council to authorize enforcement action by member states under Chapter VII of the Charter when it determines that a threat to international peace and security exists. Although Resolution 688 did determine that such a threat existed in respect of Iraq, that Resolution did not appear authorize any enforcement measures by other states. First, it is even doubtful that Resolution 688 was adopted under Chapter VII, a condition precedent for a resolution envisaging enforcement measures. Although it is not unknown for the Security Council to act under Chapter VII without specifying this expressly, the fact that Resolution 688 was not stated to have been adopted pursuant to Chapter VII was a notable omission when almost all the preceding resolutions adopted in respect of Iraq had clearly stated that the Council was acting under Chapter VII. Second, Resolution 688 contained none of the usual open-ended formulations that would permit "all necessary measures" to be taken to enforce it. Only the Secretary-General had been urged to use "all resources at his disposal" to address the needs of the Iraqi population and he certainly did not interpret this, without more, as authorizing any UN enforcement measures. Otherwise there was only an appeal to other states to contribute to the relief efforts.

The question of enforcement measures was not addressed during the debate on the adoption of Resolution 688 as this pre-dated the plan to set up the safe havens in Iraq. However, the doubts about the nature of the resolution expressed by a number of countries during the debate suggest that not only did

---

[65] See, for example, Alston, n. 36 above, and Roberts "Humanitarian war: military intervention and human rights" Int'l Aff. 69, 3 (1993) 429.

most countries certainly not interpret or understand the Resolution to authorize enforcement measures, but that they would not have agreed to this had the issue been put before them.

It might be argued that Resolution 688 could be linked to earlier resolutions, either to bring it under the umbrella of Chapter VII or to tie it to enforcement measures that had already been authorized. Resolution 678 (1990), for example, authorized member states "to use all necessary means to uphold and implement Resolution 660 (1990) and all subsequent relevant resolutions and to restore international peace and security in the area". However, again in a break from the usual pattern of the Council's other resolutions on Iraq, Resolution 688 did not refer to any preceding resolutions in its preamble.

It might also be argued that Iraq eventually consented, at least by acquiesence, to the coalition's intervention. Iraq had protested against Resolution 688 and also lodged a forceful protest against the military intervention by the coalition forces. However, in its April letter to the UN Secretary-General, calling the action an attack on its sovereignty and territorial integrity, Iraq stated that, while it opposed the safe haven operation, it had not hindered it:

> because it is not opposed to the provision of humanitarian assistance to Iraqi citizens who are in need of it and because it wishes to avoid any complication that may prevent the return of all Iraqi citizens in security to their places of residence.[66]

This is rather a thin basis on which to ground "consent". The threats of forcible military action against it if it interfered with the operation left Iraq very little choice. While it agreed to the UN's humanitarian aid programme in the Memorandum of Understanding, Iraq refused to consider any UN military presence on its territory to replace the coalition forces and continued to make clear its absolute opposition to the military intervention. In a further letter to the UN on 14 May it said:

> The United States and the European States cooperating with it...have brought their armed forces into northern Iraq on the pretext that resolution 688 authorizes them to engage in such obvious military intervention in the internal affairs of Iraq and to violate its territorial integrity. This claim could not be farther from the truth, and the resolution does not grant any party any such authorization.[67]

---

[66] UN Doc. S/22513.

[67] UN Doc. S/22599.

An examination of the strict legality of the initial establishment of the safe havens is, in some respects, primarily of historical interest. The bulk of the coalition forces withdrew in 1991 and the UN assumed responsibility for the humanitarian programme and deployed the Guards Contingent on the basis of its agreement with Iraq. Iraq itself withdrew from most of the northern area in October 1991 and so far has not made any determined overt attempts to regain control by force or otherwise. Only Iraq continues to protest the no-fly zone and the overflights of its territory by the coalition Task Force.

These issues do still have importance and relevance for the future protection of Iraqi Kurdistan, however. First, existing protection rests on an unstable legal foundation. This is of particular concern given that Iraq has refused to renew the Memorandum of Understanding with the UN since early 1993. It also makes the protection measures much more open and vulnerable to challenge, which may well happen as pressure builds to lift sanctions and normalise international relations with Iraq. Secondly, it is clear that Resolution 688 was stretched to its furthest limits as the basis for the action taken in 1991. It is difficult to conceive that it could again be invoked as the basis for more extensive measures. While the determination in Resolution 688 of a threat to international peace and security ought to be sufficient to keep Iraqi Kurdistan very much on the Security Council agenda, a new comprehensive UN plan of action will almost certainly require further Security Council authorization. Difficult though this may be to obtain, it is the nettle that must be grasped in order to move from an ad hoc crisis response to a long-term political settlement backed by effective and durable international protection.

V. THE INTERNATIONAL HUMANITARIAN AID PROGRAMME

V.1 HUMANITARIAN NEEDS OF THE IRAQI POPULATION

In the immediate aftermath of the Gulf War Iraq faced a desperate economic situation. Eight years of war with Iran had already taken a heavy toll on the country. Several days after Iraq's initial invasion of Kuwait comprehensive mandatory sanctions were imposed by the Security Council in Resolution 661 (1990) which were maintained as part of the cease-fire conditions in Resolution 687 (1991). Only the importation of medical supplies, foodstuffs and other humanitarian supplies to meet essential civilian needs are exempted from the sanctions regime.

The impact of sanctions has been heavy on a country which, even in a good year, imports 70% of its of its food needs and is dependent on oil exports as its primary source of revenue.[68] The situation was exacerbated by the massive destruction of infrastructure during the Gulf War in January and February 1991. The internal uprisings in March 1991 and the Iraqi counter-offensive resulted in further damage and destruction, on a scale "comparable or even greater" than the Gulf War, according to one UN report.[69] Under-Secretary-General Ahtisaari stated after his mission to Iraq:

> the recent conflict has wrought near-apocalyptic results upon the economic infrastructure of what had been, until January 1991, a rather highly urbanized and mechanized society. Now most means of modern life support have been destroyed or rendered tenuous. Iraq has, for some time to come, been relegated to a pre-industrial age, with all the disabilities of a post-industrial dependency on an intensive use of energy and technology.[70]

Staple foods were at critically low levels or exhausted and essential commodities were rationed at less than subsistence levels. Many families did not have access to rations and food prices had hugely increased, reflecting shortages and

---

[68] See generally Abbas Alnasrawi "Economic Devastation, Underdevelopment and Outlook" in Hazleton (ed.) Iraq Since the Gulf War - Prospects for Democracy (1994).

[69] Report of the Inter-Agency Mission headed by the Executive Delegate for Iraq, Kuwait and the Iraq/Turkey and Iraq/Iran border areas from 29 June - 13 July 1991, UN Doc. S/22799.

[70] For "security reasons", Ahtisaari's mission was not able to travel to areas in the north or the south of the country but it considered it likely that conditions were at least the same, if not "substantially worse in some locations".

transportation difficulties. There were acute shortages of fuel. Water supplies were heavily polluted and all electrically-operated installations had ceased to function. Garbage was not collected and sewage treatment plants were virtually at a stand-still. Health conditions were precarious and the oil and electricity sectors were virtually paralysed. Livestock farming was badly affected and imported seed stocks had been destroyed or exhausted. The agricultural sector and internal transportation was further threatened by lack of fuel and spare parts for machinery. Communications networks no longer functioned, affecting many other aspects of daily life. Social support and care systems were badly disrupted and there was a homeless potential of 72,000 persons following the destruction of houses.

Following the UN's grim assessment, the UN Sanctions Committee determined that "humanitarian circumstances apply with respect to the entire civilian population of Iraq in all parts of Iraq's national territory". In addition to food and medical supplies, already exempt from sanctions under a simple notification procedure, essential civilian and humanitarian imports integrally related to the supply of foodstuffs and medical supplies would also be permitted, subject to a "no-objection" supervisory procedure.

When the mass exodus of refugees and displaced persons took place in March 1991, Security Council Resolution 688 (1991) immediately called on the Secretary-General to pursue his humanitarian efforts in Iraq and to report on the plight of the Iraqi population, particularly the Kurds. It authorized him to use all the resources at his disposal to address the critical needs of the refugees and displaced and appealed to other states and humanitarian organizations to contribute to the relief effort.

As a result of this new emergency the needs already identified were radically revised upwards in a hugely expanded humanitarian program. On 8 April the Secretary-General made an Emergency Humanitarian Appeal for Iraq of US $178 million. This was only to address minimal immediate needs for the coming six months and aimed at the most vulnerable sectors of the population. Within three days of the first appeal, however, the number of refugees in the region had tripled and a new Appeal was made on 12 April for US $400.2 million for refugees and displaced persons on the borders of Iraq and Turkey and in Iran. The two Appeals were consolidated on 15 May and, on 12 June, a revised and updated appeal issued for US $448.9 million.

V.2 THE MEMORANDUM OF UNDERSTANDING

Although the country was in desperate straits, Iraq was highly reluctant to agree to a significant international presence on its territory. Resolution 688, however, insisted that Iraq allow immediate access by humanitarian organizations to all those in need and that it facilitate an aid operation. The UN opened negotiations with Iraq and on 18 April a Memorandum of Understanding was signed by the UN and Iraq as the operating basis for a humanitarian assistance programme throughout the country.

This first Memorandum of Understanding recorded that the Iraqi Government "welcomed" the UN's efforts to promote the voluntary return of the refugees and displaced. Iraq pledged support and cooperation to the UN in the operation and supervision of the humanitarian aid programme. It agreed to facilitate the access of UN staff to all parts of the country where assistance was required. Under the agreement a high level UN official was based in Baghdad as Coordinator of the Programme and UN humanitarian centres (UNHUCS) and sub-offices, staffed by UN civilian personnel and staff co-opted from non-governmental humanitarian organizations, were set up. These were to take charge of the provision of humanitarian assistance and organize routes of return with relief supplies for refugees and the displaced. The safe passage of supplies was to be guaranteed as well as the impartial provision of assistance for all those in need. The Memorandum also provided that other intergovernmental organizations and NGOs would be encouraged to participate under the terms of special agreements with the Government. The Government was to organize a distribution and monitoring structure, with the UN, and was to make cash contributions to the operational costs of the programme.

The more controversial arrangements for a UN security presence took longer to negotiate and it was not until 25 May that a supplementary agreement was signed with the Iraqi Government providing for the deployment in Iraq of 500 UN Security Guards. They were to be assigned to any UN transit centre, UNHUCS and sub-offices where their presence might be needed.[71]

It has been suggested that the "acceptance of such comprehensive arrangements is probably without precedent in such a situation".[72] Although it was stated to be without prejudice to Iraq's independence, sovereignty and territorial integrity,

---

[71] The Memorandum of Understanding and the Annex relating to the Guards Contingent is contained in UN Doc. S/22663.

[72] Alston, n. 36 above at p.150.

the Memorandum of Understanding provided for a very significant UN presence throughout Iraq, backed by special security measures. These were measures clearly consented to by Iraq, although the coalition's plan to establish the safe havens by force if necessary was undoubtably a highly persuasive factor. It was also clearly preferable to Iraq to have the large numbers of UN aid personnel in its territory rather than the coalition forces and to accept the lightly armed guards in lieu of a UN military presence.

The first Memorandum of Understanding was expressed to expire on 31 December 1991. Negotiations to renew it proved to be extremely difficult but it was eventually renewed in substantially the same form to cover the period 1 January - 30 June 1992. Renewal proved impossible, however, at the end of this period and for about six months there was no official agreement in place. The UN Secretary-General announced at this time that the aid programme would continue on essentially the same basis but, in practice, it was very badly affected. UN staff were not granted visas or travel permits, attacks and harrassment of aid workers intensified and many aspects of the programme slowed or halted. The non-governmental agencies urged that the UN programme should be operated through Turkey and, as time dragged on, key government donors also threatened a substantial cross-border operation if the Memorandum was not renewed.[73] The UN was highly reluctant to do this and continued its attempts to negotiate for several more months.

Eventually a new Memorandum was signed on 22 October 1992. This was in rather different terms and reflected a greater flexing of authority by Iraq. The emphasis on Iraq cooperating and facilitating implementation of the programme was missing and instead the onus was more on the UN to collaborate and consult with Iraq. The size of the Guards Contingent was reduced almost by half to a maximum of 300 and the Memorandum referred to their deployment only in the northern governorates, reflecting Iraq's insistence that the UN withdraw its operations in the south of the country. The size of Iraq's cash contributions was reduced by half. More stringent requirements were imposed on the operations of the non-governmental agencies.

The third Memorandum of Understanding expired on 31 March 1993 and, to this day, further renewal has proved impossible. The humanitarian programme has continued; UN officials say that it is understood to operate on the same basis as before and that Iraq has continued to grant visas and permits, indicating its continued consent. However, without an official written agreement the

---
[73] Keen at pp. 46-48.

programme is even more vulnerable to obstruction, unilateral amendment of the terms and even outright refusal to cooperate further on the part of the Iraqi authorities.

V.3 FOOD FOR OIL

A UN Inter-Agency mission in June/July 1991, which confirmed the desperate situation of the Iraqi population, concluded that the primary need was for the supply of material goods. It considered that problems with importing these lay more with financing than with the operation of the sanctions regime. It estimated that to restore even a greatly reduced level of services over a one-year time frame would cost some US $6.8 billion. Not only was this vastly in excess of what any UN programme could be expected to generate, but the Iraqi Government itself was in a position to finance these needs if it were permitted to unfreeze assets held abroad or to resume the sale of oil, prohibited under the sanctions regime.

In response to this report the Security Council adopted Resolution 706 (1991) on 15 August 1991. Pursuant to this Iraq would be permitted to export over a six-month period petrol and petroleum products up to a certain amount, not exceeding US $1.6 billion, to finance the purchase of food, medicine and essential supplies and materials to meet the humanitarian needs of the population. Each transaction would be notified and approved by the Sanctions Committee and payments would be made directly into an Escrow Account administered by the Secretary-General.

The Escrow Account was intended to finance a number of activities in relation to Iraq - the UN's humanitarian activities; payments into the Compensation Fund and the carrying out of the UN weapons inspections, both established by Resolution 687 (1991); costs incurred by the UN in facilitating the return of Kuwaiti property seized by Iraq; and half the costs of the Iraq/Kuwait Boundary Demarcation Commission. The resolution called for the Secretary-General to report on the methods of its implementation, following which Resolution 712 of 19 September 1991 approved his recommendations and specified in more detail the modalities of operation of the Escrow Account.

Iraq has, however, refused to utilize the so-called "food for oil" formula set out in these resolutions in protest at the degree of international control they impose over its oil revenues. As a result this source of financing for the humanitarian programme has not been available. Iraq has been strongly and repeatedly criticised for this failure by the Security Council and there is increasing frustration on the part of the major aid donors in having to fund such a massive programme when significant funding could be generated by Iraq itself. Concerned at the deteriorating situation in the country, Security Council Resolution 778 of 2 October 1992 called for frozen Iraqi assets based in other states, deriving from the sale of Iraq's oil and petroleum products, to be paid into the Escrow Account up to a certain maximum limit. This has generated some additional funding using Iraqi oil proceeds without the Government's consent.

V.4 THE OPERATION OF THE AID PROGRAMME

The humanitarian aid programme implemented in Iraq over the past four years has been very significant. The main UN and other agencies involved have been UNHCR, UNICEF, WFP, UNDP, WHO, ITU, UNESCO, FAO, ICRC and IOM. Since its establishment in 1992, the UN Department of Humanitarian Affairs has provided central coordination, policy guidance and operational support. Inside Iraq coordination, planning and liaison with the authorities are handled by the UN's Inter-Agency Relief Coordinator in Baghdad. At the end of 1991 there were more than 1,000 UN international and local staff engaged in the programme, although this had dropped to 590 between April and July 1994 and was further reduced in August that year when the 300-strong Guards Contingent was cut by half.

In addition a large number of international and local non-governmental organizations have been actively involved in humanitarian activities, the vast majority of them working in the north of the country. There were some 40 international organizations operating there in 1994. Most of these organizations have opted not to enter into any formal arrangements with the Iraqi Government because of its stringent operating requirements and control measures which would compromise and undermine their work. Instead these organizations have been able to gain direct access to Iraqi Kurdistan through Turkey. This means that the presence of the international non-governmental organizations in Iraqi territory is technically illegal but they have been able to enter Iraqi Kurdistan and to operate fairly freely as a result of the protected status of the area. Recently, however, Turkey has begun to tighten up customs and other regulations on the movement of personnel and goods across its border with Iraq, making it more difficult to gain access to the northern area through Turkey. Turkey has said that its requirement that those seeking entry to Iraq through its territory have Iraqi visas does not apply to aid personnel, but delays and difficulties have been reported.[74]

Initially the humanitarian programme concentrated on providing emergency relief and assistance to the most vulnerable groups in the form of food, clean water, fuel, medical care and shelter. By 1993 the UN was saying that the emergency phase had largely ended with the resettlement of most of the refugees and displaced and that the focus of the programme should shift to the rehabilitation of community infrastructure since "an enhanced capacity for self-sufficiency will enable the Iraqi population to meet a greater proportion of their own needs on a sustainable basis in future years".[75] The emphasis was to be on education, road construction and repair, agricultural support, mines-related work and income-generating activities for women. In fact, continuing emergency needs and the lack of adequate funding for the programme has greatly hampered any change in focus.

The UN's programme extends to the whole country but the bulk of operations and resources are concentrated in Iraqi Kurdistan. Needs there have been particularly acute, not least as a result of the combined effects of international sanctions and internal embargo imposed by the government. It has also been easier to operate the programme in these areas outside government control and there have been more resources available for projects there. Many donors earmark funds for projects in the north where there is greater international supervision and accountability, in contrast to the government-controlled areas. The presence of a large number of non-governmental agencies in the north has also greatly assisted the implementation of the UN's programme.

Implementation of the programme has, however, been constantly obstructed by the Iraqi Government. Even when the Memoranda of Understanding were in force, Iraq failed to comply fully with the terms of these agreements. The UN has not been permitted to operate freely throughout the country and has largely been prevented from implementing the programme in the south of Iraq. Restrictions have been imposed by the Government on non-governmental agencies. In addition to its refusal to implement the food for oil arrangements, Iraq has rarely made its required monthly cash contributions to the UN programme; in 1992 the Special Rapporteur noted that the Government had made its contribution in only three of the past 14 months.[76] The Special Rapporteur on Iraq has also sharply criticised the Government in many of his reports for its deliberate unequal distribution of scarce resources, favouring

---

[74] This move by Turkey is more directly aimed at journalists and other non-governmental organizations, such as those working in the human rights field, to prevent their free access to Iraqi Kurdistan.

[75] The UN Inter-Agency Humanitarian Programme in Iraq - April 1991-March 1993, DHA (April 1993).

[76] UN Doc. A/47/367/Add. 1, at para. 12.

Ba'ath Party loyalists, the military and government officials while imposing punitive measures in the south and the north.[77]

In addition, UN and other aid workers have experienced a disturbing catalogue of incidents of attack, assault and harassment.[78] Although it has been impossible in many of the attacks to attribute responsibility beyond doubt, a large number of incidents are reported to have occurred in government-controlled areas and sometimes in the presence of government security personnel who failed to intervene. In one case a magnetic bomb was attached to a UN vehicle as it passed through a government check-point. In November 1992 the Special Rapporteur on Iraq reported that well over 100 such incidents had occurred consisting of personal threats, searches, interrogation, restraint and detention, extortion of money, attacks on and confiscation of property, including vehicles, physical assaults, gun-shots, grenade attacks and even rocket-launched grenades.

At least one UN Guard has been killed in the northern area and other aid personnel have also been killed and seriously injured.[79] On 6 January 1993 an aid worker with CARE-Australia was killed in an attack on his vehicle. A couple of months later, on 22 March, a senior staff member of Handicap International was shot and killed in Sulaimaniya. In December that year a huge bomb exploded inside a centre run by the same organization, killing 20, injuring many more and destroying the building. On the same day another bomb, also in Sulaimaniya, exploded at an office of CARE, injuring two staff. In January 1993 in Dohuk a man found with a time bomb claimed he had been instructed by the Iraqi secret police to place it in a UN vehicle for a reward. These incidents have seriously impeded and undermined the aid programme and have led to some aid agencies suspending or terminating their activities in the northern area.

The UN has also been quite heavily criticized for inefficiencies, a lack of coordination, inadequate planning and other failures of the aid programme.[80] The UN is perceived, particularly by the NGO community, as having been over-conciliatory to the Iraqi Government and unwilling to confront its lack of cooperation. The major problems, however, stem from the Government's

---

[77] Iraq confirmed to the Special Rapporteur in 1991, for example, that salaries of current and retired government employees had been increased by 30-55% and 15-20% respectively, merely noting that the incomes of private sector employees usually rises in proportion to the cost of living. It also noted that government warehouses were only available to state employees as other people could join consumer associations (UN Doc. A/46/647 at para. 55).

[78] Keen, at p. 24, gives details of 35 separate incidents between March 1992 and May 1993.

[79] UN Doc. A/47/367/Add. 1 at para. 13

[80] See, for example, Keen, Chapter 3 and the LCHR Report.

obstructions and restrictions, the failure of the international community to provide adequate security and the gross under-funding of the programme as donors have become increasingly frustrated with the Government's intransigence. All these factors have led to wild fluctuations in the programme and an inability to move to projects aimed at long-term development and reduction of dependency.

V.5 THE FUTURE OF THE AID PROGRAMME

The situation in Iraq remains desperate. At the end of 1994 UNICEF reported that "living conditions continue to be on a state of decline for the majority of the Iraqi population".[81] The availability of food supplies gave UNICEF the greatest cause for concern. Although the food ration had gradually been increased (but still providing only 70% of energy requirements), in October 1994 the Government suddenly announced a drastic reduction in food rations by almost 40%. At the same time it introduced a monthly allowance of ID 2,000 but only for civil servants and the armed forces. According to UNICEF, this would benefit only 3.5 million people, leaving 16.5 million ineligible (including, of course, the Kurds in the northern area who anyway receive little if any supplies through government rations).[82] Dwindling food supplies, rising prices and rocketing inflation means that the majority of families cannot possibly make up their nutritional requirements by purchasing food. Domestic food production remains gravely constrained by shortages of seeds, pesticides, fertilizers, and spare parts for machinery.

Other UN agencies also painted a grim picture: a sharp and significant increase in severe malnutrition; safe water supplies at only just over one-third of 1990 levels with water treatment capacity reduced by 20% due to lack of spare parts; severe reduction in the waste disposal system; deterioration in the health care system with shortages of medical supplies and equipment; the increased risk of disease and climbing morbidity and mortality rates; a sharp decline in the education sector with a 7 per cent primary school drop-out rate; and a lack of motivation in the public sector resulting in many leaving their jobs, jeopardising social and public services still further.[83]

---

[81] UNICEF Progress Report 1 April 1994-11 September 1994 UN Inter-Agency Humanitarian Cooperation Programme for Iraq (September 1994) at p.1.

[82] Impact of the Food Ration on the Most Vulnerable Women and Children UNICEF (October 1994).

[83] See UNICEF Progress Report, n.81 above, and the Summary of the UN Inter-Agency Programme in Iraq Consultation Meeting of 11 October 1994.

The humanitarian programme faces an ever-more acute funding crisis. The programme has, in fact, never been fully funded since its inception. Now there is increasing evidence of "donor fatigue". Attention has shifted to more high-profile emergencies elsewhere in the world and there is increasing frustration at the Government's refusal to utilize the food for oil formula. Internal conflict between the Kurdish political parties is also fast eroding political and economic support. At an Inter-Agency consultation meeting in October 1994 the UN indicated that only 25% of funds requested for the period April 1994 - March 1995 had been received. It called for urgent donations of US $78 million, the bare minimum needed to provide vital assistance to some of the most vulnerable groups and to keep essential services operating. Even so, this amounted to only half of estimated requirements overall. The UN Guards Contingent has been steadily cut owing to lack of funds - in October 1994 it was down to 148 and further reductions were anticipated.[84]

Iraqi Kurdistan is still in desperate straits even though it has received more from the humanitarian programme than other areas of the country.[85] From the outset it was a region with acute needs, devastated by the social, economic and physical effects of years of conflict.[86] The internal economic blockade has resulted in steep price rises, the exhaustion of local assets, the withdrawal of government services and a decline in the health, water, sanitation and education sectors. Living standards have drastically fallen; the UN has reported that 10 per cent of the poorest households can meet only 3 per cent of their needs.[87] Some 140,000 people remained displaced in 1994, including 30,000 re-displaced in Sulaimaniya, necessitating continued emergency assistance.[88]

Agricultural production is hampered by government attacks and shelling, the degradation caused by chemical weapons and the ever-present danger of mines. Both the agricultural and industrial sectors suffer from the lack of necessary materials and spare parts. Short-term projects to provide immediate necessities have been resorted to which are economically and environmentally destructive

---

[84] Planned Activities UN Inter-Agency Humanitarian Cooperation Programme for Iraq 1994/5, Office of the UN Coordinator, Baghdad (September 1994).

[85] The south is perhaps the most serious casualty, subjected to severe military and economic repression by the Government which has also largely prevented the implementation of humanitarian programmes there.

[86] See, generally, Keen, Chapter 3 and the reports of the Special Rapporteur on Iraq for accounts of the economic and social deprivation in Iraqi Kurdistan.

[87] Mid-Term Implementation Report, UN Inter-Agency Humanitarian Cooperation Programme for Iraq 1994/5, Office of the UN Coordinator, Baghdad (September 1994) at p. 2.

[88] Ibid.

in the long-term, such as wide-spread deforestation to provide fuel. The lack of capacity for longer-term development and rehabilitation increases the Kurds' dependency on international aid. Economic and social deprivation is having a detrimental effect on the struggling democratic administration It has been suggested that the imbalance in international aid and assistance to the different areas of Iraqi Kurdistan controlled respectively by the KDP and the PUK has sharpened the internal conflict.[89]

The implementation of the humanitarian aid programme in Iraqi Kurdistan is further undermined by the uncertain status of the area. In the absence of any formal recognition, the Kurdish administration is not in a position to negotiate the terms or scope of the programme nor to be the direct beneficiary of funds. The Kurds themselves can have little say in the assistance they receive or when and how it is delivered.

The UN's presence in Iraqi Kurdistan is dependent on and governed by its relationship with the Iraqi Government. Having secured Iraqi consent for the aid programme in the form of the Memoranda of Understanding, the UN has been reluctant to act in any way outside the terms of these agreements, even though there has been no formal agreement in place for two years. The frustration of NGOs at this formalistic position is understandable, especially when it is considered possible in practice to secure access to the region without Iraqi consent.[90] However, it is difficult for UN officials to act without Iraqi consent in the absence of any authorization from the UN member states. There is no general internationally-recognized right to intervene to impose a humanitarian assistance programme against the wishes of the government concerned. General Assembly Resolution 46/182, setting out guiding principles for the provision of humanitarian assistance, may have taken the first tentative step in 1991 towards the development of such a concept by recognizing that assistance need not depend on a prior request initiated by the government concerned. However, this resolution clearly affirmed that "humanitarian assistance should be provided with the consent of the affected country and in principle on the basis of an appeal by the affected country". During the debate on the resolution many UN member states emphasized the principles of territorial integrity and non-interference.

---

[89] Ofteringer and Backer A republic of statelessness (1994) at p. 10.

[90] However, even if access across the Turkish border is possible (and this might not be assured for long if there were very strong objections by Iraq), the UN has pointed out that there would still be enormous distribution difficulties in the north where some areas are still government-controlled. Also the present security arrangements are grossly inadequate to protect UN convoys and the local population in the face of likely Iraqi retaliation or attack.

The limitations of Resolution 688 as authorization for enforcement action have already been discussed in the previous section. It "insists" on and "demands" Iraq's full cooperation and urges the Secretary-General to use all resources at his disposal but does not otherwise provide for direct enforcement measures which were certainly not contemplated at the time it was adopted. The Secretary-General was already doubtful as to whether the coalition military action was justified; certainly it could hardly be expected that UN officials would seek to impose a humanitarian programme in the face of Iraqi opposition without clear approval or further express authorization by the Security Council, backed by adequate security measures.[91]

Donor governments have gone somewhat further in by-passing the need for Iraqi consent for the provision of aid. The USA Office of Foreign Disaster Assistance is based in Arbil and Zakho and funds projects directly. Germany has a semi-official presence also and a EC diplomatic representative was based in Arbil during the winter and spring of 1992/3 to look for ways to fund non-governmental projects. A number of other government donors have channelled funds for projects directly to non-governmental agencies in the region rather than through the UN programme.[92] When negotiations stalled on the renewal of the Memorandum of Understanding in 1992, key donors made their own needs assessments and threatened a substantial cross-border operation if Iraq failed to cooperate further.[93]

At the same time the UN's humanitarian assistance programme has played an important role in the development of Iraqi Kurdistan as a de facto autonomous region outside the control of the Iraqi Government. It has established a significant UN presence in the area, including special security measures, which has undoubtably contributed to holding back the Iraqi Government from resuming control there. It has been instrumental in resettling refugees and the displaced and in helping to rebuild communities, including in areas from where they had been driven out by Government policies and military activity. It has take some steps towards the rehabilitation of the area and has cushioned it from some of the worst effects of the Government's embargo, thereby strengthening it internally. The UN has, de facto, recognized the Kurdish administration as the governing authority. It has made some attempts to work with and through local officials and states that it has urged non-governmental agencies to do so

---

[91] See also Alston, n.36 above, at pp. 148-150.

[92] Keen at p. 51.

[93] Ibid. at p. 48.

in the interests of maximum efficiency and improved coordination.[94] To fill the vacuum left by the dwindling Guards Contingent, for example, the UN has sought to set up and train a local police force.[95]

The collapse of the programme, whether through lack of funding or total opposition to its continuation by the Iraqi Government once sanctions are lifted, would place the Kurds in an intolerable situation economically, socially and politically. It is believed that if and when sanctions are lifted and oil revenues flow again, Iraq will significantly scale down the aid programme which will become no more than another bilateral UN in-country operation wholly dependent on the consent of the Government for its continuation. Given the punitive economic measures already imposed on the Kurds by Iraq, it certainly seems likely that the Government would hugely reduce international aid to the north, if not terminate it completely.

---

[94] In fact, the non-governmental agencies already do work with the Kurdish administration as far as possible and have been critical of the UN for not doing more to support and strengthen it.

[95] UNGCI Operations and Security, Un Inter-Agency Humanitarian Cooperation Programme for Iraq 1994/5, DHA Geneva (September 1994) at p.4. This report stated that of the 132 police requested for the Arbil governorate, 90 were in training and assignment was anticipated to begin before the end of September.

VI. THE ESTABLISHMENT OF A DEMOCRATIC ADMINISTRATION IN IRAQI KURDISTAN

In 1988 an alliance of seven political parties backed by the pesh merga armies formed the Kurdistan Front - the Kurdistan Democratic Party (KDP); the Patriotic Union of Kurdistan (PUK); the Kurdistan People's Democratic Party (KPDP); the Kurdistan Socialist Party/PASOK; the Kurdistan Branch of the Iraqi Communist Party; the Assyrian Democratic Movement; and the Kurdistan Toilers Party. When the Iraqi Government withdrew from the north of Iraq in October 1991, the Kurdistan Front stepped into the vacuum, operating as the regional government through a series of local committees and organizing a de facto administration. Political difficulties were exacerbated by the ad hoc nature of the Front's authority at a time when it was the only authority administering the region and the fact that each constituent party maintained a veto over proposed decisions. In May 1992 it was decided to formalise a regional government by the holding of democratic elections.[96]

In the context of Iraq this amounted to an act of open defiance of the Government which has denounced the elections as illegal. The Kurdish experiment in democracy was only made possible by the internationally protected status of the area. This gave the Kurds the necessary political space and protection from Government retaliation to allow them to proceed. The prolongation of protection has enabled the Kurdish administration to function and to begin to consolidate its authority, to the extent that fresh elections are planned for 1995.

At the same time the uncertainty surrounding the status and future of Iraqi Kurdistan is highly destabilizing. The new government is excluded from the support and assistance that the UN is able to offer other emerging democracies, including election monitoring and assistance, the drafting of laws, training of police and other officials and technical advice on the development of institutions and procedures to guarantee the rule of law, respect for human rights and the democratic process. The internal conflict between the Kurdish political parties is also seriously weakening and undermining the fledgling administration. Local institutions and political structures are not yet capable of addressing and resolving this and again no outside assistance has been forthcoming.

---

[96] See Falaq al-Din Kakai MP "The Kurdish Parliament" in Hazelton (Ed.) Iraq Since the Gulf War - Prospects for Democracy (1994) for an account of the elections and the setting up of the administration.

If the international community is serious about supporting democracy in Iraqi Kurdistan, it must take positive and rapid steps to put in place a more comprehensive plan that combines continued protection and the strengthening and consolidation of democracy within the context of reaching a durable political settlement on the future of Iraqi Kurdistan.

VI.I INTERNATIONAL STANDARDS

International standards provide a clear basis for the legitimacy of a government elected pursuant to free and fair democratic elections. Article 21 of the Universal Declaration of Human Rights states that:

> Everyone has the right to take part in the government of his country, directly or through freely chosen representatives...
> the will of the people shall be the basis of the authority of government; this will shall be expressed in periodic and genuine elections which shall be by universal and equal suffrage....

Article 25 of the International Covenant on Civil and Political Rights reiterates this and guarantees the right and opportunity of every citizen, without unreasonable restrictions:

> To take part in the conduct of public affairs, directly or through freely chosen representatives;
> To vote and to be elected at genuine periodic elections which shall be by universal and equal suffrage....

Democratic government, described by the UN Secretary-General as "the imperative of democratization",[97] is increasingly recognized by the UN as the most effective and durable way to protect all human rights and freedoms and integrally related to the preservation of global peace and security. The General Assembly has stressed in Resolution 45/150 of 1990 "its conviction that periodic and genuine elections are a necessary and indispensable element of sustained efforts to protect the rights and interests of the governed...". Democratic elections have been the goal of a number of UN-supervised peace-keeping and peace-building operations. In <u>Agenda for Peace</u> the Secretary-General noted:

> There is a new requirement for technical assistance which the United Nations has an obligation to develop and provide when requested: support for the transformation of deficient national structures and capabilities, and for the strengthening of new democratic institutions. The authority of the United Nations system to act in this field would rest on the consensus that

---

[97] Opening Statement by the UN Secretary-General to the UN World Conference on Human Rights, Vienna, 14 June 1993.

social peace is as important as strategic or political peace. There is an obvious connection between democratic practices - such as the rule of law and transparency in decision-making - and the achievement of true peace and security in any new and stable political order. These elements need to be promoted at all levels of international and national political communities.[98]

The 1993 World Conference on Human Rights, which took as its theme democracy, development and human rights, concluded that:
> Democracy, development and respect for human rights and fundamental freedoms are interdependent and mutually reinforcing. Democracy is based on the freely expressed will of the people to determine their own political, economic, social and cultural systems and their full participation in all aspects of their lives....The international community should support the strengthening and promoting of democracy, development and respect for human rights and fundamental freedoms in the entire world.

It also urged that:
> Special emphasis should be given to measures to assist in the strengthening and building of institutions relating to human rights, strengthening of a pluralistic civil society and the protection of groups which have been rendered vulnerable. In this context, assistance provided upon the request of Governments for the conduct of free and fair elections, including assistance in the human rights aspects of elections and public information about elections, is of particular importance. Equally important is the assistance to be given to the strengthening of the rule of law, the promotion of freedom of expression and the administration of justice, and to the real and effective participation of the people in the decision-making processes.[99]

International standards which affirm the principles of democracy do not, of course, deal with the conditions for or forms of local or regional self-government, either on a geographical or ethnic basis. Although the 1992 UN Declaration on the Rights of Persons Belonging to National or Ethnic, Religious or Linguistic Minorities, does not provide as such for autonomy or self-government either, its provisions on participation in public life, national and regional decision-making and economic progress and development as well as on the formation of associations do envisage a democratic process in which minorities have a full and effective opportunity to participate and to make their voices heard. In some situations, autonomy may be the most effective way to secure minority rights.

---

[98] Agenda for Peace, UN Doc. S/24111 (1992) at para. 59.

[99] Vienna Declaration and Programme of Action at Part I, para. 8 and Part II, para. 67.

VI.2 THE DOMESTIC LEGAL BASIS FOR THE ELECTIONS

The concept of an elected local government in Iraqi Kurdistan was not a new or radical departure. Periodic elections had been held in the 1980s, under the strict control of the Government, pursuant to the 1974 Autonomy Law. There was, however, no express constitutional or other appropriate existing legislative basis available to the Kurds for the holding of these elections.

Kurdish autonomy is guaranteed by the 1970 Iraqi Constitution, but stipulates that it shall be in accordance with the law and does not specify the institutional structures of self-government. The 1970 Autonomy Agreement had envisaged some form of local self-government for the region but does not spell out in detail the institutional structures nor any electoral process. The 1974 Autonomy Law provided for an elected Legislative Council but Kurdish political leaders have never accepted the validity of this Law and the severe constraints it imposes on Kurdish autonomy.

The Kurds simply asserted that they were acting in accordance with the spirit of earlier autonomy arrangements which envisaged self-rule through an elected body, although some sought to rely on the 1970 Autonomy Agreement as the basis for the elections.[100] The Iraqi Government dismissed the elections as illegal and has refused to recognize or deal with the Kurdish administration. However, notwithstanding the lack of clear legislative authority, there are a number of factors which serve to reinforce the legitimacy of these elections. First, the Government had already withdrawn its military and civil control leaving a total vacuum of governing authority in the region which had to be filled.[101] Second, the holding of democratic elections was certainly more in keeping with international standards on democratic governance and public participation than the alternative of maintaining the ad hoc political authority of the Kurdistan Front. Third, there was no freely elected democratic government in Iraq in which the Kurds could participate fully and effectively as Kurds or as Iraqi citizens. They were not, therefore, setting up local governmental institutions which were outside of or at odds with an existing democratic system through

---

[100] International Human Rights Law Group Ballots Without Borders (1992) at pp. 15-16 (hereinafter cited as the "IHRLG Report"). Some of those who purported to rely on the 1970 Autonomy Agreement were in fact citing provisions from the rejected Autonomy Laws while other Kurdish political figures claimed that the 1970 Agreement was irrelevant to the 1992 elections. Jalal Talabani, for example, relied on international treaties, including the Treaty of Sevres which had envisaged eventual independence for the Kurds but which was never implemented.

[101] According to the IHRLG Report (p. 17), the existing Kurdish Legislative Council in Mahkmour, "elected" under the terms of the Autonomy Law, denounced the 1992 elections as a usurpation of their authority. However, the Kurdish leadership claimed that this body was a sham and a puppet of Baghdad and that its actions were null since it had never convened in Arbil and it lacked a quorum.

which they could have expressed themselves and sought to secure their rights and defend their interests.

In the absence of clear legislative authority, the Kurds were careful to ensure that the elections were held on the basis of adequate and fair electoral laws. Two such laws were adopted by the Kurdistan Front - dealing with elections for the National Assembly and for the Leader of the Kurdistan Liberation Movement respectively. They were drafted by a High Commission for the Supervision of the Elections, chaired by a judge and composed mainly of jurists. This body, which also had the task of supervising and organizing the electoral process, drew on the laws and practices of other democratic countries in drafting the electoral provisions. One of the laws set out at some length the basis for the election. It cited the "unique legislative and official gap" left by the withdrawal of the central government from the region; it expressed a commitment to democracy and respect for human rights in accordance with international instruments; it articulated the aim of ensuring that the Kurds were governed by "real representatives freely elected and entitled to practise all powers"; and it ensured separation of powers of the legislature, executive and judiciary.

In an further effort to establish international legitimacy the Kurds actively sought supervision of the electoral process by outside independent observers. Had this been a state struggling to make the difficult transition from years of authoritarian rule marked by gross human rights violations to democracy and the rule of law, other UN member states would no doubt have been have falling over themselves in their eagerness to assist and observe. As it was, there was almost no help forthcoming for the Kurds from other governments. A number of non-governmental international observers were, however, present during the election process and have reported on their findings.[102]

The Kurds also made it clear that they were operating within the framework of local autonomy for the region within Iraq and were not attempting to set up wholly independent structures or laying the foundation for secession. The newly-elected Kurdistan National Assembly expressly stated in October 1992 that it had unanimously decided "to define its legal relationship with the central government, at this juncture in [the Kurdish people's] history, on the basis of a federal union within a democratic and parliamentary Iraq which believes in a

---

[102] See, for example, the IHRLG Report; Report of a Delegation sponsored by Pax Christi International, Interchurch Peace Council and the Netherlands Kurdistan Friendship Society Elections in Kurdistan - An Experiment in Democracy, 1992 (hereinafter cited as the "Pax Christi Report"); and Electoral Reform Society Kurdistan - Elections for Iraqi Kurdish National Assembly and Leader of the Kurdistan Liberation Movement, 1992 (hereinafter cited as the "ERS Report").

multi-party system and which respects human rights as recognized by international covenants and treaties".[103]

The ministries created when the Council of Ministers began functioning on 4 July 1992 covered principally those areas of responsibility which legitimately fall within the concept of local self-government - such as the ministries of the interior and justice - rather than those normally associated with the responsibilities of a national state, such as foreign affairs. The Council stated as one of its political objectives "to make efforts to establish the relationship of the Regional Government with the future central government on the basis of a voluntary union and respect for a framework of a federal and democratic Iraq in which all the rights of our people are safeguarded".[104]

VI.3 THE ELECTORAL PROCESS

The elections were held in extremely difficult circumstances. Many people were slowly reestablishing themselves in their homes after the 1991 exodus while others remained displaced. Basic living conditions remained desperate for many, exacerbated by the effects of international sanctions against Iraq and the economic embargo imposed on the region by the central government. This was the first "free" election the Kurds had ever experienced and much education and publicity was needed at a time when most communications systems were hardly functioning. There were no voter records and no institutions or systems for holding democratic elections. Everything had to be done for the first time and from scratch. Security was of great concern in view of reported threats of sabotage by the Iraqi Government.

It is a remarkable achievement that elections took place at all and more remarkable that they were largely perceived to have been free and fair. Certainly some concerns were raised. Principal among these were inadequacies in the electoral law, concerns about the lack of secrecy in voting, the lack of safeguards against multiple voting, discrepancies in registration and the inadequate number of polling stations. In general, however, international observers concluded that, in all the circumstances, the elections had generally been free and fair and had

---

[103] "Statement of the Announcement of the Federal Union" issued by KNA Decree No. 22 on 4 October 1992 and cited in Amnesty International's report, Human Rights Abuses in Iraqi Kurdistan Since 1991, AI Index: MDE 14/01/95 at p. 16 (hereinafter cited as the "AI Report").

[104] Ibid. at p. 15. The Kurds did create a ministry for Pesh Merga Affairs, which might be considered akin to a ministry of defence, but this was necessary to deal with the large numbers of armed pesh merga attached to the political parties. The Ministry of Humanitarian Affairs and Cooperation has also, of necessity, carried out some foreign relations functions in the absence of any central government authority.

not been fatally flawed by any of the issues which they noted as having been problematic.[105]

One observer concluded that his criticisms of the process "did not affect the overall fairness and freedom of the election. They must also be read in the context of an extremely difficult security and administrative situation in Iraqi Kurdistan".[106] Another delegation noted that, even though flaws had probably existed on a larger scale than acknowledged or observed by outside monitors, there was no conclusive evidence that this had significantly affected the results.[107] A third observer group stated:

> The elections in Iraqi Kurdistan represent a significant achievement towards providing the people of Iraqi Kurdistan with meaningful opportunity for democratic choice in the way they are governed...the Kurdish people's enormous accomplishments in this respect outweighed the shortcomings of the election procedures. The conduct and completion of the electoral process were remarkably fair and, on balance, free. The people of Iraqi Kurdistan showed restraint, patience and flexibility. Although the election day procedures were not without flaws, the elections offered an opportunity for the will of the people to be expressed. Election officials should, however, improve procedures in the future to rectify the irregularities identified by the delegation.[108]

Elections were held for a 105-seat Kurdistan National Assembly and for the Leader of the Kurdistan Liberation Movement on the basis of the electoral laws adopted by the High Commission for the Supervision of Elections. The Assembly was to serve a three-year term and would have the task of electing an executive Council of Ministers to over-see the civil administration in the region. The Leader would be elected for a four-year term and would be Commander-in Chief of the pesh merga forces with the task of bringing them under unified command. He would convene the Assembly and issue laws proposed by it, and have a residual power to enact laws in an emergency or when the Assembly was not in session. There was considerable disagreement among the various parties over the status and functions of the post of Leader.

---

[105] The Pax Christi Report notes, however, at p. 25, that monitoring had to be hastily organized by NGOs and it was hampered by language difficulties, the short time monitors could spend in each place and the delay in holding the elections.

[106] ERS Report at p. 9.

[107] Pax Christi Report at p. 30.

[108] IHRLG Report at p. 3

The geographical electoral area consisted of the four regions of Dohuk, Arbil, Sulaimaniya and Kirkuk and included the internally-displaced within these areas. An attempt was made to include substantial numbers of Kurdish refugees in Turkey and Iran but this was not accepted by the governments of those countries. The Kurds relied on the 1957 census and voter registration was open to anyone over 18 possessing accepted forms of identification. A special registration process was instituted for those without the requisite identification. This seemed "orderly and fair" to observers[109] and did not give rise to allegations of unfair treatment or arbitrary refusal to register, although there were considerable local variations in the way registration guidelines were implemented.

The extent of internal displacement and other difficulties did mean, however, that voter registration lists could not be drawn up. This, coupled with the subsequent difficulties in marking those who had voted (see below), gave rise to the possibility that double or multiple voting may have taken place. Observers could not confirm or deny that this had occurred but did not consider that it constituted a fatal flaw in the process.

Eight parties contested 100 seats in the Assembly. The five remaining seats were reserved for the smaller Christian parties. Election was by proportional representation with a threshold of seven per cent required for election. Some of the smaller parties complained that the threshold was too high and it also led to some political deals between parties and joint lists. In fact, on the basis of the results only one party - the Islamic Movement - would have gained seats if the threshold had been set at four per cent but one observer noted the possible impact of narrowing the choice for voters.[110] Notice of the campaign and the preparation of voters lists "seemed orderly and adequate to provide the voters a meaningful opportunity to familiarize themselves with each party's platform".[111] Any party could submit a list of at least three candidates within the required deadline, although some criticized the system as unfair to independent candidates who had to appear on recognized party lists. Any candidate who was rejected for failing to meet the legal criteria had the right to appeal to a court for a review of the decision.

Campaigning was enthusiastic, vigorous and generally free from intimidation

---

[109] IHRLG Report at p. 28.

[110] ERS Report at p.5.

[111] IHRLG Report at p. 33

and from personal attacks on other candidates or parties. There were many political meetings and rallies. The parties had access to radio and newspapers to broadcast their platforms and, although only the larger parties owned TV stations, the views of other parties were periodically broadcast. Observers found voters remarkably well informed and aware of the main issues at stake. Despite fears of sabotage from outside as well as conflict between the parties, there was very little violence reported although some incidents did occur.

Elections were originally scheduled for 17 May but had to be postponed until 19 May when it transpired that imported indelible ink to be used to mark those who had voted (in the absence of voter registration lists) could be easily removed. A new batch was refused customs clearance by the Turkish authorities and polling was delayed for two days while a new ink solution was hastily prepared by Kurdish chemists. Even this, although utilized, did not appear to be indelible, giving rise to the concerns noted earlier that multiple voting might have occurred in some areas.

It is estimated that as many as 88-90 per cent of eligible voters cast their ballots. Polling stations were administered by a judge and run by locally recruited and specially trained electoral officers. The voting observed by international monitors was reasonably well-organized, despite difficulties of the very large numbers, the absence of formal voting booths at some stations and the closure of some polling stations at the designated time before everyone in the long queues had voted. Party representatives were able to observe polling and there were no significant allegations of interference or intimidation, although one observer delegation expressed some concern about subtle pressure under the guise of assisting people to vote.[112] It also noted that some complaints of irregularities by political parties had not met with an adequate response and that such incidents had occurred on a larger scale than officially acknowledged by the supervisory High Commission.[113]

International observers expressed some disquiet at the lack of secret voting, contrary to the electoral law. In some cases private booths were not available while elsewhere they were unused. It appeared that a great deal of communal and family voting took place, especially where a family member was illiterate. Yet neither voters nor officials seemed unduly concerned by the lack of secrecy and the observers concluded that, in general, those who had wanted to vote in secret had been able to do so and the lack of secrecy had not caused any sense

---

[112] Pax Christi Report at p. 27.

[113] Ibid. at p. 28.

of unfairness or undue pressure on voters. One political party was much more concerned and considered that the lack of secrecy would have particularly affected the smaller parties.

VI.4 THE OUT-COME OF THE ELECTIONS

Initially there was considerable disquiet and frustration from many of the parties at the results which were not announced for several days. None of the smaller parties had reached the seven per cent threshold so that the remaining votes were divided proportionately between the two larger parties - the KDP and the PUK. This resulted in the KDP winning 50.8 per cent of the votes, giving it 51 seats in the Assembly and the PUK winning 49.2 per cent, giving it 49 seats. After heated internal debates and in the interests of harmony and preserving the credibility of the elections, it was agreed that the two main parties would each take an equal 50 seats in the Assembly. The Assyrian Democratic Movement took four of the five reserved seats for the Christian parties and the remaining seat went to Kurdistan Christian Unity. Four candidates had run for Leader of the Kurdistan Liberation Movement - Masoud Barzani (KDP); Jalal Talabani (PUK); Othman Abdulaziz Muhammad (Islamic Movement) and Mahmoud Ali Othman (Socialist Party). However, none of the candidates received an absolute majority necessary for election. A run-off election should have been held within 15 days but this was post-poned and to date has not yet been held.

The National Assembly held its inaugural session on 4 June 1992 in Arbil. The Council of Ministers began functioning on 4 July. Fifteen ministries were created: interior, justice, industry and electricity, culture and information, humanitarian aid and cooperation, finance and economy, agriculture, tourism, health and social affairs, pesh merga affairs, reconstruction and development, religious affairs, education, housing and public works and transport and communications. Six each were allocated to the KDP and PUK, one each to the two other parties represented in the Assembly and one to a non-affiliated candidate.

VI.5 THE REACTION OF THE INTERNATIONAL COMMUNITY

The UN itself kept a low profile with regard to the elections although the Sanctions Committee permitted the German Government to supply ballots, ink, plastic bottles and rubber stamps for voting purposes, apparently on the basis that these materials were necessary to prevent violence erupting. One observer group was told that the UN Guards would not react to any incidents of violence unless UN personnel were at risk. UNHCR maintained it took no position on the elections but would deal with the de facto authorities after the event.[114]

Some governments explicitly or implicitly welcomed and encouraged the elections, at least as an important step towards democracy in an otherwise highly authoritarian state, while making it clear that they would not support the emergence of an independent political entity. The US Government issued a statement saying:

> On May 17, the people of northern Iraq will vote in free elections to choose an executive leader and members of a legislative body. We hope the voting will proceed in a secure and peaceful atmosphere and help lead to a better life for all the people of northern Iraq - Turcomans, Assyrians and Kurds. We welcome public and private assurances by the Iraqi Kurdish leadership that these elections deal only with local administrative issues and do not represent a move towards separatism....We would like to see all the people of Iraq taking part in a democratic system and enjoying the freedoms which have so long been denied to them by Saddam Hussein. As we have said many times, we do not support the emergence of an independent political entity in northern Iraq.[115]

A British military officer in Operation Provide Comfort stated that the UK Government "is content for the elections to take place on the clear understanding they are not for the purpose of creating Kurdistan".[116] A number of parliamentarians from other countries participated as international observers, although not, apparently, in any official government capacity. The European Parliament adopted a resolution on 19 June 1992 expressing its approval of the elections and encouraging the Kurdish leadership to pursue the path to autonomy.

While direct assistance from governments was generally not forthcoming, voices of protest at the elections were few and isolated. Only Iraq actually condemned the elections as illegal. Turkey expressed the fear that they could lead to violence and Turkish planes reportedly attacked villages in the border

---

[114] IHRLG Report at pp. 20-21.

[115] Statement by Margaret Tutwiler/Spokesman, US Department of State, 15 May 1992.

[116] Quoted in the IHRLG Report at p. 21.

areas just before they took place while Iran, initially favourable, also later adopted a stance of opposition.

Following the elections and the establishment of the ministries, the Kurdish administration has been generally accepted as the de facto governing authority in the area by all except Iraq itself. UN officials administering the aid programme deal as far as possible with Kurdish ministers and officials and are keen to do so in an effort to create greater stability and coherence in the aid programme.

VI.6 THE KURDISH ADMINISTRATION[117]

After assuming power the National Assembly promulgated a number of new laws aimed at dealing with security and control of weapons as well as opening up various aspects of public life such as freedom of expression and association. Although in areas where the Assembly does not have express authority to legislate, Iraqi law would still theoretically apply, in August 1992 the Assembly ordered that no existing Iraqi laws, decrees and regulations should be enforced until their legitimacy had been confirmed by the Assembly. Some existing laws have been declared unenforceable as being incompatible with the welfare of the Kurdish people and it appears that no Iraqi legislation adopted after 23 October 1991 is being enforced.

The elections were based on a commitment to democracy and respect for human rights and Kurdish political leaders initially professed themselves to be in favour of measures to protect human rights and to prevent abuses. Some positive steps were taken by the administration. The independence of the judiciary was secured, separating it from the executive. Special courts, which had been set up to deal with political cases and which had not operated in conformity with international fair trial standards, were abolished. Prisoners were transferred to recognized places of detention under the jurisdiction of the police and security forces, rather than the political parties.

However, the administration has encountered considerable difficulties in functioning effectively since the elections. The 50-50 power-sharing arrangement, which was mirrored in the ministries with top officials being selected from different parties, has frequently paralysed decision-making and action. The vacuum in the leadership post also created problems. Initially the President of the Assembly carried out the functions of Leader but this was

---

[117] This section draws primarily on information contained in the AI Report which describes in much greater detail the political context and the administration's activities, particularly in the areas of law enforcement and the judicial system.

challenged. In December 1993 an eight-member Presidential Body was created pending a leadership election but it ceased to function within a few weeks, although the law creating it remains in force.

The situation has been further destabilized by the fact that the two main political parties, the KDP and the PUK, have continued to exercise considerable power and authority outside the institutional structures created after the elections. They have maintained their own security structures and militia and there are reports that they have interfered with the judicial process and that some judges and lawyers have been the victims of targeted assassinations. The monopoly of power concentrated in the two major parties has also impeded the development of other parties which have experienced intimidation and harassment. The only significant third party - the Islamic Movement - has moved away from mainstream politics and operates its own system of law enforcement without central accountability, with serious implications for further destabilization and fragmentation of power structures.

The human rights situation within the region remains very precarious. Amnesty International's recent report documents a range of human rights violations committed both by the political parties and the Kurdish administration since 1991. These include arbitrary arrests and detention without charge or trial; holding detainees in unacknowledged and unofficial places of detention; torture and ill-treatment and the failure to investigate such incidents; the extension of the death penalty to new offences; the deliberate and arbitrary killings of unarmed prisoners and targeted assassinations of political activists and other civilians; and the failure to bring perpetrators to justice.[118]

In addition there have been serious outbreaks of internal armed conflict between various political parties since the elections. Weapons control and plans to unify the pesh merga forces have not been effective and these forces still owe primary loyalty to the political party to which they are attached. The conflicts between the political groups have not only gravely destabilized the administration and the political alliances on which it depends, but have also resulted in many deaths and serious injuries, including of unarmed civilians. The internal conflicts are also undermining international support for the Kurds and leaving them even more vulnerable to central government intervention and exploitation of their political differences.

---

[118] See, generally, the AI Report, Chapters 4 and 5.

In December 1993 fighting broke out between the PUK and the Islamic Movement and this was followed by renewed conflict in May 1994 between the two main parties relating to a land dispute which quickly escalated into widespread violence. During these periods of fighting there have been reports of deliberate killing of prisoners, mutilation of bodies and the abduction, torturing and killing of civilians on account of their political affiliations. Attempts under the auspices of the French Government to broker an agreement between the two political leaders foundered, although an Alliance Covenant was finally signed by both of them in November 1994 agreeing a series of political and legal reforms, including the criminalization of armed conflict between the two parties.

Repeated cease-fire agreements have not been respected, however, and serious fighting has again erupted in early 1995. Many Kurdish political figures and much of the population have expressed intense frustration and despair over these continued conflicts but the governmental and judicial institutions are too weak to provide a framework for addressing and resolving political differences peacefully. The atmosphere of impunity is rife and no steps have been taken to bring those responsible for violations to justice. Plan to hold new elections in 1995 and to further consolidate and reinforce the democratic structures are being jeopardized by the continuation of conflict.

VII. THE FUTURE OF THE SANCTIONS REGIME AGAINST IRAQ

Throughout the four years since the adoption of Security Council Resolution 687 (1991), laying down the conditions for a formal cease-fire, international sanctions against Iraq have remained in full force and effect. Although Iraq officially (but reluctantly) accepted the terms of Resolution 687, its defiant and uncooperative attitude to the conditions imposed on it, and particularly its obstruction of the weapons inspections, has been repeatedly condemned by the Security Council. During 1994, however, greater cooperation by Iraq on certain issues have met with a more conciliatory attitude towards it on the part of some other states, raising questions about how long sanctions may remain fully or partially in place.

This question has a direct bearing on the situation in Iraqi Kurdistan and the continued international protection of that area. Resolution 688 (1991), pursuant to which the safe havens and the no-fly zone were established, was not expressly linked to Resolution 687 or the other package of resolutions relating to the invasion of Kuwait. However, it has been treated as a relevant resolution in many respects and, in practice, the measures taken pursuant to it are integrally linked to the whole package of conditions and international supervisory measures, backed by sanctions, to which Iraq is currently subject.

This linkage has been reinforced by some countries, particularly the USA, which have been calling for the full implementation of all Security Council Resolutions, including Resolution 688, before sanctions can be lifted. Others have argued that Resolution 688 is worded too vaguely and there is no means by which Iraqi compliance with it can be effectively monitored so as to make it a condition precedent to the lifting of sanctions.

Insofar as the sanctions regime provides significant international political leverage on Iraq and in light of recent pressures to begin to lift sanctions, the extent to which compliance with Resolution 688 can be measured and linked into the lifting of sanctions is very relevant. At the same time, the continued imposition of sanctions is by no means an effective long-term solution to the situation in Iraqi Kurdistan nor, indeed, to the human rights situation in the rest of the country. A more comprehensive settlement plan is necessary and this must be agreed and be put in place before sanctions are lifted as an integral part of the resolution of all outstanding issues relating to Iraq and its international obligations.

VII.1 THE MAIN POINTS OF RESOLUTION 687(1991)

Security Council Resolution 687 of 3 April 1991, adopted under Chapter VII of the Charter, established the grounds for the cease-fire at the end of the Gulf War and was formally accepted by Iraqi on 6 April 1991.[119] It is a complicated resolution which imposes a number of different conditions on Iraq. It does not address the issue of human rights inside Iraq and makes no reference to any human rights instruments. Its essential elements are as follows:

1. The guarantee of the inviolability of the international boundary of Kuwait. A five-member Iraq-Kuwait Boundary Demarcation Commission was set up and submitted its final report in May 1993. Resolution 833 (1993) affirmed this Commission's decisions as final and demanded that Iraq and Kuwait respect the boundary and the right to navigational access.

2. A demilitarized zone on the Iraq/Kuwait border monitored by UNIKOM, whose work is reviewed every six months and its mandate continued in the absence of any decision to terminate it. The most recent review took place in October 1994.

3. An extensive ban on Iraq in respect of the development, production and use of weapons of mass destruction. Iraq has to accept unconditionally and under international supervision the destruction and removal of all chemical and biological weapons and all ballistic missiles with a range of more than 150 kms, as well as any capacity for research and production of such weapons. Extensive on-site inspection is carried out by a Special Commission, UNSCOM, which is authorized to eliminate Iraq's weapons capability. Iraq is prohibited from using, developing or acquiring such weapons in the future and a future ongoing monitoring and verification plan must be established. In addition, the acquisition or development of nuclear weapons and related materials or components is prohibited and, under the auspices of the International Atomic Energy Agency, a similar regime of on-site inspection, surrender and removal of such weapons and related materials, as well as future monitoring and verification, is required.

---

[119] In so doing Iraq protested that it had no choice and that the resolution was "an unprecedented assault on the sovereignty, and the rights that stem therefrom, embodied in the Charter and in international law and practice", UN Doc.S/22456, Annex.

A number of subsequent resolutions relating to weapons inspection and monitoring have been adopted. In accordance with Resolution 715 (1991) the Secretary-General reports every six months on progress and on Iraq's compliance with the relevant parts of Resolution 687.

4. Iraq is held responsible for any loss or injury to foreign governments, nationals and corporations in connection with its invasion and occupation of Kuwait and a Compensation Fund has been established to which Iraq is required to pay an appropriate amount based on a percentage of its oil revenues. Approval by the Council of the compensation arrangements was expressed to be one of the conditions precedent for the lifting of sanctions on Iraqi exports. In Resolution 705 the Council agreed that compensation payable by Iraq should not exceed 30% of its annual oil revenues, although this amount is to be reviewed from time to time in light of further information and other relevant developments.

5. Sanctions imposed on Iraq pursuant to Resolution 661 (1990) are maintained with foodstuffs and supplies to meet "essential civilian needs" exempt. Procedures for the review and conditions for lifting of sanctions are specified.

6. Iraq has to cooperate fully with the International Committee of the Red Cross (ICRC) in providing lists of those still detained and facilitating the search for those unaccounted for. A Special Committee, meeting every few months, was set up under the auspices of the ICRC. Some 5,700 civilians and prisoners of war were returned from Iraq between 1991-1993 but there remain a substantial number still unaccounted for. In November 1994 the ICRC proposed establishing a technical sub-committee able to conduct a more thorough and ongoing investigation of the whereabouts and fate of these persons.

VII.2 CONDITIONS FOR THE LIFTING OF SANCTIONS

There are two separate components to the lifting of sanctions. Pursuant to paragraph 22 of Resolution 687, the prohibition on Iraqi exports (principally and most importantly oil) is to be lifted once the Compensation Fund plan is approved and the Security Council is agreed that Iraq has complied with all the conditions relating specifically to weapons control and future monitoring. These conditions stand alone and are not expressed to require prior compliance with other Security Council resolutions. Pursuant to paragraph 28 of Resolution 687 the Council periodically reviews its decisions under a number of paragraphs, including paragraph 22.

Under paragraph 21 of Resolution 687 the ban on the sale or supply to Iraq of commodities or products is subject to review every 60 days in light of "the policies and practices" of the Iraqi Government as well as its implementation of all "relevant resolutions" of the Council. The "relevant resolutions" are not enumerated. So far no modifications to the sanctions regime have been proposed at these reviews. The most recent review took place in January 1995 and the next one is scheduled for mid-March.

VII.3 GROWING PRESSURE TO LIFT SANCTIONS

There are a number of elements which have contributed to bringing the lifting of sanctions against Iraq to the forefront of the international agenda. In November 1994 Iraq finally officially recognized the sovereignty and the established borders of Kuwait, thereby removing a major obstacle to any normalization of relations with the international community. In July and September 1994 Iraq attended, for the first time since 1991, the Special Committee investigating the fate of the unaccounted Kuwaitis and others. Although Iraq denies it is holding any of these persons it indicated some readiness to assist in determining their whereabouts following the submission of files by Kuwait on 609 missing persons.[120]

The considerable economic stresses and strains of four years of sanctions are also intensifying pressure for their relaxation. The economic interests of some other states, such as Turkey, have been particularly hard-hit by the impact of sanctions. Heavy pressure is also coming from the private commercial sector for a resumption of trade and other business relations with Iraq. There are an increasing number of trade delegations travelling to and from Baghdad laying the foundations for commercial activity as soon as sanctions are lifted.

There are grave concerns for the political and social impact of the extreme and steadily worsening hardship suffered by the Iraqi people as a result of sanctions. There is particular concern in this regard about the situation in the north and the south of the country, where the inhabitants are suffering under the combined effects of external sanctions and a punitive internal embargo imposed by the Government. The growing reluctance of the major donors to continue to fund an adequate humanitarian assistance program in Iraq to meet the massive needs is exacerbating the progressively worsening situation. There has

---

[120] The Special Rapporteur on Iraq has also been following the cases of missing persons and has been highly critical of Iraq's lack of cooperation. See, for example, UN Doc. A/49/651, at paras. 12-33.

been particular pressure for the lifting of the international sanctions in respect of Iraqi Kurdistan as this would benefit the struggling democratic administration and would not represent any easing of the pressure on the Iraqi Government. The USA has said that this would undermine the sanctions regime and encourage the breaking of sanctions elsewhere in Iraq since it would be impossible for the international community to police the internal frontier between Iraqi Kurdistan and the rest of Iraq.

The most immediate impetus for the lifting of sanctions is, however, the fact that the work of weapons inspection and their destruction or removal and the implementation of ongoing monitoring is approaching completion. Although, by itself, this only opens the way for the lifting of the export embargo, the resumption of oil exports is by far the most important issue, politically and economically, in the whole debate. In the latest periodic report to the Security Council in October 1994, the Secretary-General noted that:

> ...the Commission's ongoing monitoring and verification system is provisionally operational. While certain elements are not yet in place, so much of the preparatory work is complete, with gaps being filled for the time being by alternative measures, that the Commission can with confidence commence the testing of the thoroughness and efficacy of its system. The remaining elements should be in place shortly.[121]

In November, however, UNSCOM indicated that work still was being hampered by important missing and contradictory information and by a desperate lack of funding which was threatening the program with closure by February 1995. Then in March 1995 UN inspectors ascertained that Iraq had covered up a biological weapons program with the capacity to be developed on a much larger scale than had been thought. This is of particular concern given the potential for biological weapons to be used against the civilian population. Iraq maintains that documents about its importation of 3.3 tons of bacteria in the 1980s were destroyed in the Gulf War - these excuses were "a joke" and "the most fanciful so far" according to one UN official.[122]

Unravelling the truth about the biological weapons program is probably the last main obstacle to the completion of UNSCOM's task. UNSCOM is due to submit its next report on 10 April 1995. If it reports the satisfactory conclusion of its work, including arrangements for on-going monitoring, the Security Council would have to confront the lifting of the export embargo. It has been proposed that once the mechanisms and procedures for weapons monitoring

---

[121] UN Doc. S/1994/1138 at para. 2.

[122] "UN uncovers Iraqi germ warfare plan", The Guardian 1 March 1995.

are in place, there should be a testing period perhaps of six months before the oil embargo should be lifted. This is not provided for in Resolution 687 and it would be a matter for the Security Council to decide whether a test period is needed and how long it should last.

VII.4 THE IRAQI TROOP BUILD-UP IN OCTOBER 1994

The momentum that built up in the second half of 1994 for some easing of sanctions was thrown considerably off course in the first week of October 1994 when reports broke that Iraq was building up its troop strength close to the Kuwait border. These belligerent moves came hard on the heels of threats by Iraq that it would not continue to cooperate with the UN unless there was some modification of the sanctions regime within a specific deadline.

The USA responded immediately to the troop build-up by preparing to send significant reinforcements of troops and airpower to the area with the support of some other countries. At the height of the crisis it was reported that Iraqi had up to 80,000 troops on the border, including 14,000 of the elite Republican Guards. The USA indicated that it had sent almost 40,00 troops to the area and had, in total, over 200,000 troops there or on alert. The USA also made it clear that it was considering various options, including a pre-emptive strike if necessary which its UN ambassador insisted was authorized under unspecified existing Security Council resolutions.[123] Within a few days Iraqi began to withdraw its troops.

The USA initially proposed establishing an exclusion zone for Iraqi ground troops and heavy weapons south of the 32nd parallel (the area in respect of which the coalition forces already operate a no-fly zone). Although the exclusion zone did not meet with support from other key countries, the Security Council did adopt Resolution 949 unanimously on 15 October 1994. This resolution demanded that Iraq withdraw its troops to their original positions and that it should not use its forces again in a hostile or provocative manner to threaten its neighbours or UN operations in Iraq. The preamble noted that there would be "serious consequences" of any failure to comply.

Adopted under Chapter VII, the resolution did not otherwise specify enforcement measures but the USA indicated that it interpreted the resolution as sanctioning the use of force if necessary. Russia publicly rejected such an interpretation and

---

[123] "US wary of Iraq may seek exclusion zone" and "Pre-emptive strike on Iraq seen do-able, effective", Reuters report, 11 October 1994.

France indicated that it would be up to the UN to decide on any use of force, not any individual state. Following the adoption of the resolution the USA and the UK made a joint demarche to Iraq outside the Security Council making it clear that force would be used if Iraq enhanced its military capabilities below the 32nd parallel. A US official also said that its ambassador to the UN had made it clear to Iraq that the USA "would not remain indifferent should Iraq use military force to suppress the Iraqi people in the north or the south".[124]

VII.5 THE IMPACT ON MOVES TO LIFT SANCTIONS

Although Iraq's threatening move was widely condemned, the incident highlighted the political divisions between some key states regarding future relations with Iraq. Russia played a key role in defusing the crisis, issuing a joint statement with Iraq on 13 October which noted Iraq's withdrawal of its troops and its intention to recognize the international borders of Kuwait. It also set out an undertaking by Russia to support the start of weapons monitoring with a limited test period not exceeding six months and to advocate the lifting of other sanctions subject to Iraq's implementation of relevant resolutions. Russia insisted on explicit recognition of these moves in Resolution 949 before it would agree to its adoption. Its role as a key diplomatic player was reinforced when Iraq officially recognized Kuwait's borders a month later. China was also more positive, welcoming the announced recognition of Kuwait and stating its view that "given the recent developments, the international community shall now consider the gradual lifting of sanctions against Iraq so as to ease the Iraqi people's sufferings".[125]

France was initially ambivalent. It insisted that Iraq's troop movements had not broken any Security Council resolutions and intimated that the USA had over-reacted to the crisis for domestic reasons. France has also taken the view that the Security Council must set clear objectives for Iraq, such as scheduling the test period for weapons monitoring, with a view to lifting sanctions on Iraqi exports once Iraq has complied. In November France initially reacted more cautiously following Iraq's recognition of Kuwait's borders. Its Defence Minister indicated that other measures would be needed and that France would take into consideration the treatment of minority groups in deciding whether to improve its relations with Baghdad.[126] In early January, however, in a move sharply

---

[124] "US, Britain warn Iraq on future troop movements", Reuters report, 21 October 1994.

[125] "China urges lifting of sanctions against Iraq" Reuters report, 11 November 1994.

[126] "France reacts cautiously to Iraqi move on Kuwait", Reuters report, 10 November 1994.

criticized by the USA and the UK, France took the first steps towards a resumption of diplomatic relations with Iraq by announcing it would open an interests section in the Romanian Embassy in Baghdad. The French Foreign Minister also met with Iraq's deputy Prime Minister to discuss the easing of sanctions.

The USA has maintained its position that all relevant resolutions must be complied with, including Resolution 688, before the lifting of sanctions can be discussed. In the after-math of the troop build-up the US Secretary of State reiterated this and noted that this would be unlikely as long as Saddam Hussein was in power.[127] The UK has been broadly supportive of this tougher position and has also stressed the need for all Council resolutions to be complied with. Addressing the Security Council on the occasion of the adoption of Resolution 949 (1994), the UK ambassador to the UN noted that confidence in Iraq had been seriously undermined and that, before sanctions were lifted, the Council had to ensure that Iraq would cooperate with weapons monitoring, that it would not divert oil income to illegal arms purchases, and that it would not turn again on its own people or its neighbours. He stated in no uncertain terms that steps required by Iraq to demonstrate its peaceful intentions not only extended to cooperation with the weapons inspections but also included remedying the appalling human rights situation in the country as called for by Resolution 688.

In March 1995 it was reported that Russia and France may seek to introduce a resolution to lift the export embargo when the next UN report on weapons monitoring is published on 10 April. To head off such a move the US ambassador to the UN toured some of the countries on the Security Council to secure support for maintaining the full sanctions regime until a "pattern of compliance" is demonstrated on a range of issues. She stressed that "Iraq still abuses its own people in the north and the south of the country".[128]

VII.6 THE RELATIONSHIP OF RESOLUTION 688 TO THE SANCTIONS REGIME

Resolution 688 (1991) was not expressly linked to the other package of resolutions on Iraq. It did not refer to any of these in its preamble, in contrast to other resolutions which have generally recalled relevant previous Council decisions by express reference. It was, however, cited and reaffirmed in Council Resolutions 706 and 712 which set out the "food for oil" formula as a special

---

[127] "US upholds right to use force against Iraq" Reuters report, 16 October 1994.

[128] "US insists sanctions on Iraq must stay", The Guardian 25 February 1995.

modification of the oil embargo to finance humanitarian needs. In practice, the measures which have been taken pursuant to Resolution 688 are integrally linked to the whole package of resolutions on Iraq. Furthermore it appears to have been treated as a "relevant resolution", the implementation of which must be considered in the periodic reviews of the sanctions regime.

In 1992, for example, statements by the President on behalf of the Council reviewing Iraq's obligations under the relevant resolutions included a specific review of Resolution 688. It was recorded in November 1992 that "the Council remains deeply concerned at the grave human rights abuses that, despite the provisions of Resolution 688 (1991), the Government of Iraq continues to perpetrate against its population, in particular in the northern region of Iraq, in southern Shi'a centres and in the southern marshes". The Council took note of the reports of the Special Rapporteur on Iraq in this context.

In any event, even if it were to be argued that Resolution 688 is not a relevant resolution for the purpose of the consideration of the lifting of sanctions, pursuant to paragraph 21 of Resolution 687, the issues it deals with certainly fall within the much broader and open-ended concept of the Iraq Government's "policies and practices". These policies and practices must also be taken into account under the terms of paragraph 21.

Some states have argued that Resolution 688 is too broadly worded and that compliance with it cannot satisfactorily be measured. Yet objective standards by which compliance could be judged do exist. The UN's own human rights treaties to which Iraq is a party and other relevant UN instruments, such as the Declaration on the Rights of Persons Belonging to National or Ethnic, Religious and Linguistic Minorities, provide an objective set of internationally-agreed norms and standards by which the UN can assess the extent to which Iraq is acting to end internal repression and ensuring the protection of the human rights of all its citizens.

A monitoring mechanism could also be established now by the Security Council, pending a more comprehensive settlement which should also include a monitoring component. The USA has said, after all, that "Because the Government of Iraq is not credible, it must be judged by what it verifiably does, not by what it says".[129] It is simply not credible to neglect the monitoring of human rights obligations. Human rights monitoring components have been established in the context of a number of UN operations, such as those in El

---

[129] Press release of the Security Council debate on Resolution 949 (1994), SC/5915 of 15 October 1994.

Salvador, Cambodia, Haiti, the former Yugoslavia and, most recently, in Rwanda. The Special Rapporteur on Iraq made detailed proposals some considerable time ago, endorsed by the General Assembly and the Commission on Human Rights, for a human rights monitoring operation in Iraq. The Security Council found no difficulty with imposing in Resolution 687 an intrusive and long-term supervisory mechanism for the monitoring of Iraq's weapons capability.

It is more difficult to tie compliance with Resolution 688 to the lifting of the oil embargo. This is dependent on the specific conditions laid down in paragraph 22 of Resolution 687 which do not include general compliance with all other relevant resolutions. The USA and the UK seem to take the view, however, that as long as Iraq continues its flagrant disregard of its other obligations under Council resolutions and international law, the Government cannot be trusted to comply in good faith with the weapons monitoring mechanism. If real progress is made on weapons monitoring, however, and the UN inspectors confirm that they are satisfied with Iraqi compliance, this position will be increasingly difficult to sustain.

This only underscores the fact that sanctions alone cannot be a long-term solution and cannot be a guarantee of on-going security for Iraqi Kurdistan. In any event, international sanctions have intensified hardship and deprivation in the northern region (as elsewhere in Iraq) and are impeding its economic, social and political development in ways that only perpetuate insecurity and conflict. Steps must be taken now, while the leverage of the sanctions regime is still in place, to secure a comprehensive UN plan for Iraqi Kurdistan and one that is not solely dependent on sanctions as an attempt to force its implementation.

VIII. GROSS VIOLATIONS OF HUMAN RIGHTS IN IRAQ

The international protection of Iraqi Kurdistan has to be viewed in the wider context of Iraq's shocking human rights record and, in particular, its persistent and brutal repression of the Kurds over many years.[130]

Iraq is clearly obligated under international law to protect the rights of all its citizens, including the special rights of minority groups, and to abide by the rules of humanitarian law in situations of armed conflict. Yet the Iraqi Government has repeatedly flouted its international obligations and responsibilities and has demonstrated its contempt for the international monitoring mechanisms that supervise the implementation of human rights in UN member states. Many of these violations affect the entire population of Iraq, but it is the Kurds who have suffered some of the worst abuses over the years and who have been the targets of particularly violent measures.

The primary responsibility under international law for the observance and respect of human rights must lie with individual states. However, when a state is not willing to protect its own citizens and itself becomes the instrument of repression, then the international community has a responsibility to step in. The history of gross violations perpetrated by the Iraqi Government, although ignored for many years, was certainly the driving force behind the safe havens and the subsequent continuation of international protection for Iraqi Kurdistan.

There can be no question that special protection for the region must continue. The Iraqi Government has continued its flagrant breaches of international human rights and humanitarian law. Even the universal condemnation and the punitive measures imposed by the international community since 1991 have not resulted in the smallest indication of a change of attitude. On the contrary, the characteristic pattern of gross and systematic violations has continued in the government-controlled areas, particularly in the south of Iraq where brutality and repression have reached new heights.[131] The Iraqi Government must be held to its international legal obligations; but as long as it shows no intention of observing these the Kurds can look only to the international community to secure the protection of their rights.

---

[130] Chilling accounts of the nature and extent of repression in Iraq can be found in Kanan Makiya (Samir Al-Khalil) Republic of Fear (1989) and Cruelty and Silence (1994).

VIII.I IRAQ'S OBLIGATIONS UNDER INTERNATIONAL LAW

VIII.1.1 INTERNATIONAL HUMAN RIGHTS LAW

The promotion and protection of human rights is a founding principle of the UN. As a UN member state, Iraq is obligated under Articles 55 and 56 of the UN Charter to take joint and separate action to promote "universal respect for, and observance of, human rights and fundamental freedoms for all without distinction as to race, sex, language or religion".

Furthermore, Iraq is legally bound to implement detailed and specific human rights obligations by virtue of its voluntary ratification of a number of key international treaties. These require Iraq to respect and safeguard a wide range of civil, political, economic, social and cultural rights as well as to respect the principles of humanitarian law in times of armed conflict. It is also required to comply with the various international supervisory procedures established under these treaties.

Iraq is a party to the following international treaties:
The Convention on the Prevention and Punishment of the Crime of Genocide (accession: January 20 1959)

The International Convention on the Suppression and Punishment of the Crime of Apartheid
(ratification: 9 July 1975)

The International Covenant on Civil and Political Rights
(ratification: 25 January 1971)
Iraq has not made the declaration under Article 41 of this Convention recognizing the competence of the Human Rights Committee to consider inter-state complaints. Neither has it ratified the Optional Protocol to the Convention recognizing the Committee's competence to consider complaints of violations submitted by individuals.

---

[131] Severe reprisals in the south following the 1991 uprisings intensified in 1992, apparently as a preconceived policy of destruction. The predominantly Shi'a population has been subjected to a barrage of indiscriminate bombings and military attacks on civilian settlements, killings, disappearances, arbitrary arrest and detention, forced relocation and the almost total destruction of the livelihood and culture of the Marsh Arabs by a massive water diversion project which is drying the marshes and rendering them uninhabitable. The area is under a de facto blockade and neither the UN nor international aid agencies have been able to operate there. A second no-fly zone imposed south of the 32nd parallel has not halted the onslaught. This situation not only demands an emergency response, but serves as a grim and urgent reminder of the likely fate of the Kurds if international protection were to be removed. See, generally, the reports of the Special Rapporteur on Iraq, particularly UN Doc. A/47/367, and Stapleton The Shias of Iraq (1993), issued by the UK Parliamentary Human Rights Group.

The International Covenant on Economic, Social and Cultural Rights
(ratification: 25 January 1971)

The International Convention on the Elimination of All Forms of Racial Discrimination
(ratification: 14 January 1970)
Iraq has not made the declaration under Article 14 of this Convention recognizing the competence of the Committee on the Elimination of Racial Discrimination to consider complaints of violations submitted by individuals. It has also made a reservation to Article 22 indicating that it does not accept the jurisdiction of the International Court of Justice over disputes between states parties as to the interpretation or application of the Convention.

The Convention on the Elimination of All Forms of Discrimination against Women
(ratification: 13 August 1986)
Iraq has made reservations to substantive Articles 2 (f) and (g); 9 (1) and (2); and 16. It has also made a reservation in respect of Article 29(1) indicating that it does not accept the jurisdiction of the International Court of Justice over disputes between states parties as to the interpretation or application of the Convention.

The Convention on the Rights of the Child
(accession: 15 June 1994)
Iraq has made a reservation to substantive Article 14(1) of this Convention.

Iraq has also made a unilateral declaration undertaking to comply with the terms of the 1975 UN Declaration on the Protection of All Persons from Being Subjected to Torture or Other Cruel, Inhuman or Degrading Treatment or Punishment and to implement its provisions. The General Assembly urged states in 1977 to demonstrate voluntary compliance with the Declaration in this way. A unilateral declaration can be a way of entering into treaty obligations with another state[132] and it has been suggested that these declarations of compliance may represent legally binding commitments.[133]

In addition to the human rights treaties which impose legal obligations on Iraq,

---

[132] Eastern Greenland Case, (1933) PCIJ, Ser. A/B, No. 53.

[133] Rodley, The Treatment of Prisoners Under International Law (1987) at pp. 58-59. Rodley also demonstrates that the basic content of the Declaration against Torture probably already reflects general international law and, as such, is binding on all states.

the UN has adopted a wide range of other norms and standards in the form of declarations, principles and guidelines. These are not per se legally binding, but do represent authoritative statements by UN member states as to the norms and standards by which they should be guided in their conduct. As such, these instruments carry significant political and moral weight. Their value and impact rests on their acceptance and recognition by a large number of states; they are frequently cited in UN resolutions and comprise broadly accepted principles that form part of the body of international human rights standards and contribute to fleshing out the terms of the human rights treaties.

The UN norms and standards which are particularly relevant in the Iraqi context include the Body of Principles of the Protection of All Persons Under Any Form of Detention or Imprisonment; The Declaration on the Protection of All Persons from Enforced Disappearance; the Principles on the Effective Prevention and Investigation of Extra-Legal, Arbitrary and Summary Executions; the Safeguards guaranteeing the Protection of those Facing the Death Penalty; the Code of Conduct for Law Enforcement Officials; the Basic Principles on the Use of Force and Firearms by Law Enforcement Officials; and the Declaration of the Rights of the Child.

VIII.1.2 INTERNATIONAL HUMANITARIAN LAW

Iraq has ratified and is legally bound by the terms of the four Geneva Conventions of 1949:
The Geneva Conventions for the Amelioration of the Condition of the Wounded and Sick in Armed Forces in the Field

The Geneva Convention for the Amelioration of the Condition of Wounded, Sick and Shipwrecked Members of the Armed Forces at Sea

The Geneva Convention relative to the Treatment of Prisoners of War

The Geneva Convention relative to the Protection of Civilian Persons in Time of War
(ratification: 14 February 1956)
Iraq has not, however, ratified the two Additional Protocols to the Geneva Conventions dealing with the protection of victims of international and non-international armed conflicts respectively.

The four Geneva Conventions of 1949 to which Iraq is a party are primarily

applicable in situations of international armed conflict between two or more states. However, Article 3, which is common to all four Conventions, requires states parties to respect minimum humanitarian standards in cases of armed conflict occurring in that state's territory and which is not of an international character. A state is required to ensure that persons taking no active part in the hostilities, such as civilians and members of armed forces placed <u>hors de combat</u> for any reason, are treated humanely and without discrimination and that the wounded and sick are collected and cared for. In particular the following acts are absolutely prohibited:
(a) violence to life and person, in particular murder of all kinds, mutilation, cruel treatment and torture;
(b) taking of hostages;
(c) outrages upon personal dignity, in particular humiliating and degrading treatment;
(d) the passing of sentences and the carrying out of executions without previous judgment pronounced by a regularly constituted court, affording all the judicial guarantees which are recognized as indispensable by civilized peoples.
Common Article 3 also states that the parties to the conflict should endeavour to bring into force by special agreements all or part of the other provisions of each Geneva Convention.

A state responsible for the acts prohibited by Common Article 3 commits very serious breaches of international humanitarian law. Such acts are a flagrant violation of Common Article 1 by which states parties "undertake to respect and to ensure respect for the [Geneva Conventions] in all circumstances". They are also in contravention of the general enforcement provisions common to all four Conventions that oblige states parties to take the "measures necessary for the suppression of all acts contrary to the [Geneva Conventions]...".[134] It should be noted, however, that violations of Common Article 3 are not classified under the terms of the Geneva Conventions as "grave breaches" and do not, therefore, fall within the special enforcement rules governing grave breaches.

It is also necessary for conflict to reach a certain degree of severity before it would be considered to fall under Common Article 3. Riots and other civil disturbances, even if suppressed with lethal force, would not generally fall within its scope. There is no doubt, however, that much of the conflict waged between the Iraqi Government and the Kurds is certainly of a level to which Common Article 3 would apply. Excessive and illegal use of force in quelling

---

[134] Article 49 of Geneva Convention I; Article 50 of Geneva Convention II; Article 129 of Geneva Convention III; and Article 146 of Geneva Convention IV.

lesser disturbances would, in any event be caught by the provisions of international human rights law which continues to apply in a state of emergency or other civil conflict.

Although Iraq is not party to the two additional Protocols to the Geneva Conventions dealing with the protection of victims of armed conflict, attacks against civilians are widely condemned and prohibited by the customary laws of armed conflict. General Assembly Resolution 2444 (1968) reaffirms principles that must be observed by all parties in armed conflict, including the prohibition of attacks on the civilian population and the requirement to distinguish at all times between civilians and persons taking part in hostilities. Similarly, the Declaration on the Protection of Women and Children in Emergency and Armed Conflict prohibits and condemns "attacks and bombings on the civilian population, inflicting incalculable suffering".[135]

The use of chemical weapons by Iraq is already outlawed by the 1925 Protocol for the Prohibition of the Use in War of Asphyxiating Poisonous or Other Gases, and of Bacteriological Methods of Warfare to which Iraq is a party. In 1986 the Security Council strongly condemned Iraq's use of chemical weapons in the Iran-Iraq war and in 1988 adopted a resolution condemning the use of such weapons in that conflict. Although this Protocol only applies to international conflicts, it reflects three important customary principles of international humanitarian law: i) the right to adopt methods of warfare is not unlimited; ii) methods and weapons that cause unnecessary suffering and superfluous injury, whether to civilians or combatants, are prohibited; and iii) non-combatants must always be protected and, in particular, the indiscriminate targeting of civilians is outlawed. These same principles are reflected in Protocol II of the 1980 UN Convention on Prohibitions or Restrictions on the Use of Certain Conventional Weapons Which May be Determined to be Excessively Injurious or to have Indiscriminate Effects, to which Iraq is not yet a party. Protocol II, <u>inter alia</u>, prohibits the indiscriminate use of mines against civilians and the laying of mines without a record of their location.

In view of their international regulation, resort to chemical weapons and the indiscriminate laying of mines in civilian areas may well amount to serious violations of the laws and customs of war, even in an internal conflict.[136] The Statute of the International Tribunal for the former Yugoslavia, for example,

---

[135] Proclaimed by General Resolution 3318 (XXIX) of 14 December 1974.

[136] Chemical weapons, which are necessarily indiscriminate in their effect, are probably unlawful per se whereas land mines are unlawful if they are used in ways that cause indiscriminate harm.

expressly includes the "employment of poisonous weapons or other weapons calculated to cause unnecessary suffering" as a violation of the laws and customs of war. Article 22 of the draft Code of Crimes against the Peace and Security of Mankind also includes the use of unlawful weapons as an exceptionally serious war crime. The use of such weapons against non-combatants would certainly fall within the general prohibition of violence, murder and cruel treatment in Common Article 3. The Declaration on the Protection of Women and Children in Emergency and Armed Conflict also strongly condemns the use of chemical and bacteriological weapons as "one of the most flagrant violations" of the Geneva Conventions and the principles of humanitarian law.

VIII.2 THE GENERAL HUMAN RIGHTS SITUATION IN IRAQ

Iraq's invasion of Kuwait in 1990 and the events which followed turned the spotlight on Iraq's human rights record in an unprecedented way. Still international attention has tended to focus on current human rights violations in the country and those which occurred in the relatively recent past, about which a great deal of new information has now come to light. Yet extensive and brutal human rights violations have been the pattern in Iraq for many years. Indeed, the information now available about the human rights situation only serves to confirm the veracity of past allegations to which the international community largely turned a blind eye or dismissed as exaggerated.[137]

In its 1990 report on human rights violations by Iraqi forces in occupied Kuwait, Amnesty International stated:

> Those violations which have been reported since 2 August [1990] are entirely consistent with abuses known to have been committed in Iraq over many years...Amnesty International has repeatedly placed such information on the public record and regrets that, until the invasion of Kuwait, the international community did not see fit to apply serious pressure in an attempt to put an end to these abuses.

Drawing attention to human rights violations in Iraq has been exacerbated by the difficulty in gathering accurate information. The Iraqi Government has not generally permitted access to human rights organizations, journalists or others to carry out independent investigations and assessments. Its typical response to all allegations of violations is to dismiss them as totally unfounded and biased

---

[137] The systematic breaches by Iraq of its international obligations have been extensively documented and are only briefly summarized in this section. It should also be noted that some of these violations would amount to war crimes and crime against humanity and, as such, would incur individual criminal responsibility as well as state responsibility. The implications of this are discussed more fully in Section XII.3 below.

and to point to provisions of the Constitution or domestic law which, on paper, guarantee and protect human rights. The web of fear and distrust that pervades the country, the constant threat of reprisals and restrictions on communications with the outside world has severely limited information coming from inside Iraq. The main sources have been exiles and refugees, many of whom have also been unwilling to speak freely for fear of reprisals against family and friends left in Iraq.

Nevertheless there is no shortage of reliable documentation of a seemingly endless catalogue of human rights violations in Iraq. These include reports by reputable non-governmental organizations, such as Amnesty International, the Federation Internationale des Droits de L'Homme, Middle East Watch and the International Commission of Jurists,[138] as well as reports by the UN's thematic mechanisms dealing with disappearances, summary or arbitrary executions and torture. In 1991, following Iraq's invasion of Kuwait, the UN Commission on Human Rights appointed a Special Rapporteur on the human rights situation in Iraq. His twice-yearly reports to the Commission and the General Assembly - provide extensive and chilling documentation of recent and on-going violations in Iraq.

Iraq is governed by a repressive one-party political and security apparatus which exercises tight control over virtually all aspects of life.[139] It perpetuates "an all-pervasive order of repression and oppression which is sustained by broad-based discrimination and wide-spread terror".[140] The Arab Ba'ath Socialist Party has ruled Iraq since it seized power for the second time in 1968, under the authority of General Ahmad Hassan Al Bakr. Since 1979 Saddam Hussein has occupied a position of unrivalled political power and authority at the apex of the party hierarchy as President of the Republic, Chairman of the highest legislative and executive body, the Revolutionary Command Council (RCC) and Secretary General of the Arab Ba'ath Socialist Party.

Saddam Hussein consolidated his position through a series of bloody purges of the Ba'ath Party, by establishing a complex and ruthless security apparatus and

---

[138] See, for example, Amnesty International's Annual Reports, which have documented human rights violations in Iraq for over 20 years; Human Rights Watch World Reports; Amnesty International Torture in Iraq 1982-1984 (1985), Torture and Executions in Iraq (1986), Iraq - Children Innocent Victims of Political Repression (1989), Middle East Watch Human Rights in Iraq (1990) and Bureaucracy of Repression (1994); International Commission of Jurists Iraq and the Rule of Law(1994); Federation Internationale des Droits de L'Homme/Fondation France Libertes Rapport de la Mission D'Enquete - Kurdistan Irakien (1993) and the other reports cited later in this section.

[139] See, generally, CARDRI Saddam's Iraq - Revolution or Reaction? (1989).

[140] Report of the Special Rapporteur on Iraq, UN Doc. E/CN.4/1993/45 at para. 179.

by building up a personal cult admitting of no criticism or challenge. The party apparatus pervades all walks of life and membership is essential for any positions of political influence and, effectively if not explicitly, for positions and advancement in many other professional posts. It operates through a web of police and intelligence agencies and party members are expected to play a key role in surveillance, creating a nation of informers and an atmosphere of constant fear, intimidation and suspicion.

The RCC, the cadre of top party officials presided over by Saddam Hussein, wields absolute political, executive and legislative power. Provisions of the Constitution and domestic laws guaranteeing and protecting rights are routinely ignored or deliberately flouted with no prospect of challenge or redress. Other institutions, such as the judiciary and the National Assembly, which, in theory, might represent some checks and balances on the RCC are effectively powerless. The National Assembly, for example, has very limited powers and although it can review draft laws it has no power of review over the decrees frequently issued by the RCC.

A whole range of fundamental rights, including freedom of expression, association and movement, are tightly circumscribed or non-existent under this authoritarian regime. The introduction in 1986 of life imprisonment or death for insulting the President or top state institutions as well as the network of Ba'ath Party informers has effectively silenced any free political discussion, much less any expression of dissent. By far the most chilling characteristic of the regime, however, is the ruthless brutality of its suppression of any opposition. In his first report to the Commission on Human Rights the Special Rapporteur on Iraq concluded:

> Having studied further the situation in Iraq, after having been to Iraq and after having met numerous persons inside and outside the country (at least such persons as would dare to speak), the Special Rapporteur concludes that the violations of human rights which have occurred are so grave and are of such a massive nature that since the Second World War few parallels can be found. Nor is it likely that these violations will come to an end as long as the security forces have the power to decide over the freedom and imprisonment, or even life or death, of any Iraqi citizen. With every day that passes, new names will be added to those of the thousands of Iraqi citizens who have been victims of human rights violations.[141]

---

[141] UN Doc. E/CN.4/1992/31 at para. 154.

Political killings are commonplace; Amnesty International has estimated that hundreds of thousands of people have been extra-judicially killed during the 1980s. The Special Rapporteur on Iraq noted in 1994 that "arbitrary executions and killings remain widespread throughout the country" and affect "all strata of the population, irrespective of ethnicity, religion, language or geographical location".[142] In a recent report Amnesty International stated:

> the perpetration of extrajudicial executions has been developed into a fine art [in Iraq]. The methods used include the use of chemical weapons against civilians; mass executions by firing squad; burying people alive or tying heavy weights to their feet and pushing them into rivers while alive; poisoning through the use of thallium (a substance used in rat poison) and other poisons; bleeding prisoners and detainees to death; assassinations by shooting; and "accidental deaths" supposedly occurring in car accidents or helicopter crashes. In addition, thousands of people have died in custody in unknown circumstances or as a result of torture.[143]

There have also been a number of instances of assassinations or attempted assassinations which have taken place abroad and in respect of which Iraq security agents have been held responsible or heavily implicated.

The death penalty serves as another tool of political and social repression and is been applied to an ever-increasing list of broadly-defined offences. It is a capital offence, for example, for Ba'ath Party members to hide previous party affiliations, maintain ties with other parties or enter into a relationship with another party after leaving the Ba'ath Party or for others to recruit members of the Ba'ath Party to another party. In 1980 affiliation to the Al Da'wa Al Islamiya party was retroactively made punishable by death, as is membership of the Communist Party. More recently, following the Gulf War, the death penalty was extended to a range of economic crimes such as looting, hoarding food for commercial purposes, harbouring Western nationals, trading in banned goods, and car theft. Death sentences, including against minors under 18 years old, are often carried out after secret trials with inadequate or no legal defence and with no possibility of appeal.

Disappearances are commonplace; many remain unresolved while, in other cases, the victim's body has been returned, often bearing appalling injuries, and a fee demanded for "state expenses", including the cost of bullets used in the execution. Amnesty International believes several hundred thousand people

---

[142] UN Doc. E/CN.4/1994/58 at paras. 20 and 25.

[143] Amnesty International "Disappearances" and Political Killings - Human Rights Crisis of the 1990s. A Manual for Action, (1994).

disappeared in the 1980s:
Kurds, Arabs, Turcomans, Assyrians; Sunni and Shi'a Muslims, Christians and others; men, women and children; members of prohibited political parties and their families; military personnel and deserters; disaffected members of the ruling elite; relatives of deportees; Iraqis returning from abroad to benefit from officially-declared amnesties and others.[144]

The UN Working Group on Enforced or Involuntary Disappearances first took up cases of disappearance in Iraq in 1984 and has over 15,900 unresolved cases on its books, the majority of them involving Kurds. Of the 5,335 new cases submitted in 1994, for example, 4,982 concern Kurds reported to have disappeared in the region of Khalar during the 1988 Anfal campaign. According to the Working Group, Iraq is the country with the highest number of disappearances on its files and the climate of continuing retaliation and intimidation in the country makes it impossible for relatives to take steps to establish the whereabouts of their family members.[145]

Torture is routine and systematic for political and security prisoners and is also used against common criminals. The Special Rapporteur on Iraq stated in 1994 that "it appears that hardly anybody kept in an Iraqi detention centre escapes subjugation to physical or psychological abuse".[146] In a number of cases torture has resulted in deaths in custody or bodies have been found bearing marks of torture, sometimes with eyes gouged out. In 1981 Amnesty International issued a report documenting the personal torture testimonies of 15 Iraqi exiles which proved to be entirely consistent with the signs and symptoms revealed when they underwent medical examinations in London.[147] Methods of torture include beating on the body or soles of the feet, electric shock, threats of death or rape, mock executions, and burning with cigarettes. Sexual assault and rape are frequently used to extract information or as an insult against the woman's family. The UN Special Rapporteur on Torture has raised a number of torture cases with the Iraqi authorities and has never received a satisfactory response, other than a routine denial of the veracity of the allegations.[148]

---

[144] Ibid.

[145] Report of the Working Group on Enforced or Involuntary Disappearances, UN Doc. E/CN.4/1995/36 at paras. 237-245.

[146] UN Doc. E/CN.4/1994/58 at para. 34.

[147] Amnesty International Iraq: Evidence of Torture (1981).

[148] See, for example, UN Doc. E/CN.4/1994/31, paras. 348-351.

Any suspicion of political opposition is immediately repressed. Most opposition parties are banned and suspected political opponents are routinely and arbitrarily arrested, detained without trial or tried and sentenced to lengthy prison terms. Political arrests carried out by the various security officials typically ignore any procedural safeguards and those arrested may be taken to secret locations or simply disappear without trace. In a number of cases family members, including young children, have been arrested and detained as hostages in lieu of a suspect who cannot be found. Amnesty International has estimated there to be thousands of political prisoners in Iraq, although it is impossible to gauge the exact figures with any accuracy.

One of the most recent examples of the brutality of the current regime is the 1994 promulgation by Saddam Hussein of a series of punitive decrees. Decree No. 59 requires amputation of the right hand for certain property crimes and theft, and amputation of the left foot for repeat offences. If the perpetrator is armed or the crime results in death, the death penalty is imposed. Decree No. 92 provides for amputation for falsification of official documents and Decree No. 109 requires that anyone punished by amputation is to be branded with a tattooed "x" on their forehead. Decree No. 93 prohibits army deserters or those who evade military service from a range of commercial, industrial and agricultural activity (thereby effectively precluding them from earning a living). Such persons are also to have an ear amputated and a tattooed "x" branded on their forehead, as will anyone who harbours a deserter or draft evader (Decree No. 115). A second offence results in amputation of the other ear and a third offence carries the death penalty. In order to force medical personnel to comply with these decrees, Decree No. 117 provides that anyone removing a tattooed brand or carrying out cosmetic surgery following an amputation will be subject to the same punishments. Public records and identity documents must specify any such punishments suffered. The Special Rapporteur on Iraq reports that these punishments are already being widely implemented throughout the country.[149]

VIII.3 HUMAN RIGHTS VIOLATIONS AGAINST THE KURDS

While the general climate of repression and the perpetration of a range of gross violations has affected whole sectors of the Iraqi population, the Kurds have been subjected to a history of particularly severe oppression clearly aimed at stamping out political dissent and crushing their aspirations towards autonomy. The cumulation of these persistent efforts to force the Kurds into submission

---

[149] In his November 1994 report to the General Assembly the Special Rapporteur discusses these Decrees and includes the translated text of their provisions, UN Doc. A/49/651, Section IV and Appendix.

came with the Anfal campaign in 1988 in which between 50,000 and 100,000 Kurds are believed to have lost their lives. This campaign has demonstrated that there is no apparently no limit to the methods the Iraqi Government is ready to use against the Kurdish people. When the Iraqis moved in to crush the 1991 March uprisings with excessive and indiscriminate military force, it was hardly surprising that thousands of people fled for their lives and finally precipitated international intervention to save them.

Kurdish political groups have, of course, themselves taken up arms against the Government in their struggle for autonomy. Armed Kurdish pesh merga have attacked government forces and officials in conflicts which have sometimes been bloody and prolonged. However, Iraqi retaliation has typically been far in excess of what might be considered permissible by a government countering an armed insurgency. Unarmed civilians, including women and children, have frequently been targeted in massive reprisals and subjected to a consistent wave of violations of fundamental rights.

VIII.3.1 A HISTORY OF OPPRESSION

Kurdish aspirations to greater autonomy have always been regarded with the deepest suspicion. The government's moves to provide for some form of autonomy in the 1970s were accompanied by continuing efforts to crush Kurdish political movements and to force the Kurds into quiet submission with weak autonomous structures that would remain tightly controlled by the central government.

Periodic heavy military offensives against the Kurds have involved illegal and excessive methods of warfare and the indiscriminate targeting of civilians. Chemical weapons have been widely used, particularly during the Anfal campaign as described below. It is also estimated that as many as 20 million mines were laid in Iraqi Kurdistan during the 1980s, both in response to pesh merga uprisings as well as during the Iran-Iraq war.[150] It has been reported that mines were laid carelessly without mapping, often in agricultural areas and other non-war zones to render them uninhabitable. The many different types of mines used, a large number of them light-weight plastic mines, makes detection and clearing extremely difficult and hazardous. They constitute the largest single cause of unnatural death and injury in the area; in early 1992 figures indicated an average of 600 mine casualties a month. The Iraqi Government has made no attempts at demining the area. In May 1993 the UN Coordinator of the

---

[150] UNHCR Report on Northern Iraq - April 1991-May 1992 at Annex V-1.

humanitarian aid programme requested a visa for a UN demining expert to advise and prepare a plan to address the problem, but this was refused by the Government.[151]

Both in times of conflict and of relative peace the Kurds have consistently been subjected to a range of human rights violations including political killings, disappearances, arbitrary arrest and torture. Although the Autonomy Law guaranteed cultural and political freedom of expression, suspected Kurdish political activists have been singled out for repression. Ordinary civilians, including children, have also been targeted.

After the 1975 Algiers Agreement was concluded with Iran, for example, the Iraqi Government cracked down on Kurds suspected of political activities, including distributing leaflets, holding meetings or forming organizations. In 1976 Kurdish sources alleged that at least 60,000 men suspected of links with the banned KDP were detained in camps in the south of the country while 23 students and teachers suspected of membership in a secret organization affiliated to the PUK were tried before the Revolutionary Tribunal and three were sentenced to death. A year later Amnesty International reported that it had received information about 760 Kurdish political prisoners held in Iraq.[152]

When wanted suspects could not be found the Government instead arrested their relatives and detained them without charge - including the elderly, pregnant women and young children.[153] In 1985 300 children and young people were arrested in Sulaimaniya apparently in retaliation for pesh merga activities. There were reports that they had been tortured and that 29 of the group were executed without trial. That same year 300 people were reported to have been killed in northern Iraq after two air force officers were killed by Kurdish pesh merga. Twenty-three suspects were rounded up in Sulaimaniya and shot by firing squad - eight others were alleged to have been buried alive. Demonstrations against these measures in Sulaimaniya and other cities were violently suppressed, with soldiers firing directly into the crowd leaving many more dead. A further 80 people were killed in Arbil when the Citadel was destroyed by aerial bombardment.[154]

---

[151] Report of the UN Special Rapporteur on Iraq, UN Doc. E/CN.4/1994/58 at paras. 104-108.

[152] Amnesty International Report 1977

[153] Amnesty International Report 1978

[154] Amnesty International Report 1986

There were numerous other reports of summary executions of Kurds, after unfair trials or without any pretence of legal proceedings at all. Many of them were suspected of acts of sabotage or membership of banned organizations - others were students. In 1987 there were reports of 360 people executed in a two-month period. They included Kurdish political prisoners - among them 17 children aged between 14 and 17; between 100-150 Kurds from Jiman rounded up in house-to-house searches and summarily executed; and 32 Kurds from Shaqlawa arrested and summarily executed without trial after pesh merga forces had killed eight Iraqi officials. Thirty-one suspected KDP sympathizers were executed after summary trials and 150 prisoners in Abu Ghraib prison executed in two days in December including Kurds from Sulaimaniya and Dohuk. There were also reports that year of 40 Kurdish opponents of the government poisoned by thallium poisoning - among them 10 from the town of Marga in Sulaimaniya province aged 14-60 years.[155]

Other Kurdish opponents of the Government simply disappeared without trace. One of the most notorious incidents of disappearance was that of 5,000-8,000 Kurds, 315 of them children, in 1983. All were male members of the Barzani clan. At that time Barzani had forged a new alliance with Iran, by then at war with Iraq, and the KDP had supported the Iranians in their take-over of the strategic border town of Haj Omran. In an early morning military raid on the Qushtapa resettlement camp, between 5,000-8,000 men were rounded up and taken south to unknown destinations.[156] These disappearances have never been clarified although it is feared the victims were executed.

Those that were put on trial were typically denied any fundamental rights. A special court was set up in Kirkuk to try Kurds charged with political offences. Trials in special courts are summary and held in camera before members of the executive rather than the judiciary. There is no right of defence and no appeal and conviction often relies on confessions extracted by torture from detainees held incommunicado.

During the 1970s and 1980s the Government periodically announced amnesties for Kurds who had been involved in armed conflict. It was never possible to determine with any accuracy the numbers who sought to benefit from such measures but there were ample reports of some of those who attempted to do so being arrested, disappeared or executed.

---

[155] Amnesty International Report 1988

[156] Amnesty International Report 1989

Alongside this pattern of political persecution, the Government has consistently sought to maintain control in the northern area by a policy of forced relocation of Kurds and "arabization" of predominantly Kurdish areas, offering Arab settlers financial inducements to move into these areas. Attempts to re-draw the map of Kurdistan and to resettle Kurds in areas under central government control intensified after the Kurdish uprising of 1974-5. Hundreds of Kurdish villages in the governorates of Nineveh and Dohuk were destroyed and 150 more in Diyala. Those uprooted were sent to government-controlled camps along the main highways and restrictions were imposed on the residence and employment of Kurds in Kirkuk. Large numbers of Kurds were expelled altogether from the northern area and despatched to barren desert areas in the south of the country. Even when some were allowed to return a few years later they were barred from their former villages and were resettled either in the urban areas of Sulaimaniya, Arbil and Dohuk or in "new towns" which were then little more than make-shift camps but promoted by the Government as part of the development and modernisation of Kurdistan.

From about 1978, following the Algiers Agreement with Iran, the Government began to clear a cordon sanitaire along the borders with Iran and Turkey, which eventually extended to 30 kilometres. Kurdish villagers living in these border areas were forcibly removed and resettled in the "new towns". As many as 500 villages were destroyed and, according to the Ba'ath Party newspaper, in one two-month period some 28,000 families were forcibly expelled from their homes.

Expulsions ceased during the early years of the Iran-Iraq war, when army garrisons in Kurdistan had to be reduced and the pesh merga were able to reclaim their territory and establish Kurdish control, at least in the more inaccessible mountainous region. Kurds seized large areas adjacent to the Turkish and Iranian borders, those expelled began to return to their villages and proved remarkably resilient even in the face of continued Iraqi bombardments. The government's policy towards the Kurds hardened and by 1987 it was laying the basis for the Anfal campaign a year later - a campaign that went far beyond re-settlement and control and envisaged whole-scale extermination of the Kurds who continued to defy its authority.

VIII.3.2 THE CONTEXT OF THE ANFAL CAMPAIGN

The so-called Anfal campaign is the name given to a series of military actions against the Kurds carried out with ruthless planning and precision between

February and September 1988. It represents the most brutal and destructive government campaign against the Kurdish people to date - a campaign which resulted in the deaths of between 50,000 and 100,000 people and the whole-sale destruction of the Kurdish rural economy and infrastructure.

The Anfal campaign must be seen in the context of the Iraqi Government's long-standing attempts to control its Kurdish population and the political situation at the end of the 1980s. The struggle for Kurdish autonomy represented both an internal threat of on-going armed insurgency and an external one as long as Kurdish groups forged alliances with hostile foreign powers. Periodic cosmetic concessions to limited Kurdish autonomy had always been underpinned by a determination to quash the military capacity of the Kurds, to limit the extent of any autonomous area, in particular to exclude valuable oil resources, and to keep the area firmly under ultimate government control. Foreshadows of the Anfal campaign can be seen in the policy of enforced removal and re-settlement of Kurds as well as in the harsh repression of political activity and the widespread use of arrest, disappearance, torture and execution against suspected Kurdish political activists.

In the late 1980s the Iraqi Government was counting the heavy cost of its eight-year war with Iran, during which it had seen both of the major Kurdish parties adopting dangerous alliances with the enemy as well as coming to an equally threatening agreement between themselves. The Kurds had regained effective control in many of their traditional strong-holds in the strategic border areas, in defiance of the government's attempts to move them into government-controlled areas.

At the same time the Anfal campaign cannot be explained away simply as a particularly harsh counter-insurgency operation. The aims of the campaign, its huge scale, the methods used, the indiscriminate targeting of entire civilian village populations and the subsequent rounding up and treatment of survivors were not only far in excess of legitimate counter-insurgency measures under international law, but also indicated a more sinister intent to destroy whole sectors of the Kurdish population, their culture and livelihood.

Such a conclusion is not based on mere speculation or hear-say about the events of the campaign. During the March uprising in the Kurdish areas in 1991, access was obtained to the offices of the security services and other government agencies and an extraordinary volume of materials were discovered, documenting in great detail the aims, planning and execution of the campaign. This volume of evidence - consisting of 14 tons of documents, audiotapes, videotapes, films and photographs - has since been secured in archives in the USA. The Special Rapporteur on Iraq has reviewed some of this evidence and has reproduced some of the documents in his reports. A more detailed analysis of this huge volume of material has been carried out by the US-based human rights organization, Middle East Watch, which also conducted extensive field research and forensic investigations in northern Iraq and has published a very detailed account and analysis of the Anfal campaign.[157]

VIII.3.3 THE CONDUCT OF THE ANFAL CAMPAIGN

The Anfal campaign was characterized by gross violations of human rights and humanitarian law committed on a massive scale and, in the words of the Special Rapporteur, "accomplished in a clearly systematic fashion though the intentional use of obviously excessive force". These included:
 deliberate mass executions and indiscriminate killings on a huge scale of non-combatants as well as those captured and disarmed;
 the extensive and indiscriminate use of chemical weapons;
 mass disappearances of men, women and children, many of whom have never been seen again;
 mass arbitrary arrests and detention without any legal basis or legal proceedings;
 cruel and inhuman treatment, including denial of food, medical attention and neglect, of those detained;
 forced re-settlement of whole communities in appalling conditions that resulted in further deaths; and
 looting and destruction of property and the complete destruction of some 2,000 villages, including civilian habitation, schools, mosques and other infrastructure.

The Anfal campaign was well-planned, meticulously organized and extensively documented. It was master-minded by Ali Hassan al-Majid (now Minister of Defence) who was appointed Secretary General of the Ba'ath Party's Northern Bureau in 1987. While it was ostensibly directed against Kurds who continued to defy the government - "saboteurs", "traitors" and "subversives" - it is clear from the documentary evidence that it was aimed indiscriminately at destroying whole sectors of the Kurdish population who had not been brought under strict government control and who refused to "return to the national ranks". The

---

[157] Middle East Watch Genocide in Iraq - The Anfal Campaign Against the Kurds (1993). This section of the report draws extensively on this study.

target areas were the rural villages which were beyond government control and were designated "prohibited areas".

The basis for the campaign was laid in 1987 with a series of orders tightening the already repressive measures directed against the Kurds. "Saboteurs" lost all property rights, the legal rights of the residents of the prohibited villages were suspended, and the execution of first-degree relatives of saboteurs and of wounded civilians considered hostile to the government was ordered. More chilling were two directives issued by Ali Hassan al-Majid. The first authorized the killing of anyone found in prohibited areas which were placed under strict economic embargo. The second called for bombardment of these areas "in order to kill the largest number of persons present in those prohibited areas" and stated that all those captured there should be detained and "those between the ages of 15 and 70 shall be executed after any useful information has been obtained from them".

In April 1987 the first chemical weapon attack was launched against the KDP headquarters in Dohuk governorate and the PUK headquarters in Sulaimaniya governorate. Chemicals were also dropped on the civilian villages of Sheikh Wasan and Balisan; in addition to those killed in the attack a large number of victims being treated in the hospital in Arbil were taken away and have not been seen again. In the ensuing couple of months 700 villages were burned and bulldozed.

The target group of the campaign was further defined by a national census held in October 1987. This required people to register as Arabs or Kurds and only those Kurds who moved out of the prohibited areas and aligned themselves with the government were eligible. Families of unrepentant "saboteurs", however, could not remain in government-controlled areas and were expelled to the prohibited areas, except males between 12 and 50 who were to be detained. Anyone who did not participate in the census would lose Iraqi citizenship and be regarded as an army deserter, thereby at risk of the death penalty - the punishment for desertion after one year or for a repeat offence.

In February 1988, four months after the census, the Anfal campaign began with a massive attack on the PUK headquarters and strong-holds in the governorate of Sulaimaniya. It was carried out in eight distinct stages until an amnesty was declared on 6 September. The pattern of each onslaught was similar - an initial massive assault using chemical weapons and other conventional weapons was directed indiscriminately against the target areas. The initial assault was followed by ground troops who swept through the villages looting and destroying everything. Survivors were rounded up and taken away to holding centres and detention camps or prisons. Those who attempted to escape were pursued and captured. One of the most notorious and the largest chemical weapon attacks which finally attracted the world's attention was that on the town of Halabja in March in which between 3,200 and 5,000 people lost their lives.[158]

In the aftermath of the Anfal military sweeps, large numbers of those rounded up simply disappeared - men, women and children. Some were taken from camps to execution sites and killed en masse. Eyewitnesses have described mass executions and have indicated the location of at least three grave sites. Detention conditions were appalling and many are believed to have died in detention from neglect, starvation and disease. In the September amnesty many of the women, children and the elderly who had managed to survive were released from detention but the majority of the men arrested in the campaign have never reappeared and many of them are believed to have been executed.

Between 50,000 and 100,000 are believed to have died during the Anfal campaign. Some 2,000 villages were completely destroyed as well as a dozen larger towns and administrative centres. Those released in the amnesty were not, of course, allowed to return to the ravaged villages which were sown with landmines. Instead they were dumped in barren relocation areas or simply abandoned without shelter or infrastructure of any kind and with no means of support. Many more died there from disease, exposure, and malnutrition. Political rights and employment were denied to the amnestied Kurds until their loyalty had been established, which included a pledge that they would remain in the re-settlement camps on pain of death.

According to Middle East Watch the arrests, executions, forced re-location and destruction of villages continued beyond the amnesty. That organization has documented three cases of mass executions in late 1988; in one instance 180 people were executed. Dozens more villages, even those with pro-government sympathies - were razed to the ground in late 1988 and 1989.

VIII.3.4 THE CRUSHING OF THE MARCH 1991 UPRISING

The uprisings which began inside Iraq shortly after its forces were finally driven from Kuwait represented the most serious threat to the very survival of the Iraqi

---

[158] Middle East Watch points out in its report on the Anfal campaign that, in fact, the attack on Halabja was not technically part of the Anfal but was a reprisal for its capture by peshmerga supported by Iranian Revolutionary Guards.

Government. It had lost control to rebel forces of key cities in the south and north of the country and it was to be expected that there would be a determined attempt to put down the rebellion. The conflict was fierce and there were reports of violations on all sides.

However, the Iraqi Government reacted to the uprising with characteristic ruthlessness and brutality, far in excess of what might be considered legitimate under international human rights and humanitarian law in countering civil conflict. Indiscriminate and heavy ground and aerial bombardments resulted in a high civilian death toll. As people in the north began to flee towards the borders in huge numbers, helicopter gun-ships deliberately strafed columns of terrified civilians. As security forces advanced into the cities there were numerous reports of summary executions on the streets and in hospitals and homes. There were widespread arrests, sometimes of entire families, and some of those arrested simply disappeared. Torture, mass summary executions and the killings of unarmed civilians fleeing the advancing onslaught were widely reported. Several refugees from Kirkuk reported the rounding up and arrest of 5,000 males in that city alone.[159]

The terrified flight from this offensive of some 1.8 million people in Iraqi Kurdistan finally prompted the adoption of Security Council Resolution 688 (1991) and the setting up of the safe havens, as described in Section IV above. These measures have significantly inhibited but have not terminated continuing violations against the Kurds:

> Iraq's continuing embargo and military build-up, the periodic shelling and skirmishes along the frontline, the uncertain future of the Allied and UN presence, the harassment of UN workers and apparent acts by saboteurs have all helped to keep hundreds of thousands of Kurds ready to take flight at a moment's notice.[160]

VIII.4 UN ACTION IN RESPECT OF HUMAN RIGHTS VIOLATIONS IN IRAQ

Iraq has been subject to some forms of UN scrutiny for many years. It is required, for example, to submit periodic reports on its implementation of a number of the human rights treaties which are examined by expert monitoring

---

[159] More detailed accounts of the crushing of the March uprisings, and particularly the devastating violence perpetrated in the south of the country which is beyond the scope of this report, can be found in the reports of the Special Rapporteur on Iraq; Amnesty International Iraq: Human Rights Violations Since the Uprisings (1991); and Middle East Watch Endless Torment - The 1991 Uprising in Iraq and Its Aftermath (1992).

[160] Middle East Watch Endless Torment. n. 159 above at p.21.

committees. However, Iraq has precluded the full application of the treaty supervisory system by its refusal to accept provisions allowing for the consideration of individual or inter-state complaints and its reservations precluding the jurisdiction of the International Court of Justice. Its periodic reports are generally restricted to a pro forma description of legislative provisions and it refuses to acknowledge, much less address, any allegations of violations. The increasingly critical stance of the treaty-monitoring bodies towards Iraq appears to have had no appreciable impact at all.[161]

A number of the thematic mechanisms of the Commission on Human Rights have also raised cases and concerns with Iraq for a number of years and continue to do so. However, these are generally met with a bland response denying the allegations. These mechanisms and the treaty bodies do contribute to keeping violations by Iraq on the international agenda and calling it to account. They can provide an additional source of information and some measure of longer-term periodic scrutiny. Beyond this, they are not at all equipped to address gross and systematic violations on the scale occurring in Iraq. They cannot alone provide an adequate international response to a situation of such urgency and gravity and should not be expected or relied upon to do so.

Deeply disturbing reports of grave human rights violations in Iraq raised by human rights organizations and reinforced by the findings of the UN mechanisms were otherwise ignored by the UN for many years. An attempt to have a critical resolution adopted by the Commission on Human Rights in 1989 was headed off by Iraq itself which successfully proposed a motion to take no action. It was only Iraq's invasion of Kuwait in August 1990 and the ensuing events that finally prompted the UN to reverse its shameful record of inaction. At least Iraq's human rights record is now firmly established on the UN agenda in the Security Council, the Commission on Human Rights, the Economic and Social Council and the General Assembly.

Security Council Resolution 688 (1991) has determined that the consequences of Iraq's repression of its citizens constitutes a threat to international peace and security and the Council has demanded that Iraq end that repression and cooperate fully with the UN. Compliance with this resolution has been increasingly linked to the sanctions regime but it also stands alone on its own

---

[161] In April 1991 the Human Rights Committee unusually called for the immediate submission of Iraq's third report and required that this pay particular attention to certain articles of the International Covenant on Civil and Political Rights. The Committee on Economic, Social and Cultural Rights and the Committee on the Elimination of Racial Discrimination have also been increasingly critical of Iraq and both have recently insisted on the submission of supplementary information.

terms. It provides the basis for consideration of Iraq's human rights record by the Security Council and for further action to address continuing violations. The Security Council took the highly unusual step in August 1992 of inviting the Commission's Special Rapporteur on Iraq to appear before it to brief members on the deteriorating situation in the country, particularly in the south. This is an indication that the human rights situation in Iraq is still very much on the Council's agenda.

The appointment by the Commission on Human Rights of a Special Rapporteur to investigate the human rights situation in a country is its strongest measure of censure. The Commission appointed the Special Rapporteur on Iraq in 1991 to "make a thorough study of the violations by the Government of Iraq" using all information that the Rapporteur deemed relevant, including information from non-governmental organizations.[162] The Commission's Resolution 1991/74 made specific reference to the use of chemical weapons by Iraq against the Kurdish population, the forced displacement of hundreds of thousands of Kurds, the destruction of Kurdish towns and villages, the situation of tens of thousands of displaced Kurds living in camps in Iraqi Kurdistan and the deportation of thousands of Kurdish families.

The Special Rapporteur on Iraq, Max van der Stoel of the Netherlands, reports both to the General Assembly and to the Commission on Human Rights. His mandate has been renewed every year since his appointment, most recently at the Commission's 51st session in February/March 1995. His detailed reports constitute the most comprehensive catalogue of the violations which continue to be perpetrated in Iraq and he has continually pressed for further action by the UN to address these. The Government of Iraq does not permit him to visit Iraqi Kurdistan but he regularly includes in his reports a special section on the area drawn from information he has received.

Since the appointment of the Special Rapporteur both the General Assembly and the Commission have regularly adopted annual resolutions strongly condemning the "continued massive and grave violations of human rights by the Government of Iraq". These resolutions have noted in particular summary executions, political killings and orchestrated mass executions and burials; the

---

[162] At its 1991 session the Commission on Human Rights also took the unprecedented step of appointing a second Special Rapporteur to investigate Iraq's violations in respect of its invasion and occupation of Kuwait. This is the only occasion on which two Commission Rapporteurs have been appointed to investigate the acts of one government. The Special Rapporteur on occupied Kuwait submitted an extensive final report to the 48th session of the Commission in 1992 and his mandate was then terminated. Unresolved issues and concerns arising out of the invasion and occupation, such as the large numbers of persons disappeared and unaccounted for, were taken over by the Special Rapporteur on Iraq.

routine and systematic practice of torture; cruel and unusual punishments such as mutilation for certain offences; disappearances; arbitrary arrest and detention; the consistent and routine failure to respect due process and the rule of law; suppression of freedom of thought, conscience and association and the violation of property rights; failure to respect economic and social rights, especially access to food and health care; and the general repression of the civilian population and particularly the political opposition. The persistent failure of Iraq to cooperate fully with the Special Rapporteur has also been repeatedly criticised.

All these resolutions make specific reference to violations against the Kurdish population which indicates that the international community has no illusions that the special measures of protection in Iraqi Kurdistan place the Kurds entirely beyond the reach of continuing violations by the Iraqi Government and recognizes that they continue to be particularly at risk of repression and reprisals.

VIII.5 HUMAN RIGHTS MONITORS FOR IRAQ

From the very first, the Special Rapporteur on Iraq warned that the human rights situation was so dire that unusual measures were needed and he proposed setting-up an on-site human rights monitoring operation in Iraq.[163] In his first full report to the Commission on Human Rights in February 1992 he stated that "this exceptionally grave situation demands an exceptional response - a response that would have to be considered disproportionate in most other cases of human rights violations".[164]

He proposed a number of mobile teams of three monitors each who would establish local offices and a public presence in the main cities throughout Iraq (including the north). The monitors would travel regularly to the surrounding area, investigate violations, visit places of detention and hospitals, observe trials and make representations to local authorities in the event of defined urgent matters. The monitors would liaise closely with other UN agencies operating in Iraq and depend on the UN Department of Humanitarian Affairs for transport, communications and security. The monitors would report directly to the Special Rapporteur who would evaluate the information and formulate

---

[163] A year earlier, in July 1991, Amnesty International had called on the UN urgently to send human rights monitors to Iraq before the coalition forces were withdrawn. See Amnesty International The Need for Further UN Action to Protect Human Rights in Iraq, AI Index: MDE 14/06/91.

[164] UN Doc. E/CN.4/1992/31, para. 156.

recommendations to the Government.[165]

In a predictable and somewhat hysterical response the Iraqi Government stated that it "peremptorily rejects the idea of sending human rights monitors". They would have "very wide powers, in a manner blatantly incompatible with the concepts of sovereignty, independence and non-interference in internal affairs". The Government asserted that the Special Rapporteur "would make of the monitors something resembling the political agents of the colonialist States, in total disregard of the authority of the Iraqi State to exercise its full powers in full sovereignty and independence". This would establish a precedent "that would become a tool in the hands of the hegemonistic international forces with which to threaten third world peoples...".[166]

Both the General Assembly and the Commission on Human Rights eventually endorsed the proposal to send monitors to Iraq and have repeatedly called on the Government to permit the immediate and unconditional stationing of monitors throughout the country. Beyond this, however, the UN has taken no further steps to implement the proposal. The Rapporteur has only been able to send small investigative missions to neighbouring countries to assist in the gathering of information, particularly from refugees. In 1994 the General Assembly actually called on the Secretary-General to approve the necessary funding to send human rights experts to such locations as would improve the information flow and help in its assessment and verification. This may finally prompt the appointment of long-term monitors but still does not address the crucial problem of having monitors stationed inside Iraq. Given the extremely intrusive weapons inspection provisions imposed by the Security Council in Resolution 687(1991), which include indefinite on-site monitoring of an extremely sensitive area of governmental policy and practice, it is scandalous that the UN has not moved with equal vigour and firmness on the question of human rights monitoring.

---

[165] UN Doc. A/47/367, para. 17 et seq.

[166] UN Doc. A/47/367/Add.1 at para .45

IX. IRAQ'S OBLIGATIONS TO PROTECT THE RIGHTS OF MINORITIES

IX.1 THE INTERNATIONAL PROTECTION OF MINORITY RIGHTS

In addition to international obligations to ensure the universal respect for and observance of the human rights of all individuals, international law also recognizes and requires the special protection of the rights of minorities. Minority protection in international law comprises two main elements:
(i) the concept of equality of treatment, including the equal enjoyment of rights, and non-discrimination of members of the minority within the state in which they live; and
(ii) protection and promotion measures particular to the minority group to enable them to preserve and develop their identity as a minority, their culture and other distinct characteristics.

It should be recalled that the ending of the British mandate and Iraq's emergence as an independent state were conditioned on the international guarantees to protect the minority rights set out in the 1932 Iraq Declaration. The Declaration guaranteed non-discrimination and the equal enjoyment of all rights for minorities within Iraq as well as measures to safeguard the distinct characteristics of minority groups. Its provisions were expressed to constitute internationally supervised obligations and fundamental laws of Iraq which could not be undermined by any subsequent laws, regulations or official action (see Section II.2 above).

Subsequent international instruments have further developed and amplified international obligations in respect of minority groups within the territory of a state, both in terms of non-discrimination and of special measures to protect the identity and characteristics of a minority group.

IX.2 NON-DISCRIMINATION

The equal enjoyment of rights and the absolute prohibition of discrimination are among the founding principles of the United Nations and are fundamental concepts of international human rights law. These principles constitute legally binding obligations on Iraq and are important in ensuring that members of a minority group, such as the Kurds, are treated equally to the majority population.

Article 1 of the UN Charter includes among the purposes and principles of the UN:
> ...to develop friendly relations among nations based on respect of the principle of equal rights and self-determination of peoples...
> to achieve international cooperation...in promoting and encouraging respect of human rights and for fundamental freedoms for all without distinction as to race, sex, language or religion...

These principles of equality and non-discrimination are reiterated in Article 55 of the Charter.

Article 1 of the 1948 Universal Declaration of Human Rights states that "All human beings are born free and equal in dignity and rights". The principle of non-discrimination is set out in Article 2 in broader terms than appears in the Charter:
> Everyone is entitled to the rights and freedoms set forth in this Declaration, without distinction of any kind, such as race, colour, sex, language, religion, political or other opinion, national or social origin, property, birth or other status.

As a state party to the International Covenant on Civil and Political Rights and the International Covenant on Economic, Social and Cultural Rights, Iraq is also obligated by Article 2 of these treaties to ensure that there is no discrimination in the exercise of the rights guaranteed by both Covenants. The International Covenant on Civil and Political Rights also contains a specific non-discrimination clause in Article 26:
> All persons are equal before the law and are entitled without any discrimination to the equal protection of the law. In this respect, the law shall prohibit any discrimination and guarantee to all persons equal and effective protection against discrimination on any ground such as race, colour, sex, language, religion, political or other opinion, national or social origin, property, birth or other status.

The International Convention on the Elimination of All Forms of Racial Discrimination, to which Iraq is a party, prohibits any distinction, exclusion, restriction or preference based on "race, colour, descent, national or ethnic origin". States parties are required to take positive steps to eliminate such discrimination and to guarantee equal enjoyment of rights, including "special and concrete measures" to ensure the adequate development and protection of certain racial groups or individuals. Iraq is also legally bound to eliminate and prevent any discrimination in employment and in education on grounds of, inter alia, race, national or social origin or political opinion by virtue of its ratification of the 1958 ILO Convention (No. 111) Concerning Discrimination in Respect of Employment and Occupation and of the 1960 UNESCO Convention against Discrimination in Education.

IX.3 THE INTERNATIONAL COVENANT ON CIVIL AND POLITICAL RIGHTS

International law is increasingly recognizing obligations on states for the specific protection of the rights of members of a minority group as such, aimed at securing the preservation and development of the identity, culture and other distinct characteristics of minority groups.[167]

Article 27 of the International Covenant on Civil and Political Rights requires states parties to ensure that members of ethnic, religious or linguistic minorities are not denied the right to enjoy their own culture, profess and practice their religion or to use their own language. The Human Rights Committee, the UN body charged with supervision of the implementation of the Covenant, has elaborated on state obligations under this article in General Comment No. 23, adopted in 1994.[168] The Committee has stressed that Article 27 is aimed at ensuring "the survival and continued development of the cultural, religious and social identity of the minorities concerned" and that it requires states to take "positive measures of protection" against acts of public officials or private persons. These may require steps to protect the identity of a minority and may legitimately involve positive discrimination if based on reasonable and objective criteria. The Committee has also reiterated that Article 27 is distinct from and in addition to the non-discrimination provisions and all the other rights in the Covenant which members of minority groups are equally entitled to enjoy.

---

[167] One of the main impediments to the development of minority rights protection is that states are still reluctant to accept the notion of minority rights as "group" rights and insist on dealing with these only on the basis of the rights of individual members of minorities. This does not, however, undermine the validity of the rights which have been recognized but it affects strategies and procedures for their implementation.

[168] UN Doc. CCPR/C/21/Rev.1/Add.5 of 26 April 1994.

IX.4 THE UN DECLARATION ON THE RIGHTS OF PERSONS BELONGING TO NATIONAL OR ETHNIC, RELIGIOUS AND LINGUISTIC MINORITIES

The protection of minorities has been further advanced by the UN Declaration on the Rights of Persons belonging to National or Ethnic, Religious and Linguistic Minorities. This instrument was adopted by the General Assembly by consensus in 1992. It is the first international human rights instrument devoted solely to minority rights and represents an important step forwards in the development of international standards relating to minorities. Although this Declaration is not a legally binding Convention, its unanimous adoption represents an authoritative statement of internationally-accepted principles concerning minority rights that all states are expected to respect and implement.[169]

The over-arching principle of the Declaration, set out in Article 1, is that states shall protect, by legislation and other measures, "the existence and the national or ethnic, cultural, religious and linguistic identity of minorities" and shall encourage conditions for the promotion of that identity. This principle, expressed in mandatory terms, has two important elements. First, it prohibits any acts which threaten the very existence of the minority - genocide would be the most extreme example of such an act but it encompasses many less serious acts of violence, deprivation of basic resources or services, destruction of homes and means of livelihood and the like, whether the intent to destroy a group is evident or not. Second, it calls for the protection and promotion of the group's identity, which requires a state to take positive steps to secure the development of minority groups and to enable them to preserve their livelihood, traditions and distinct characteristics.

Article 2 of the Declaration protects not only the more "traditional" minority rights - culture, religion, language - but also guarantees minorities important rights to participate in cultural, religious, social, economic and public life; to participate in national and regional decisions concerning them and the areas where they live; to establish their own associations; and to have "free and peaceful" contacts with other members of their group and with persons belonging to other minorities. It is particularly significant for the Kurdish people that these contacts are to include contacts across frontiers with members

---

[169] For a full commentary on the Declaration and the obligations contained in it, see Thornberry "The UN Declaration on the Rights of Persons Belonging to National or Ethnic, Religious and Linguistic Minorities: Background, Analysis and Observations" in Phillips and Rosas (eds.) The UN Minority Rights Declaration (Abo Akademi University Institute for Human Rights -Minority Rights Group 1993).

of their group in other states.

Positive obligations are imposed on states in Article 4 to ensure that minority groups can exercise all their rights without discrimination and in full equality before the law; to create favourable conditions to enable minorities to express their characteristics and develop their culture, language, religion, traditions and customs; to enable minorities to learn and have instruction in their mother tongue; to encourage through education knowledge of the history, traditions, language and culture of minority groups and to enable those groups to gain knowledge of the society as a whole; and to consider appropriate measures to enable minorities to participate fully in the economic progress and development in their country. Furthermore, national policies and programmes must be planned and implemented with due regard for the legitimate interests of persons belonging to minorities (Article 5.1).

The UN Declaration does not specify how states are to secure minority rights but it is clear that in some states genuine and effective fulfilment of the Declaration - particularly its provisions for effective participation in social, economic and public life, in economic progress and development, in national and regional decision-making and in the creation of any kind of minority associations - may well require some form of autonomy arrangements.

IX.5 IMPLEMENTING MINORITY PROTECTION IN IRAQ

In characteristic fashion Iraq continues to assert to the international community that minority rights are fully protected in the country. The gap between its rhetoric and the harsh reality for the Kurds serves as yet another example of the way in which Iraqi repeatedly flouts its international obligations and demonstrates its utter contempt for human rights guarantees.

In 1993, in response to a UN Sub-Commission questionnaire on minority protection, Iraq made the following assertions:
  i) There are several minorities in Iraq which have been coexisting with the Arab majority for a long time;
  ii) All the minorities enjoy their cultural rights...in addition to all other rights enjoyed by Iraqi nationals;
  iii) All Iraqi nationals are regarded as equal and are entitled to equality of opportunity in regard to access to all levels of public office. By virtue of this equality, the minorities participate effectively in national planning, administration and development; and

iv) All [Iraqis] enjoy equal treatment, without discrimination, in all spheres of national life, including the health, education and economic sectors.[170]

A year later Iraq issued its own "study" on minorities as a UN document, stating that Iraq "has actually transcended the minimum rights that international instruments are endeavouring to guarantee. In fact, a sound legal analysis shows that such minorities in Iraq enjoy "privileges", so to speak, in excess of those that are permitted by law...". It also stated that "[s]ince 1968, the Iraqi State has faithfully respected the principles of human rights in regard to minority rights by refusing to permit the development of legal, economic or social situations in which the majority would have recognized rights and privileges that were not enjoyed by the minorities living in Iraq".[171]

Clearly strong measures are required if minority rights are to mean anything for the Kurds. The above statements make it clear that Iraq has no intention of recognizing or protecting minority rights. Existing supervisory mechanisms at the UN for the protection of minority rights are virtually non-existent and are certainly not capable of holding a defiant country like Iraq to its obligations. Yet the minority rights framework can provide a starting point for the development of an acceptable form of autonomy and should be drawn on by the international community in moves towards a long-term settlement for Iraqi Kurdistan.

---

[170] UN Doc.E/CN.4/Sub.2/1993/34/Add.1 at paras. 16, 72, 151 and 175.

[171] Note Verbale from the Permanent Mission of Iraq to the UN in Geneva enclosing a study entitled "Iraq's experience in dealing with minorities", circulated at the 46th session of the Sub-Commission in 1994 in UN Doc. E/CN.4/Sub/2/1994/54.

X. SELF-DETERMINATION AND AUTONOMY

X.1 SELF-DETERMINATION

Self-determination - the right of peoples freely to determine their political status and to pursue their economic, social and cultural development - is a compelling legal concept for many groups seeking greater autonomy, protection and freedom from a repressive authoritarian regime. The precise scope of the principle of self-determination - both as to its substantive content, the legal rights it confers and the entities to which it applies - is still vaguely defined.[172] This tends to make it particularly attractive as an elastic principle which can be moulded to fit a variety of very different situations and aspirations.

Yet its very lack of precise definition and application have made self-determination a highly controversial, politicized and confused concept. This, coupled with the tendency to associate claims by non-state entities to self-determination as capable of being met only by the achievement of full independence as a sovereign state, has limited its value as an objective legal basis for the protection and defence of human rights and as the impetus for political change within a state. This is regrettable since the objective and fair application of the elements of the principle of self-determination could provide the basis in many situations for measures to protect human rights, to guarantee the fair treatment of minority groups, to foster democratic institutions and to serve as an engine for political, social and economic development without necessarily bringing about the dismemberment of a state.

The right of self-determination is now generally accepted as a recognized international legal principle, even if its precise scope is unclear. The UN Charter includes as one its basic purposes in Article 1(2):

> To develop friendly relations among nations based on respect for the principle of equal rights and self-determination of peoples...

The same phrase occurs in Article 55 which calls for the promotion of economic and social cooperation, including observance of human rights, in order to create the conditions necessary for "peaceful and friendly relations among nations

---

[172] For a fuller discussion of self-determination see, for example, Crawford The Creation of States in International Law (1979) and Hannum Autonomy, Sovereignty and Self-Determination (1990) and the numerous further references cited in those publications.

based on respect for the principle of equal rights and self-determination of peoples".

The right to self-determination and the duty on all states to promote it is also incorporated as Article 1 in both International Covenants on Civil and Political Rights and on Economic, Social and Cultural Rights. This common article states that:

> 1. All peoples have the right of self-determination. By virtue of that right they freely determine their political status and freely pursue their economic, social and cultural development.
> [...]
> 3. The States Parties to the present Covenant, including those having responsibility for the administration of Non-Self-Governing and Trust Territories, shall promote the right of self-determination, and shall respect that right, in conformity with the provisions of the Charter of the United Nations.

The principle of self-determination has been most commonly invoked in respect of colonial territories, in particular the two types of territory placed under a special regime by the UN Charter - trust and non-self-governing territories. The Declaration on the Granting of Independence to Colonial Countries and Peoples, contained in General Assembly Resolution 1514 (XV) of 1960, reaffirmed the right of peoples to self-determination in the context of calling for a speedy and unconditional end to colonialism in all its forms. It recalled the important role of the UN in assisting the movement for independence in trust and non-self governing territories. The International Court of Justice has also held that the principle of self-determination applies to all colonies.[173]

Trust territories and non-self-governing territories are terms of art developed by the UN; there is no comprehensive legal definition of such territories. The Trusteeship System, established in Chapter XII of the UN Charter, essentially replaced the League of Nations' system of mandate territories. The Charter states that the trusteeship system applies to existing mandate territories; territories "detached from enemy states as a result of the Second World War"; and territories voluntarily placed under the system by the states responsible for their administration. The purpose of the trusteeship system was four-fold and underscored the linkage between the different elements: i) the furtherance of international peace and security; ii) the progressive development of the territories towards self-government or independence in accordance with the freely expressed

---
[173] The Namibia Case, ICJ Reports 1971, 16.

wishes of the people; iii) encouraging respect for human rights and recognition of global interdependence; and iv) equality of treatment for all UN member states and their nationals. With the recent termination of trusteeship over the Pacific Islands Trust Territory, administered by the USA, the trusteeship system is formally at an end.

It was initially left up to states to determine which territories they considered to be "non-self-governing" and thereby subject to the provisions of Chapter XI of the Charter. In 1959 the General Assembly established a Special Committee to study the criteria and in 1960 adopted Resolution 1541 (XV) setting out some rather restrictive guidelines as to which territories should be included in the definition. The principal characteristic was a territory that was "geographically separate" and "ethnically distinct" from the country administering it. If that was met, other historical, political, economic and other factors which arbitrarily placed the territory in a subordinate position became relevant. The General Assembly has, on several occasions, determined that a particular territory qualified as non-self-governing with or without the approval of the administering state but it has generally followed the basic criterion of geographical separateness which would exclude from the concept many groups struggling for some form of autonomy within the territorial borders of a state. States responsible for such territories were expected to protect the people against abuses, ensure their political and social advancement and to develop their self-government and free political institutions taking account of their political aspirations.

The 1960 Colonial Declaration, which reaffirmed the right of "all peoples" to self-determination suggested, however, that self-determination is not limited to colonial territories but might have a wider application. Ten years later the Declaration on the Principles of International Law concerning Friendly Relations and Co-operation among States in accordance with the Charter of the United Nations, annexed to Resolution 2625 (XXV) of 1970, stated that every State has an obligation to promote the realization of the right of self-determination and a duty to respect this right of peoples in order to promote friendly relations among states and to bring a speedy end to colonialism. Other references to self-determination in international instruments and subsequent, but inconsistent, state practice indicates that the right is not limited to colonial situations, although it is still not possible to delineate with any legal certainty a category of territories or peoples to which the right clearly applies.[174]

---

[174] See Crawford and Hannum, n.172 above, and McCorquodale "Self-Determination: A Human Rights Approach" 43 ICLQ 857.

There is no general agreement on the definition of "peoples" for the purposes of self-determination. Although common characteristics such as ethnicity, language and religion, a territorial connection, a common historical tradition and self-identification as a distinct group, would all be relevant, it is certainly not accepted that every minority or indigenous group automatically has a legitimate claim to self-determination. The territorial approach has resulted in the principle being applied to territorial units which contain a mix of different groups. It is also invoked to defend the rights of entire states to determine their own political, economic and social systems, free of external interference.

The issue is further complicated by the fact that UN references to self-determination are almost always accompanied by statements defending the territorial integrity of states. The Colonial Declaration stated that "any attempt aimed at the partial or total disruption of the national unity and the territorial integrity of a country is incompatible with the purposes and principles of the Charter of the United Nations". A similar reference appears in the 1970 Declaration on Friendly Relations but here it is limited to states "conducting themselves in compliance with the principle of equal rights and self-determination of peoples...and thus possessed of a government representing the whole people belonging to the territory without distinction as to race, creed or colour".

In as much as a claim to self-determination is sought to be exercised by secession, international law is effectively neutral. There is no generally accepted right of secession but it is not necessarily prohibited and once secession has occurred in practice it may have legal consequences. A secessionist group that is militarily successful in its attempts to break away from an existing state and that fulfils the basic criteria of statehood[175] may be able to function as a independent state and may subsequently be recognized as such by all or some of the international community, depending on the political context in which secession has occurred.

It has been suggested that, in addition to colonial territories and existing states, there may be another category of 'self-determination units': "entities part of a metropolitan State but which have been governed in such a way as to make them in effect non-self-governing territories".[176] The Committee of Rapporteurs, appointed by the League of Nations to investigate aspects of the dispute over

---

[175] Article 1 of the 1933 Montevideo Convention on the Rights and Duties of States lays down four criteria of statehood: i) a permanent population; ii) a defined territory; iii) government; and iv) capacity to enter into relations with other states.

[176] Crawford, n.172 above, at p.100.

the Aaland Islands, stated in 1921 that:
> The separation of a minority from the State of which it forms a part and its incorporation in another State can only be considered as an altogether exceptional situation, a last resort when the State lacks either the will or the power to enact and apply just and effective guarantees.[177]

There is, however, no conclusive body of legal principles or state practice to clarify application of the right of self-determination in respect of this possible third category, which remains "acutely controversial".[178]

A claim to self-determination as the basis for international action and protection for Iraqi Kurdistan, if actually or perceived to be a claim for independence from Iraq, would meet with little, if any, political support today. Iraq has consistently defended its territorial integrity and even the coalition governments who intervened to set up the safe havens have been at pains to stress that they do not challenge the territorial integrity of Iraq nor would they support an independent political entity in Iraqi Kurdistan. Such a claim would also have drastic and unacceptable political implications for the other countries in the region with Kurdish populations. Even if the case can be made out that the Kurds are a "people" for the purposes of self-determination, the legal and practical difficulties are enormous in claiming self-determination in respect of a people divided between a number of different states. It would have to be determined whether self-determination was claimed on behalf of the Kurdish people as a whole, which implies a high degree of commonality of political goals shared by the Kurdish populations in all the states they currently inhabit, or simply by the Kurds in one of these countries, a claim which might not enjoy the same degree of international legitimacy.

The principle of self-determination is not, however, relevant only to claims for full independence. The term has two distinct meanings: "the sovereign equality of existing States, and in particular the right of a State to choose its own form of government without intervention" and "the right of a specific territory ('people') to choose its own form of government irrespective of the wishes of the rest of the State of which that territory is a part".[179] Resolution 1541 (XV) envisaged the exercise of self-determination through the options of free association or integration with an independent state, with safeguards to ensure that these options were exercised by a people freely and voluntarily through

---

[177] Report of the Committee of Rapporteurs, 1921, quoted in Crawford, ibid. at p.86.

[178] Crawford, ibid., at p. 100.

[179] Ibid. at p. 90.

informed and democratic processes. Integration depended on an advanced state of self-government with free political institutions and had to be opted for in full knowledge and through impartial democratic processes. The 1970 Declaration on Friendly Relations added another option - "the emergence into any other political status freely determined by a people".

This confirms that the principle of self-determination not only has an external aspect (such as emergence as an independent state) but also internal aspects by which peoples have the right to determine their political and form of government and to pursue their development within a given territory. Free and participatory choice on the basis of equality are the conditions for the exercise of the internal aspects of self-determination. It has been noted that:

> The Covenant [on Civil and Political Rights] clearly intends to make the right of self-determination applicable to citizens of all nations, entitling them to determine their collective political status through democratic means...When the Covenant came into force, the right of self-determination entered its third phase of enunciation: it ceased to be a rule applicable only to specific territories...and became a right of everyone. It also, at least for now, stopped being a principle of exclusion (secession) and became one of inclusion: the right to participate. The right now entitles peoples in all states to free, fair and open participation in the democratic process of governance freely chosen by each state.[180]

There are close links between self-determination, the existence of a representative government and the protection of human rights. The Human Rights Committee in its General Comment on Article 1 of the International Covenant on Civil and Political Rights stated that the realization of self-determination is an "essential condition for the effective guarantee and observance of individual human rights...". A government such as that in Iraq which is not freely elected, denies its people the most fundamental human rights and has routinely suppressed minority rights of particular groups is certainly not fulfilling its obligations to guarantee self-determination for its people.

The widespread violation of rights, and particularly on a massive scale that amounts, for example, to genocide, is one of the most obvious examples of the denial of a people's right to self-determination. At the same time the right to self-determination extends beyond protection from violence and repression and implies the free determination of political status, the existence of open and participatory institutions that reflect and safeguard that status, and the

---

[180] Franck "The Emerging Right to Democratic Governance" 86 AJIL 46 at 58-59 (1992).

opportunity to pursue economic, social and cultural development.

The development of the concept, scope and legal principles of internal self-determination is still in its infancy, particularly the extent to which the concept relates to specific self-determination rights of oppressed groups within a state as opposed to the right of the state population as a whole. It has been suggested that human rights norms and standards may provide a framework of legal rules to balance the competing rights and interests inherent in claims to self-determination.[181] The advantages of reliance on self-determination is that it is a collective right of a people, rather than the sum of the rights of individuals, and one in respect of which all states share an obligation to promote its realization. The drawbacks are that it does not yet provide a firm basis of clearly defined rights applicable in identifiable political contexts and that reliance on it inevitably raises the fear of secession and the fragmentation of states. This is not to say that the principle of self-determination is irrelevant in the Kurdish context, but only that it probably does not provide a sufficiently firm basis at the present time on which to ground international responsibility or as the impetus for continued protection.

X.2 AUTONOMY

There is no generally accepted definition of the concept of "autonomy" in international law. It has been stated that:

> Autonomous areas are regions of a State, usually possessing some ethnic or cultural distinctiveness, which have been granted separate powers of internal administration, to whatever degree, without being detached from the State of which they are a part....Until a very advanced stage is reached in the progress towards self-government, such areas are not States".[182]

There is presently no generally internationally recognized right to any form of autonomous status. However, the development of minority rights protection beyond the traditional areas of language, culture and religion to encompass measures to protect and promote the identity of minorities and to secure their participation in decision-making and public life envisage far more extensive political and economic rights for minorities. The full exercise of these rights in some situations may well require a form of autonomous status.[183] According to

---

[181] McCorquodale, n. 174 above.

[182] Crawford, n. 172 above, at pp. 211-212.

[183] See the discussion of minority rights guaranteed by the 1992 UN Declaration on the Rights of Persons Belonging to National or Ethnic, Religious and Linguistic Minorities in Section IX above.

a recent UN report autonomy "represents the highest possible level of minority rights".[184]

Autonomy is, however, increasingly recognized as a useful concept and means by which to address competing claims for political and minority rights. State practice offers a wealth of different autonomy and internal self-governing arrangements to respond to a wide variety of political contexts, claims to minority protection and the realization of other international rights and obligations.[185] It has been noted that "while conventional wisdom accords regional autonomous entities only limited status under international law, the increasing frequency of claims to autonomy and the incremental effect such claims will have upon the international legal order make the concept of autonomy ripe for review".[186]

Autonomy for a group or part of a territory within a state is generally the result of an internal political and legislative arrangement, which may well enjoy entrenched constitutional or other special protection. It will not usually grant the area any internationally-recognized status or devolve powers normally associated with state-hood, such as in the areas of defence or foreign affairs. In some cases, however, an autonomous area may have a limited capacity to enter into international agreements on issues within the scope of its reserved powers, such as cultural or economic matters. It will usually encompass a local or regional executive, legislature and judiciary and may grant authority in a wide range of matters such as education, health, housing, social welfare, culture, religion, land, resources and local security as well as providing for some means of financing itself through taxation or otherwise.

Autonomy has long been accepted as a political option in Iraq and must be at least the starting point for discussions on the status of Iraqi Kurdistan. Iraq committed itself 25 years ago to the principle of Kurdish autonomy and did establish the basic parameters and institutional structures for such autonomy (whatever the shortcomings of these arrangements and however imperfectly they have been implemented since). Since then it has held out the autonomy arrangements for the Kurds as evidence of its accommodation of and commitment

---

[184] UN Doc. E/CN.4/Sub.2/1990/46.

[185] See Hannum and Lillich "The Concept of Autonomy In International Law" 74 AJIL 858 (1980). The article is derived from a two-volume report by the authors on "The Theory and Practice of Governmental Autonomy" which examined 22 case studies of non-sovereign entities and federal states offering a wide range of examples of varying degrees of governmental autonomy and internal self-government.

[186] Ibid. at pp.858-9.

to the promotion and protection of the rights of the Kurdish minority. However, an acceptable autonomy arrangement must be one which is acceptable to the Kurds, which allows them to preserve and develop their identity as a group and which fosters open and participatory institutions of self-government. It must genuinely secure the promotion and protection of all the rights guaranteed to them both under legally-binding treaties as well as the principles and standards set out in the 1992 UN Declaration on the rights of minorities. Most importantly, it must reflect the will of the Kurdish people and be developed in a process which allows them full and equal participation.

Previous experience has shown, most recently after the establishment of the safe havens, that there can be no confidence in the present Iraqi Government's commitment to any form of genuine autonomy for the Kurds. It is imperative that future negotiations be conducted under international supervision and that effective international guarantees are secured. This is neither a new nor radical departure. There are a number of previous examples of the temporary "internationalization" of a territory, in particular circumstances where its status was in dispute and/or where special protection for the population was needed. In such cases a form of autonomous status may be granted as a result of an international arrangement and be secured by international guarantees and subject to international supervision, pending a more long-term political settlement that would ideally no longer require external supervision.

There are a number of examples of territories of special international status or concern. The Free City of Danzig, for example, was placed directly under the protection of the League of Nations, which was responsible for maintaining its territorial integrity, pursuant to the 1919 Treaty of Versailles. It has been described as "perhaps the purest example of an 'internationalized territory' in which, despite almost complete autonomy and various attributes of statehood, sovereignty resided in an international organization".[187] Danzig exercised complete autonomy over its internal affairs but not over defence or foreign affairs. Poland was granted special rights, including access to the port and a customs union with Danzig. The City's Constitution was drafted by its citizens but was subject to final approval of the League Council which retained power to approve changes. The rights of Danzig and of Poland were contained in two bilateral treaties and disputes submitted to the League of Nations' High Commissioner, its executive representative.

---

[187] Hannum, n. 172 above, at p. 378. In his book Hannum describes in some detail the historical context and the arrangements adopted in respect of a number of these territories of international concern and demonstrates very well the variety of legislative and practical measures adapted to each situation.

Another example is that of the territory of Memel. After Lithuanian occupation of Memel in 1923, Lithuanian sovereignty was accepted in a 1924 Convention signed by Lithuania and the UK, France, Italy and Japan. The local population was granted full cultural autonomy and the port designated as a port of international concern administered by an international harbour board. Sovereignty over Memel could not be transferred without the consent of the contracting parties. Any breach of the founding convention could be drawn to the attention of the League Council. Individual and minority rights were guaranteed and Memel authorities enjoyed a fair degree of autonomy over local matters under the residual authority of Lithuania. The port was administered jointly by a Board appointed by Lithuania. "Memel can perhaps be most aptly described as an area of formally recognized international concern, evidenced by the right of the Principal Allied Powers to take disputes concerning the Convention or Statute to the Permanent Court of International Justice, and by the authority of the League over proposed changes with respect to the port".[188]

The proposal to establish the Free Territory of Trieste as a neutral international autonomous area under the direct authority of the Security Council remains an interesting example of a true internationalized territory under UN control even though it was never implemented.[189] The aim was to reconcile competing claims to the city after the end of the Second World War. The head of government was to be a Governor appointed by and answerable directly to the Security Council with direct authority over various aspects of the administration. These included observance of the founding Statute, a veto power over legislation and administrative rules; approval of international agreements; appointment of judges; and considerable control over public order and security through appointment of the heads of police and public security and special powers to assume greater control in emergency situations. The Governor's decisions could be appealed to the Security Council which could also promulgate laws to override the Governor's veto. Day-to-day administration was to be exercised by an executive Council of Government and an elected Assembly. The Council would have joint power with the Governor to enter into international agreements on economic, social and cultural questions.

The system of UN trust and non-self-governing territories is another example of a high degree of international supervision over territories which were expected eventually to become independent. The concept was based on the

---

[188] Ibid. at p. 383.

[189] Ibid. at pp. 400-406. East-West political divisions prevented the proposal from ever coming into being and the idea of a Free Territory was abandoned in 1954.

notion that the administering authorities were exercising a form of "sacred trust" over the territories and special obligations were imposed on them in the UN Charter itself in the exercise of that trust.

Trusteeship territories were administered under an agreement designating the terms of administration and the responsible authority, which could be one or more states or the UN itself. The UN Trusteeship Council was comprised of UN members administering territories, other members of the Security Council and members elected by the UN in order to ensure a equal balance on the Council of those administering territories and other states. The Trusteeship Council operated under the General Assembly with the Security Council retaining control over any designated "strategic areas" in the trust territories. The Trusteeship Council could, <u>inter alia</u>, consider reports by the administering authority, accept and examine petitions, and undertake periodic visits to the territories. Petitioners could be inhabitants of the territory or other parties. The Trusteeship Council has not been dissolved although it has no more territories under its jurisdiction. If its terms of reference were suitably amended, it could be adapted to play a role in respect of other territories in dispute or requiring international protection, even if these would not have fallen within its original mandate.

UN member states with responsibilities for non-self-governing territories were subject to obligations to ensure the political, social and economic advancement of the people, their protection against abuse, the development of self-government and progressive development of free political institutions, the furtherance of peace and security and constructive measures of development. A Special Committee was set up to further the implementation of the Declaration. Like the Trusteeship Council, the Special Committee has carried out missions to territories, where it could secure the cooperation of the administering authority, and has accepted petitions and heard petitioners. It has also made recommendations for political and constitutional reform and was authorized by the General Assembly to alert the Security Council to situations posing a threat to international peace and security.

More recently, a number of the UN's recent peace-keeping operations have also imposed a high degree of international protection and supervision in various countries. In Cambodia, for example, the UN established a Transitional Authority with considerable powers to oversee the process leading to elections. The 1989 Paris Conference brought together 18 countries, the Cambodian parties and the UN Secretary-General to negotiate a political settlement under

UN supervision. It included the five permanent members of the Security Council and the key regional powers. The Agreements on a Comprehensive Political Settlement in Cambodia were signed in October 1991 and endorsed by the Security Council which also approved and supervised the implementation plan. The UN Transitional Authority in Cambodia comprised military and civilian components, including an extensive human rights monitoring operation. Cambodian administrative bodies in the areas of foreign affairs, defence, public security and information were placed under the direct control of UNTAC which also had control and supervisory powers over any administrative bodies which could influence the elections and the authority to reassign or remove any government personnel. The interim national authority, the Supreme National Council, delegated to the UN all powers necessary to implement the political settlement. UNTAC remained in place until free elections had been held and a new government installed.

It is not, of course, suggested that any of these prior international arrangements can or should provide a blue-print for the future international protection of Iraqi Kurdistan. Each was tailored to a particular historical and political context. The special circumstances, characteristics and needs of each situation must dictate the form and nature of supervision and protection. These examples do, however, indicate considerable international creativity in devising special arrangements to meet the particular needs of a territory where there is the political will to act. If the international community is willing to face up to its responsibilities in Iraqi Kurdistan, it is quite possible to devise an arrangement that meets the political and security needs of this particular situation.

XI. THE RESPONSIBILITY OF THE INTERNATIONAL COMMUNITY IN IRAQI KURDISTAN

This report has shown that, historically, both Iraq itself and the international community have recognized that the Kurdish people in Iraq have legitimate claims and aspirations to some form of autonomous self-governing status as a distinct group and to special measures to protect their rights and their unique identity and characteristics.

Preceding chapters of this report have also described the shocking record of gross and systematic violations by the Iraqi Government of the most basic rights of the Kurdish people and the complete lack of any commitment by that Government to genuine autonomy and to minority protection for the Kurds. The responsibility for the protection and well-being of the Iraqi Kurds is not only that of Iraq alone, however. The international community also bears an important responsibility in this regard, most particularly when a state makes a mockery of its international obligations and flouts the international legal order so openly and repeatedly and with such appalling consequences as Iraq has done.

The responsibility of the international community in this situation has a number of facets deriving both from general international obligations and also from the actions which have already been taken by the international community. International responsibility flows firstly from obligations on all states to secure universal respect for human rights and humanitarian law, to ensure the special protection of vulnerable minorities and to uphold fundamental principles of international refugee protection. These obligations derive from the UN Charter, from the relevant international treaties and other standards which have been adopted and from state practice over the years in these areas of international concern.

There is, in addition, in this particular situation a further and over-arching political and moral responsibility that flows from the extraordinary and far-reaching intervention by the international community over four years which has created and sustained Iraqi Kurdistan as a de facto self-governing area from which the Iraqi Government is effectively excluded. The creation of the safe havens may also have imposed specific obligations on the coalition forces under the Geneva Convention IV as occupying forces in a foreign territory.

XI.1 INTERNATIONAL RESPONSIBILITY FOR THE PROTECTION OF HUMAN RIGHTS

XI.1.1 THE UN CHARTER

It has already been noted that the respect for human rights and fundamental freedoms is one of the founding principles and purposes of the UN Charter. The International Court of Justice has confirmed that the Charter imposes legal obligations in the human rights field, stating that acts amounting to a denial of fundamental human rights are "a flagrant violation of the purposes and principles of the UN Charter".[190] The Charter also makes it clear that UN member states must not only respect human rights within their own borders, but that they also bear a joint responsibility to secure the universal observance of human rights. Article 1(3) includes among the purposes of the UN:

> To achieve <u>international co-operation</u> in solving international problems of an economic, social, cultural, or humanitarian character, and in promoting and encouraging respect for human rights and for fundamental freedoms for all without distinction as to race, sex, language or religion....(emphasis added).

Further, under Article 56 all member states pledge themselves to take "joint and separate action in co-operation with the [UN]" to the achieve the purposes of the UN set out in the preceding Article 55, which includes universal respect for and observance of human rights and fundamental freedoms.

The UN Secretary-General succinctly expressed the dual nature of state and international responsibility for human rights protection in his opening speech to the 1993 World Conference on Human Rights:

> ...human rights, by their very nature do away with the distinction traditionally drawn between the internal order and the international order. Human rights give rise to a new legal permeability...[they] call for cooperation and coordination between States and international organizations.
>
> In this context, the State should be the best guarantor of human rights. It is the State that the international community should principally entrust with ensuring the protection of individuals.
>
> However, the issue of international action must be raised when States prove unworthy of this task, when they violate the fundamental principles laid down in the Charter of the United Nations. and when - far from being protectors of individuals - they become tormentors.
> [...]

---
[190] The Namibia Case ICJ Reports 1971 p. 16 at p. 57.

In these circumstances, the international community must take over from States that fail to fulfil their obligations. This is a legal and institutional construction that has nothing shocking about it and does not, in my view, harm our contemporary notion of sovereignty...Where sovereignty becomes the ultimate argument put forward by authoritarian regimes to support their undermining of the rights and freedoms of men, women and children, such sovereignty - and I state this as a sober truth - is already condemned by history [emphasis added].

XI.1.2 THE UN HUMAN RIGHTS SYSTEM

It is on this basis of joint responsibility and international cooperation that the international human rights system has been developed over the past 46 years or so. The legal instruments and the procedures that make up the system all serve to reinforce the legitimacy and the necessity of international action in response to human rights violations by a member state. Universal human rights treaties, adopted by the full UN membership and open for ratification by all states, form the legal basis of the system. These are supplemented by an extensive range of other norms and standards which lay down authoritative guidelines applicable to all states. At the same time, UN member states have developed a comprehensive international and, for the most part, public monitoring system by which they accept that their treatment of their own citizens may be subjected to international scrutiny and, where necessary, action. The development of similar regional human rights systems operating alongside the UN system has further reinforced the concept of inter-state responsibility to secure human rights protection.

The supervisory machinery developed by the UN in the human rights field permits fairly extensive and increasingly intrusive international investigation into the domestic human rights record of individual states. All states parties to human rights treaties are obliged to submit periodic reports of their implementation of the treaty provisions and are questioned on these by expert committees. A number of the treaties also permit other states and individuals to lodge complaints about violations of human rights which are investigated and adjudicated in quasi-judicial international procedures.[191]

Other human rights monitoring procedures are applicable to all UN member states, whether or not they are party to any human rights treaty. Pursuant to

---

[191] Although some of these complaints procedures are optional, others are mandatory and automatically apply to all states parties to the treaty, such as the individual complaints procedure in the American Convention on Human Rights and the inter-state complaints procedures in the European Convention for the Protection of Human Rights and Fundamental Freedoms and the International Convention on the Elimination of All Forms of Racial Discrimination.

Economic and Social Council resolutions 1235 (XLII) and 1503 (XLVIII), the Commission on Human Rights can investigate and act in respect of serious human rights violations anywhere in the world. The Commission has also developed a number of special procedures to investigate and report on human rights in individual countries or to examine on a global basis particular types of violations, such as disappearances, arbitrary detention, torture and unlawful killings.

Inter-state action in response to human rights violations has not only been confined to international bodies with an explicit human rights mandate. Exceptionally grave human rights violations that threaten international peace and security have on occasion led to action by Security Council, for example. Security Council Resolution 688 (1991), condemning internal repression by Iraq of its citizens, is one example of this. Human rights agreements and monitoring structures are also increasingly built into wider UN peace-keeping and peace-building operations. At its first Summit meeting in 1992, the Security Council's closing statement noted that:

> The absence of war and military conflicts among states does not in itself ensure international peace and security. The non-military sources of instability in the economic, social, humanitarian and ecological fields have become threats to peace and security.

It also welcomed human rights verification measures in the context of recent peace-keeping operations as being among the "integral parts of the Security Council's effort to maintain international peace and security" and noted that "lasting peace and stability require effective international cooperation for the eradication of poverty and the promotion of a better life for all in larger freedom".[192]

There is also widespread evidence of state practice in raising human rights questions bilaterally and multilaterally in the context of a whole range of inter-state relations. In their 1991 Guidelines on the Recognition of New States in Eastern Europe and the Soviet Union,[193] European Union member states confirmed their position that respect for "the rule of law, democracy and human rights" is an essential component of statehood by making this a prerequisite to their recognition of new states in Eastern Europe.

Thus, violations of human rights by a government cannot be confined to the realm of its domestic affairs but can and do engage the responsibility of other

---
[192] UN Doc. S/23500.

[193] Reprinted in 31 ILM 1486.

states. UN and state practice has long ago laid to rest any assertion that such violations are "matters which are essentially within the domestic jurisdiction of any state" in respect of which UN intervention would be prohibited under Article 2(7) of the Charter. The former UN Secretary-General stated in 1991 that "the principle of non-interference with the essential domestic jurisdiction of states cannot be regarded as a protective barrier behind which human rights could be massively or systematically violated with impunity". The case for non-interference, where it is legitimate, would be weakened, he said, "if it were to carry the implication that sovereignty, even in this day and age, includes the right of mass slaughter or of launching systematic campaigns of decimation of forced exodus of civilian populations in the name of controlling civil strife or insurrection."[194]

The 1993 UN World Conference on Human Rights expressly reaffirmed that "the promotion and protection of all human rights is a legitimate concern of the international community".[195] On the increasingly rare occasions when a state tries to invoke Article 2(7) on human rights questions, this has not prevented UN action even in the face of a total refusal by the state concerned to cooperate.[196]

XI.1.3 THE SPECIAL NATURE OF INTERNATIONAL HUMAN RIGHTS OBLIGATIONS

The responsibility of the entire international community to ensure human rights protection also derives from the special nature of human rights obligations and the unusual characteristics of human rights treaties. The International Court of Justice has described human rights rules and principles as being among a category of obligations that states have towards the international community as a whole. Such obligations are:

> [b]y their very nature...the concern of all States. In view of the importance of the rights involved, all States can be held to have a legal interest in their protection; they are obligations <u>erga omnes</u>. Such obligations derive, for example, in contemporary international law from the outlawing of acts of aggression, and of genocide, as also from the principles and rules concerning the basic rights of the human person....[197]

---

[194] Report of UN Secretary-General Perez de Cuellar on the work of the UN, UN Doc. A/46/1 (1991).

[195] The Vienna Declaration and Programme of Action, 25 June 1993, at Part I, para. 4.

[196] For a more detailed discussion of inter-state responsibility in this area see Kamminga Inter-State Accountability For Violations of Human Rights (1990).

[197] Barcelona Traction Case ICJ Reports 1970, p. 3 at p. 32.

According to the European Commission of Human Rights a state bringing a complaint of a breach of the European Convention is not enforcing its own rights but rather bringing before the Commission a "violation of the public order of Europe".[198]

Human rights treaties confer rights on individuals and thus have some special characteristics not normally attributed to other treaties. The remedies of termination or suspension of a treaty following a breach of its terms do not apply to "provisions relating to the protection of the human person contained in treaties of a humanitarian character".[199] The International Court has stated that states parties to the Genocide Convention enjoy a common, collective interest in its application, "namely, the accomplishment of those high purposes which are the raison d'etre of the convention".[200] It follows from this that other states can take formal action against an offending state even though the violations do not involve the complainant state's own nationals. The inter-state complaints mechanisms contained in the treaties confirm this as do those treaty provisions allowing recourse to the International Court of Justice or other settlement procedures to resolve disputes of interpretation or application of the treaty. The European Court of Human Rights has stated that the European Convention creates "objective obligations" which benefit from a "collective enforcement". It has said that the inter-state complaints provision in the European Convention:

> allows Contracting States to require the observance of those obligations without having to justify an interest deriving, for example, from the fact that a measure they complain of has prejudiced one of their nationals".[201]

The International Law Commission has also provided in its draft articles on state responsibility that if any right infringed arises from a multilateral treaty or under customary international law and was created for the protection of human rights then the "injured states" include all those who are also party to the treaty or bound by the rule of customary law. In certain circumstances it may be possible to ground an action in customary international law as well as pursuant to a treaty.[202]

---

[198] Austria v. Italy, 11 January 1961, 4 YECHR (1961), p. 140.

[199] Article 60(5) of the Vienna Convention on the Law of Treaties.

[200] The Genocide Convention Case ICJ Reports 1951, p. 15 at p. 23.

[201] Ireland v. the United Kingdom (1978) ECHR Series A, Vol 25, p. 91.

[202] Some commentators have doubted that disputes concerning human rights provisions that amount to rules of customary international law would be declared admissible by the International Court when brought by a state on the basis that these are "erga omnes" obligations. The International Law Commission's draft articles would certainly appear to provide for this although these are not yet adopted. It may be even more difficult when a state is also party to a treaty covering the same obligations but has not accepted the complaint procedures in the treaty and has expressly refused to accept the jurisdiction of the Court in respect of the treaty. See generally Kamminga, n.196 above, at pp.175-177.

XI.1.4 IS THERE A DUTY ON OTHER STATES TO ACT?

Given the joint responsibility on the international community to ensure the protection of human rights and the legitimacy of international scrutiny and action by other states in response to human rights violations, it is pertinent to consider to what extent there may be a <u>duty</u> under international law on states to take action to respond to human rights violations. In their 1986 Declaration on Human Rights the European Community countries stated "the Twelve seek universal observance of human rights. The protection of human rights is a legitimate <u>and continuous duty</u> of the world community and of nations individually" (emphasis added). There is little authority in the terms of most of the treaties themselves to support such a binding duty on states to act. State practice, bilaterally as well as at the UN and regional organizations, has been notoriously inconsistent in addressing situations involving breaches of human rights and humanitarian law. However, it is arguable that in cases of particularly serious violations, there may indeed be a duty on other states to act.

The Genocide Convention, for example, appears to impose such a duty on states parties to act. Article 1 of the Convention lays down a clear obligation in providing that genocide is a crime under international law "which [the states parties] undertake to prevent or punish". The Convention goes to state that persons committing genocide "shall be punished"; the reference to an international penal tribunal, although not so far set up, was clearly aimed at ensuring prosecution of suspects when national courts were unable or unwilling to act. Disputes concerning the Convention, including the responsibility of a state for genocide, "shall be submitted to the International Court of Justice" and no other method of dispute settlement is envisaged.

Article 1 common to all four of the Geneva Conventions may also impose a duty on all states parties who "undertake to respect and <u>to ensure respect</u> for the present Convention <u>in all circumstances</u>" (emphasis added). The Commentary to the Geneva Conventions stresses the importance and prominent placing of this provision which has been "deliberately invested with imperative force". It explains that the provision derives precisely from the special nature of a treaty not based on reciprocity but being a series of unilateral undertakings "solemnly contracted before the world" and imposing obligations on each state vis-a-vis itself and vis-a-vis others. According to the Commentary, the words "to ensure respect" are not redundant but were "intended to emphasize the responsibility of the Contracting parties". They are required to ensure the enforcement of the Conventions and, when a state party is in breach, "to endeavour to bring it back to an attitude of respect for the Convention".[203] The duty in Article 1 to "ensure respect" presumably extends to states parties taking all necessary measures to suppress acts contrary to the Conventions, although it is not spelt out what these should be.

It is more difficult to import this duty into the human rights treaties. Even when available, inter-state complaints procedures in the UN human rights treaties have never been used. Under Article 2 of the International Covenant on Civil and Political Rights each state party undertakes to respect and to ensure the rights guaranteed "to all individuals within its territory and subject to its jurisdiction". The Convention on the Elimination of All Forms of Racial Discrimination contains in Article 2 a more open-ended obligation on all states to pursue a policy of eliminating racial discrimination "in all its forms" and is not expressly limited to a state's own jurisdiction (in contrast with some other articles which are expressed to be so limited). However, the nature of many of the measures envisaged in the Convention could only be taken by a state within its own jurisdiction.

Even if it is difficult to find a generalised individual or collective duty on states under international law to act in response to all human rights violations, there may at least be an emerging obligation to act in respect of particularly serious or widespread violations of human rights. Treaties which impose obligations on states to prosecute anyone in their jurisdiction suspected of particular violations on the basis of universal jurisdiction create a duty to act in particular circumstances, at least in respect of states parties to those treaties. The unprecedented steps taken by the Security Council to establish two ad hoc international tribunals in two years to prosecute very serious violations of human rights and humanitarian law indicate a sense of international obligation to take special measures in respect of abhorrent acts committed on the scale of those in the former Yugoslavia and in Rwanda. The General Assembly's directives to the International Law Commission to speed up and complete its work on a draft Statute for an international criminal court is also indicative of the international community's recognition that it must create a tribunal capable of dealing with such serious violations wherever these may occur.

XI.2 INTERNATIONAL RESPONSIBILITY FOR MINORITY PROTECTION

The international community has historically assumed a special responsibility

---
[203] Pictet Commentary to Geneva Convention IV (1958) p.16.

for the rights and protection of minorities. The League of Nations took international responsibility for the protection of certain vulnerable minorities after the first World War. These measures constituted one of the earliest antecedents of the comprehensive system of international human rights protection in effect today. Minority rights were also recognized as having a special importance in the early days of the UN. More recently, with the end of the Cold War and the resurgence of bitter ethnic conflicts, minority protection is again at the forefront international concern. Recent measures include the adoption of the first UN set of standards aimed specifically at minority protection; the adoption of the first regional binding treaty on minority rights; and establishment of a regional High Commissioner on Minorities. All these steps demonstrate a heightened awareness by the international community of its responsibility in this area and an acceptance that international action and intervention is often essential to resolve minority conflicts.

XI.2.1 MINORITY PROTECTION BY THE LEAGUE OF NATIONS

The protection of the rights of certain minorities was provided for in a series of treaties and other international instruments adopted after the end of the first World War under the auspices of the League of Nations. The League's system of minority protection has been criticised for its limited scope of application and for the ineffectiveness in practice of the supervisory procedures. It did, however, establish the principle of international responsibility for the protection of certain minority groups by ensuring that the provisions of these instruments constituted international obligations overriding domestic law which were to be subject to political and judicial supervision by the League.[204]

As described in Section II, the 1932 Iraqi Declaration guaranteeing minority rights was a condition of Iraq becoming a member of the League of Nations and formed part of this system for the protection of minorities. The guarantees in all these international instruments were expressed in very similar terms. For the most part, they dealt with traditional minority rights rather than broader issues of political and economic rights. The international supervisory mechanism extended to actual and anticipated breaches. In the event of breach, the Council of the League was authorized to take any measures or give such directions as it saw fit. A dispute of law or fact arising out of the terms of the instruments could be referred for judicial determination to the Permanent Court of International Justice.

---

[204] For a fuller account of the history and content of the minority protection system established by the League of Nations see Thornberry, International Law and the Protection of Minorities (1991), Part I.

In addition to the supervisory authority of the Council of the League and the Permanent Court, the League also established a petition system. This gave the minorities themselves and other private persons direct access to bring to the attention of the League member states complaints about breaches of the guaranteed minority rights. Petitions were considered by three-member Minorities Committees who could decide to bring the issue to the attention of the Council, undertake informal negotiations with the government concerned or terminate consideration of the petition.

XI.2.2 MINORITY PROTECTION AT THE UN

The early history of the United Nations did not advance the protection of minority rights significantly in international law, yet the recognition that minority issues are of international concern was clearly marked. In 1948, immediately after the UN was established, the General Assembly adopted Resolution 217 C(III) entitled "Fate of Minorities". This clearly stated that "the United Nations cannot remain indifferent to the fate of minorities" and requested the Commission on Human Rights and its Sub-Commission to make a thorough study of the problem of minorities "in order that the United Nations may be able to take effective measures for the protection of racial, national, religious or linguistic minorities".

One of the first subsidiary UN bodies to be set up in 1947 was the Sub-Commission on Prevention of Discrimination and Protection of Minorities, a sub-body of the Commission on Human Rights, with a specific mandate to deal both with minority issues and discrimination. The Sub-Commission has carried out some land-mark studies on the question of minority rights[205] and was the catalyst for the drafting of the 1992 UN Declaration on minority rights.

The 1992 Declaration underscores the role of the international community in securing minority rights protection. Its preamble recalls that "the United Nations has an important role to play regarding the protection of minorities" and Article 9 requires UN bodies to contribute to "the full realization of the rights and principles set forth in this Declaration...".

The necessity for cooperation among states on minority questions and to promote respect for minority rights is also stressed in Articles 5, 6 and 7 of the 1992 Declaration. These provisions are a recognition that minority issues are

---

[205] See, for example, Capotorti Study on the rights of persons belonging to ethnic, religious and linguistic minorities UN Sales No. E.78.XIV.1 (1979).

not only important domestically but affect international relations between states and have implications for peaceful cooperation and global security. This is also borne out in the preamble of the Declaration which states that protection and promotion of the rights of minorities "contributes to the political and social stability of States in which they live" and "as an integral part of the development of society as a whole and within a democratic framework based on the rule of law, would contribute to the strengthening of friendship and cooperation among people and States".

The adoption of the Declaration also reflects the increasing importance and urgency of the UN's role in minority protection in recent years as minority issues have increasingly erupted in bitter and prolonged violent conflicts around the globe. In his Agenda for Peace the UN Secretary-General drew attention to the global insecurity and conflict engendered by "brutal ethnic, religious, social, cultural or linguistic strife". He said that "the time of absolute and exclusive sovereignty...has passed" and stressed that "one requirement for solutions to these problems lies in commitment to human rights with a special sensitivity to those of minorities, whether ethnic, religious, social or linguistic".[206]

The increasing preoccupation of the international community with minority protection was evident at the UN World Conference on Human Rights. The Vienna Declaration and Programme of Action adopted at the conclusion of the Conference reaffirmed "the obligation of States to ensure that persons belonging to minorities may exercise fully and effectively all human rights and fundamental freedoms without any discrimination and in full equality before the law in accordance with the Declaration on the Rights of Persons Belonging to National or Ethnic, Religious and Linguistic Minorities". It condemned genocide and ethnic cleansing and called on the Commission to consider ways to secure the implementation of the 1992 minority rights Declaration. It also urged the UN Centre for Human Rights to provide qualified expertise on minority issues and human rights, on the prevention and resolution of disputes and to assist in situations involving minorities. It stressed that measures to ensure minority rights should include "facilitation of their full participation in all aspects of the political, economic, social, religious and cultural life of society and in the economic progress and development in their country".[207]

The Sub-Commission has also had a part in this renewed focus on minorities.

---

[206] Agenda for Peace UN Doc. S/24111 (1992).

[207] Vienna Declaration and Programme of Action, 25 June 1993, at Part I, paras. 19 and 28 and Part II, paras. 25-27.

It recently carried out another major study on minority protection[208] and it is currently re-examining its mandate to give more prominence to this work and particularly to the development of international mechanisms for supervision and implementation of minority rights.[209]

XI.2.3 MINORITY PROTECTION BY OTHER INTERGOVERNMENTAL ORGANIZATIONS

Action taken within other intergovernmental organizations provides further evidence of a rapid evolution in international responsibility for minority protection and in the development of international standards concerning minority rights. The 1975 Helsinki Final Act of the Conference on Security and Cooperation in Europe (CSCE)[210] included in Principle VII dealing with respect for human rights:

> The participating States on whose territory national minorities exist will respect the right of persons belonging to such minorities to equality before the law, will afford them the full opportunity for the actual enjoyment of human rights and fundamental freedoms and will, in this manner, protect their legitimate interests in this sphere.

Common commitments to minority protection were again stressed in the Concluding Documents of the CSCE Follow-Up Meetings in Madrid (1983) and Vienna (1989) but were much more extensively developed in the final document of the 1990 Copenhagen meeting on the human dimension of the CSCE.

The Copenhagen provisions lay emphasis on multilateral state cooperation to address minority issues. The Document notes that respect for minority rights "as part of universally recognized human rights is an essential factor for peace, justice, stability and democracy in the participating States". It stresses the importance of constructive cooperation among states in this area, including through the UN and other international organizations, to promote mutual confidence, good relations and international peace, security and justice.

The Copenhagen Document is indicative of the gradual development of international standards towards the protection of a wider range of minority

---

[208] Eide Possible ways and means of facilitating the peaceful and constructive solution of problems involving minorities UN Doc.E/CN.4/Sub.2/1993/34.

[209] See UN Doc. E/CN.4/Sub.2/1994/36.

[210] The CSCE is now renamed the Organization on Security and Cooperation in Europe to reflect the institutionalization of its structures and competence.

rights than those traditionally protected. It imposes specific positive obligations on states to protect and promote the identity of minorities in consultation with them; to provide opportunities for instruction in their own language; to respect their right to participate in public affairs including those affecting their identity; and, most significantly, takes note of the establishment of "appropriate local or autonomous administrations corresponding to the specific historical and territorial circumstances of such minorities...". These commitments were further strengthened at a 1991 CSCE Expert Meeting in Geneva devoted solely to national minorities.

Conscious of the need to provide an operational mechanism in addition to developing new standards, in 1992 the CSCE appointed a High Commissioner on National Minorities with a special mandate for early warning of minority problems and for preventive action. The Commissioner is able to receive information from a wide range of governmental and non-governmental sources and reports directly to political decision-making structures within the CSCE.

A significant advance in minority protection has also come from within the Council of Europe. In November 1994 the Committee of Ministers adopted the text of a Framework Convention for the Protection of National Minorities. It is the first legally-binding international instrument aimed specifically at minority protection and builds on the 1992 adoption of the European Charter for Regional and Minority Languages by the Council of Europe. The Framework Convention, which is also open to ratification by non-member states of the Council of Europe, opens with a firm statement of international responsibility:
> The protection of national minorities and of the rights and freedoms of persons belonging to those national minorities forms an integral part of the international protection of human rights, and as such falls within the scope of international cooperation.

According to the explanatory report, the main purpose of this Article 1 "is to specify that the protection of national minorities...does not fall within the reserved domain of states." The Convention further provides in Article 18 that states parties shall endeavour to conclude bilateral and multilateral agreements with other states, particularly neighbouring states, to ensure minority protection. It also establishes a special monitoring system - state party reports on implementation are required within one year and thereafter periodically to be considered by the Committee of Ministers assisted by an expert Advisory Committee.

Although the standards and mechanisms for minority protection adopted by the

CSCE and the Council of Europe are in still in their infancy and can be criticised for weaknesses and failings in a number of respects, they do represent significant advances in the existing international framework to promote and protect minority rights. They demonstrate the evolution towards addressing minority issues on the basis of international norms and through international mechanisms in a region beset by particularly intransigent and divisive minority conflicts. It should also be noted that Turkey is a member of both these organizations so that the issue of the Kurds is very much on the agenda of the OSCE and the Council of Europe as these new minority standards and mechanisms take effect.

XI.3 PRINCIPLES OF INTERNATIONAL REFUGEE PROTECTION

The General Assembly explicitly recognized "the responsibility of the United Nations for the international protection of refugees" when it established the UN High Commissioner for Refugees (UNHCR) in 1950.[211] Refugees are one of the primary groups for which the international community has responsibility since, by definition, refugees do not enjoy the protection of their own government and must look to the international community for the protection of their rights. In the words of UNHCR:

> international protection [of refugees] begins with securing admission, asylum and respect for basic rights, including the principle of non-refoulement, without which the safety and even survival of the refugee is in jeopardy; it ends only with the attainment of a durable solution, ideally through the restoration of protection by the refugee's own country...if safe return is not possible, it involves promoting and implementing other durable solutions of resettlement or local integration.[212]

There is also a growing international awareness that some fundamental principles and practices relating to refugee protection must be extended to the internally-displaced. UNHCR is increasingly being called on to extend its protection to the internally-displaced in particular situations and in 1992 a UN Special Rapporteur on the internally-displaced was appointed to give particular attention to these problems.

The mass exodus of the Kurds from Iraq in 1991 constituted a refugee crisis of enormous proportions and presented UNHCR (designated lead agency at the height of the crisis) with one of its greatest challenges. Although it is difficult,

---

[211] See General Assembly Resolution 319(IV) of 3 December 1949.

[212] UNHCR Note on International Protection, UN Doc. A/AC.96/830 (1994) at para.12.

particularly four years later, to analyse the situation of the Kurds in Iraq solely in terms of the principles of refugee protection, these cannot be ignored and in some respects are still operative in terms of engaging international responsibility.

At the time of the mass exodus of the Kurds in 1991, events unfolded very quickly. Many Kurds did manage to flee the country and to cross a border into Turkey or Iran. However, although they would have been entitled to apply for asylum, formal and individual determinations of refugee status were never undertaken for the majority of them because of the speed at which events unfolded and the rapidity with which the safe havens were set up to encourage their return (some did refuse to return and were recognized as refugees and granted asylum elsewhere). For many others the question of asylum never actually arose as they had not actually crossed a border but were stranded in the mountains in the border area and refused entry to Turkey. Article 1.A(2) of the 1951 Convention for the Protection of Refugees defines refugees as persons outside their country of nationality. Technically, therefore, this group would not have been considered to be refugees but displaced persons, although this was only by reason of the fact that they were prevented from entering Turkey.

The fundamental cornerstone of refugee protection is that of non-refoulement. This is laid down in Article 33 of the 1951 Refugee Convention but is also understood to have the status of customary international law, applicable to all states. Under this principle a refugee may not be returned "in any manner whatsoever" to a country where his life or freedom would be threatened on account of his race, religion, nationality, membership of a particular social group or political opinion.

If it is not possible for a refugee to return to his or her country the normal method of implementing the non-refoulement principle is the granting of asylum in another country. In Iraq, the international community instead offered a unique form of protection - the setting up of internationally protected safe havens which were located inside the Kurds' country of origin but were not under the control of the Iraqi Government. This exceptional measure constituted a recognition that the non-refoulement principle was applicable and that the refugees and those still attempting to flee could not be forced back under the control of their own government.

The Refugee Convention further provides in Article 1.C that it will cease to apply to a person who "has voluntarily re-availed himself of the protection of his country of nationality" or who "has voluntarily re-established himself in the country which he left or outside which he remained owing to fear of persecution". While the Kurds who returned to Iraq and the displaced who never managed to cross the border would technically fall outside the Convention definition of refugees, these people were certainly not re-availing themselves of Iraq "protection"; on the contrary, their return was conditional on the assurances they were given that, even if they returned to their country of origin, they would be guaranteed international protection against Iraq. They understood and were encouraged to believe that they were returning not to territory controlled by Iraq but to protected safe havens that would be defended against Iraqi military incursions and control by foreign troops and the UN.

Moreover a key word in Article 1.C of the Convention is "voluntarily" and the Kurds were hardly in a position to exercise a wholly free choice. Turkey was particularly intransigent in its obstruction of relief supplies and refusal to grant asylum. The coalition countries, particularly sensitive to the concerns of a key ally like Turkey as well as to domestic public opinion, were almost frantic in their haste to get the refugees off the mountainsides and back into Iraq. Even UNHCR was encouraging return on the basis that the risk of further persecution by Iraq had been removed. The entire relief programme was geared towards return. The Kurds had little option, if they were to survive, other than to go back. It has been noted in one study that:

> the very fact that the Kurds were brought back...into the heart of a state with a proven record of hostility towards then might reasonably have been taken as an implicit promise of continuing protection....Moreover, the UN - and UNHCR in particular - has continued to encourage the return of refugees into Iraq, some into areas originally destroyed by the Iraqi Government. These were considered by the [Iraqi Government] to be forbidden areas and its opposition to resettlement in such areas was particularly obvious in Sulaimaniya governorate...Insofar as UNHCR encouraged the reoccupation of forbidden and possibly insecure areas, this must impose an additional obligation to protect those encouraged to return to their former villages in this way.[213]

It is still difficult and somewhat tortuous now to analyse this sui generis situation in terms of the international law applicable to conventional refugee situations. Subsequent events have muddied the waters still further. The coalition ground troops have withdrawn and no longer offer the immediacy of protection that induced the refugees to return. At the same time, a variety of factors resulting from the international intervention have had the effect of rendering "safe" a

---
[213] Keen at p. 10.

much larger area, enabling people to return to an area much more extensive than that which is under international protection. With the passage of time, the return of Kurds to their places of origin, the relief and rehabilitation programs to assist people in re-establishing themselves, the election of a local government and the functioning of a local Kurdish administration it becomes even more strained to continue to analyse this situation in terms of refugee protection.

However, the origins of the situation and the circumstances in which the refugees returned to Iraq should not be forgotten. As long as international protection of the area continues in some form and the Iraqi Government has not re-established control, it could not be considered compatible with international principles of refugee protection, and particularly the fundamental principle of non-refoulement, simply to remove unilaterally the special security status and international protection of the Kurdish area without replacing it with other effective protection mechanisms and international guarantees.

It is also highly likely that, if the special security arrangements for the area are simply terminated, this will immediately generate a new mass exodus of refugees at least on the same scale if not greater than occurred in 1991. In 1991 the international community was taken by surprise; some outflow of refugees had been anticipated but on nothing like the scale that actually happened. If the Kurds are again abandoned to their fate in Iraq today, no one should be surprised at the magnitude of the refugee flow that is likely to occur or the volume of human and financial resources that will needed to cope.

XI.4 RESPONSIBILITY ASSUMED BY THE INTERNATIONAL COMMUNITY IN IRAQI KURDISTAN

Resolution 688 (1991) determined beyond any doubt that the consequences of the internal repression by Iraq of its population constitutes a threat to international peace and security. The Security Council also decided to remain seized of this matter, thus retaining it on its agenda. It is expressly acknowledged by the international community that internal repression in Iraq continues on a massive scale. The periodic reports of the Special Rapporteur on Iraq confirm this and document human rights violations in considerable detail. Resolutions by the General Assembly and the Commission on Human Rights recognize and continue to condemn that repression in the strongest terms. Both these bodies have called for additional exceptional measures in the form of a human rights monitoring operation in respect of Iraq.

As long as power is retained by a Government which holds human rights in contempt and shows no hesitation in resorting to the most extreme forms of brutality to compel the submission of its citizens, the threat to international peace and security remains. As the UN organ with the primary responsibility to maintain peace and security, this imposes a continuing obligation on the Security Council to take the measures to address the threat posed by Iraq.

The threat is a real one. It is abundantly clear that there is a very substantial risk of another mass exodus if international protection is removed, or even despite the maintenance of protection if and when sanctions are partially or wholly lifted and Iraq regains its political and economic strength. The limitations and failings of the protection currently provided have been discussed in Section IV.4 above; it would be no match for a determined military onslaught in Iraqi Kurdistan just as it is of no effect now against less dramatic but equally devastating measures aimed at weakening and destabilizing the Kurds. The punitive internal embargo against the area is one example of this; history provides many other examples of the lengths to which the Iraqi Government will go to crush any challenges to its authority.

In 1991 the world was taken by surprise by the size and speed of the exodus and the suffering that resulted. Now the international community has the benefit of hindsight and knows only too well the scale of the humanitarian disaster that can occur. In 1991 almost two million people fled in a matter of days with no knowledge of what awaited them and no guarantee of international assistance. The exceptional response of the international community in 1991 has created expectations, not only among the Kurds themselves but also among the public at large, that the world cannot abandon the Kurds again. Its very success, ironically, can have only increased the likelihood of a second mass exodus to compel further international action if and when it proves necessary.

The international community created a special status for Iraqi Kurdistan. The intention to establish an internationally protected area in northern Iraq was quite deliberate as it was seen to be the only way to encourage the Kurds to return and to remove the much greater international problem of coping with a mass outflow of refugees requiring long-term protection and settlement outside their own country. The necessity of seeking a political solution to the problem, backed by international guarantees, was ignored. While the withdrawal of the Iraqi civil administration from virtually the whole of the northern area a few months later may not have been initially foreseen or intended, it was hardly surprising. It was closely connected to Iraq's loss of control in the area as a result of the international intervention and the clear threats of force if it interfered with the safe havens.

Having been instrumental in creating a protected area and actively encouraging the inhabitants to return to it, the international community has subsequently perpetuated the special status of Iraqi Kurdistan for the past four years. Over such a long period it has certainly facilitated, if not indirectly encouraged, the emergence of a de facto self-governing area independent of Iraqi control. The regular policing of the no-fly zone and the coalition's military base, coupled with a significant UN presence backed by special security measures, has maintained Iraqi Kurdistan as an internationally protected area. The humanitarian programme, provided by the UN and by non-governmental agencies, some with government backing and funding, has helped local communities to re-establish themselves and has assisted in rebuilding the area. It has cushioned the Kurds from some of the worst effects of the Iraqi internal embargo and helped them to withstand pressure to force them to submit again to central governmental control.

The special status of Iraqi Kurdistan has also made possible its political development as a functioning autonomous area. International protection provided the political space and the security necessary for the holding of democratic elections in 1992. As a democratic experiment in an authoritarian country the elections were welcomed by a number of governments. They were accepted by most others without protest. The Kurdish administration has been accepted as the de facto governing authority of the region. Efforts have been made by UN officials and others to strengthen and bolster that authority, not least as a means of countering internal conflict between the Kurdish political groups.

At the same time, by facilitating the emergence of Iraqi Kurdistan as de facto autonomous unit under a democratically elected government, the international community has fuelled long-standing Kurdish political aspirations and created expectations that international support will be forthcoming to secure a stable and long-term political settlement that accords with the freely-expressed wishes of the Kurdish people and that guarantees respect for all their internationally-recognized fundamental rights and freedoms.

The actions of the international community that have served to protect the Kurds, hold the Iraqi Government at bay and permit at least the beginnings of political, economic and social development in the region, coupled with international acceptance of or at least acquiescence in the de facto status of the area as an autonomous unit governed and administered by the Kurds, creates a situation in which some principle of estoppel would seem to apply. In principle, estoppel precludes the author of any representation or conduct from denying the express or implied 'truth' of the representation particularly when there has been good faith reliance on it by another party to his detriment. It has been said that "a considerable weight of authority supports the view that estoppel is a general principle of international law, resting on principles of good faith and consistency, and shorn of the technical features to be found in municipal law".[214] As a matter of basic equity and justice, the international community, having created a special protected status which has enabled the Kurds to rebuild their communities and establish democratic governing structures, cannot now simply abandon Iraqi Kurdistan to its fate.

The responsibility which the international community has assumed in Iraqi Kurdistan by its actions is further reinforced by the fact that it has thereby increased the vulnerability of the Kurds and intensified the risks they face if international protection is now withdrawn. The creation of a protected area facilitated and encouraged the Kurds in taking precisely the bold political steps which the present Iraqi Government considers illegal. Past history and practice of this Government have repeatedly confirmed its aim to crush the Kurds into submission and to deny them effective political autonomy. Its outright rejection of the 1992 Kurdish elections indicate that it has no intention of recognizing the authority of the present or any future democratic Kurdish administration. It will inevitably take the harshest punitive measures against the Kurds for their defiance of its authority. Political leaders and activists will certainly be singled out for massive reprisals but there is every likelihood that punishment will be directed against the general population as well for their participation.

Threatening Iraqi troop movements in the north, the pattern of bomb and grenade attacks, the shelling of agricultural areas, the resumption of arabization in Kirkuk and the internal economic embargo imposed on the area are all indicative of the Government's aggressive attitude towards the Kurds. Furthermore, according to the Special Rapporteur on Iraq:

> The Government of Iraq and personalities close to the Presidency have reportedly expressed veiled threats to reinstitute control by force and to do away with the Kurdish leadership. Such reports are given credence by the

---

[214] Brownlie Principles of Public International Law (1994) at p. 641. Brownlie also notes here, without dissenting from this observation, that "it is necessary to point out that estoppel in municipal law is regarded with great caution and that the 'principle' has no particular coherence in international law, its incidence and effects not being uniform".

massing of Iraqi military forces around the northern region and by widely published statements attributed to Saddam Hussein in December 1992 to the effect that the Government of Iraq will "apply the rule of law" again to the region once the "foreign troops are out" and certain "elements" have been removed.[215]

In such circumstances it is politically and morally unacceptable to withdraw international protection. Any steps by the international community which enable the present Government, renowned for its brutality and contempt for the rule of law, to re-establish control over the Kurds could only amount at best to international acquiesence, if not complicity, in the violations and reprisals that would certainly follow.

While the international community certainly has an obligation not to abandon the area, it is equally clear that the present measures of protection are not by themselves sufficient nor can they be prolonged indefinitely. They are integrally linked - in practice if not necessarily formally - to the conditions imposed by Resolution 687 (1991) and to the imposition of sanctions against Iraq. As and when these are modified or lifted and relations with Iraq begin to normalise, pressure to remove the special protection measures in the north will inevitably mount.

In any event, these measures have never had long-term political objectives. They are not aimed at bringing about a durable political settlement which guarantees respect for the rights of the Kurds. They simply maintain a highly unstable status quo, leaving Iraqi Kurdistan without a clear legal framework; without the possibility to participate in discussions in international fora about future political options; without adequate assistance to resolve political differences peacefully and to institutionalize respect for human rights and the rule of law; and severely crippled socially and economically by the dual effect of international sanctions and the internal embargo imposed by the Iraqi Government.

XI.5 THE RESPONSIBILITY OF OCCUPYING FORCES

The states whose forces participated in establishing the safe havens may bear special legal responsibilities under the Geneva Conventions, particularly the provisions of Geneva Convention IV which deal with a military occupation.

Article 2, common to all the Geneva Conventions, states that the Conventions

---
[215] UN Doc. E/CN.4/1993/45 at para. 84.

apply "to all cases of partial or total occupation of the territory of a High Contracting Party, even if the said occupation meets with no armed resistance". It appears that an occupation need not necessarily be in connection with a state of war or other armed conflict between the parties. Although the common perception of an occupation is a belligerent act imposed on a hostile population, the humanitarian obligations of the Geneva Conventions would still apply, as far as they are required, in a "benign" occupation where the presence of foreign troops is welcomed by the local population.[216]

The presence of foreign forces in another state's territory which is not pursuant to any agreement and which displaces that state's control over an area are strong indicators of an occupation. The commentary to the Geneva Conventions indicates that even a relatively minimalist military presence, such as a patrol penetrating enemy territory with no intention to remain, could constitute an occupation.[217] An extensive military presence or a formal declaration is not required nor that the troops exercise complete authority in all respects over the local population. Geneva Convention IV clearly envisages situations where local authorities remain in place and its provisions prohibit occupying forces from dismantling local laws and structures.

It would certainly appear that there was a military occupation by the coalition forces at the time the safe havens were set up. It is less clear whether the occupation can be said to have continued after the withdrawal of the bulk of the troops in 1991 and the assumption of control by the UN's humanitarian bodies. Article 6 of Geneva Convention IV states that the application of the Convention shall cease "one year after the general close of military operations"[218] but the commentary suggests that the Convention provisions remain fully applicable where there has been no state of war and no armed resistance to the occupation.[219] It may be that the coalition forces can be understood to have delegated their

---

[216] Roberts "What is a Military Occupation?" 55 BYIL (1984) p. 249. In this examination of military occupations, Roberts indicates the very wide range of situations which may fall within the concept and argues that the humanitarian law obligations ought to be widely and flexibly applied even where the technical legal designation of a territory as "occupied" is disputed. The crucial factors are the presence of foreign forces and a degree of control over the area rather than the intent of the foreign state(s) concerned. Motive and purpose may distinguish one type of occupation from another and have some practical implications. Strict observance of all relevant obligations may be more urgent, for example, where there is a high degree of hostility between the foreign forces and the local population.

[217] Pictet, n. 203 above, at p.60. Roberts points out in his article (n.216 above) that both the USA and UK Military Manuals also provide that the rules governing occupations should apply as far as possible even when troops are passing through foreign territory.

[218] Under the Convention certain obligations remain in force in any event for the duration of the occupation "to the extent that [the occupying power] exercises the functions of government" in the territory.

[219] Pictet, n.203 above, at p. 63.

authority for day-to-day administration to the Kurds but they would remain responsible for areas such as defence and security in the area. Alternatively it might be argued that they have delegated to the UN, although it is not clear the extent to which this is legitimate given that UN bodies are not formally bound by the Geneva Conventions.

Many of the provisions of Geneva Convention IV, which deals with the protection of civilians, are aimed at protecting the local population from hostile or violent acts and unlawful interference with daily life and public services and institutions by the occupying forces. These obligations do not raise particular problems in the case of Iraqi Kurdistan. However, there are a number of positive duties required of the occupying forces working, as necessary with the cooperation of local authorities. Protected persons must be humanely treated and protected against all acts of violence, threats and insults (Article 27); protected persons must not be deprived of the benefits of Geneva Convention IV by reason of the occupation (Article 47); protected persons must have full access to humanitarian organizations (Article 30); the occupying forces must ensure the population has necessary food and medical supplies and must bring supplies into the territory and facilitate relief programs undertaken by other states or organizations if local resources are inadequate (Articles 55 and 59); they must ensure and maintain medical facilities, public health and hygiene (Article 56); and they must facilitate the functioning of all institutions for the care and education of children (Article 50). Articles 27, 30, 47 and 59 are among the provisions which remain operative in any event for the duration of an occupation.

To the extent that the coalition forces are still in occupation and have displaced the Iraqi Government, leaving a vacuum in Iraqi Kurdistan, there may well be some continuing obligations on the coalition powers to ensure the protection of the population, at least as regards physical protection and essential food and medical needs. This may entail responsibilities to ensure that the UN aid programme can meet these needs. It may also impose a responsibility for the maintenance of security of the general population threatened by Iraqi attacks, attacks by neighbouring states and the consequences of internal conflict.

However, the Geneva Conventions offer only minimal protection as long as an occupation continues. They cannot be relied on to impose more extensive obligations on the coalition governments to address the deeper long-term needs of the Kurds nor to compel prolongation of the protective presence of the coalition. Indeed, while the coalition forces must strictly observe all obligations on them as long as they maintain a presence in the area, weighting humanitarian law responsibilities too heavily on them may prompt an over-hasty withdrawal and removal of any outside protection. The Geneva Conventions were not aimed at promoting benign and protective foreign occupations and impose no future protection obligations at all on a retreating force before or after its withdrawal from the territory.

XII. FORMAL LEGAL MEASURES AGAINST IRAQ

There are a number of possibilities open to the international community or other individual states to take formal legal measures against Iraq or Iraqi officials for violations of human rights and humanitarian law. The scope of these measures is, however, generally restricted to tackling acts which have occurred and would not necessarily prevent future violations even if the Iraqi Government were ordered to take preventive measures. Recourse to such measures is very rare or non-existent in the history of the UN and the fact that none have been resorted to so far in respect of Iraq is indicative of the great reluctance of states to use these options against other states. Furthermore, while any of them would be strong measures of international censure and would carry considerable moral and political weight, effective enforcement would be likely to be very difficult in the case of a country such as Iraq which has little respect for international law.

These measures would also not address the underlying political problems and root causes of human rights violations in Iraq and thus could not, by themselves, constitute an adequate response by the international community to the situation of the Iraqi Kurds. However, some of the measures outlined below could certainly be taken in conjunction with a more comprehensive solution and would be an important and necessary demonstration of the political will and commitment of the international community to hold the state of Iraq and individual perpetrators of gross violations accountable for their atrocious acts.

XII.1 A CASE OF GENOCIDE?

The evidence of the Iraqi Government's actions against the Kurds, particularly in the course of the Anfal campaign but not limited to events in 1988, certainly points to a prima facie case involving acts prohibited by the Convention on the Prevention and Punishment of the Crime of Genocide, to which Iraq is a state party. Article I of the Convention confirms that genocide is a crime under international law and, under Article III, conspiracy, direct or indirect incitement and attempt to commit genocide are all punishable, as is complicity in genocide.

Genocide is defined in Article II of the Convention as covering:
...any of the following acts committed with intent to destroy, in whole or in part, a national, ethnical, racial or religious group, as such:

(a) Killing members of the group;
(b) Causing serious bodily or mental harm to members of the group;
(c) Deliberately inflicting on the group conditions of life calculated to bring about its physical destruction in whole or in part:
(d) Imposing measures intended to prevent births within the group;
(e) Forcibly transferring children of the group to another group.

A key element of the crime of genocide, and one which would require very strong and precise evidence to establish, is the requisite intent to destroy a group in whole or part. The Special Rapporteur on Iraq has stated that in his view the Iraqi Government's operations against the Kurds may well amount to genocide within the meaning of the Convention. He has stated that "it would seem beyond doubt that these policies, and the "Anfal" operations in particular, bear the marks of a genocide-type design" and that "the Anfal Operations constituted genocide-type activities which did in fact result in the extermination of a part of this population and which continue to have an impact on the lives of the people as a whole".[220]

The mandatory language of Article I of the Genocide Convention whereby all states parties undertake to prevent and punish genocide suggests there may be a duty on other states to act in respect of a prima facie case of genocide. The Convention, in Article VI, envisages acts of genocide being tried by a competent tribunal in the state where the act was committed or by an international penal tribunal having jurisdiction. Neither of these options are feasible in cases such as Iraq. When senior members of the ruling government are implicated in such crimes it is inconceivable that there can be proper and impartial investigations and trials in the country itself and, at present at least, there is no international penal court which has the requisite jurisdiction.

Even in the absence of applicable criminal jurisdiction, it is possible for other states parties to the Genocide Convention to submit disputes relating to "the interpretation, application or fulfilment" of the Convention, including state responsibility for genocide, to the International Court of Justice.[221] Unlike some of the other human rights treaties, Iraq has made no reservation to the

---

[220] UN Doc. E/CN.4/1992/31 at paras. 103 and 153.

[221] A case alleging acts of genocide in breach of the Genocide Convention is currently pending before the International Court of Justice, lodged by Bosnia and Herzegovina against Yugoslavia (Serbia and Montenegro). So far the Court has not ruled on the merits of the case but has made orders for provisional measures. It has ordered, inter alia, that Yugoslavia should immediately take all measures within its power to prevent the commission of genocide and that it should ensure that "any military, paramilitary or irregular armed units which may be directed or supported by it, as well as any organizations and persons which may be subject to its control, direction or influence" do not commit any acts amounting to genocide. Genocide Convention Case ICJ Reports 1993 at p. 325.

Genocide Convention to the effect that it does not accept the Court's jurisdiction for this purpose. Although the International Court has no criminal jurisdiction as such, it is open to it to determine on the basis of all the evidence the responsibility of a state for acts of genocide or other acts prohibited by the Convention.

Even though the injury would not be to nationals of the state bringing such a case against Iraq, it would appear that appropriate measures of redress and compensation could be claimed on behalf of the Kurds, since the purpose of an international claim for reparation is that "reparation must, as far as possible, wipe out all the consequences of the illegal act and reestablish the situation which would, in all probability, have existed if that act had not been committed".[222] A state might seek Court orders for cessation of the illegal acts, for compensation for the victims or some other specific redress such as restoration of property, medical care, release of those arbitrarily detained and so on. In such a case Iraq might also be required by the Court to undertake to change legislation, policies or practices to prevent further violations and possibly also to investigate past violations and to prosecute and try those responsible.

Finally, it is also open to any state party to the Convention pursuant to Article VIII to call on the competent organs of the UN "to take such action under the Charter of the United Nations as they consider appropriate for the prevention and suppression of acts of genocide or any of the other acts enumerated in article III". The application of this provision is not dependent on any formal finding by a competent tribunal of acts of genocide having been committed or responsibility attributed to particular individuals. The Article is aimed at "prevention" and "suppression" of genocide, rather than criminal investigation and punishment. In circumstances such as Iraq, where there is at least a prima facie case that genocidal acts have been committed and a substantial risk that these may recur, Article VIII of the Convention provides another legislative basis for international action to protect the Kurds in future from the kinds of acts to which they have already been subjected.

XII.2 FORMAL MEASURES UNDER OTHER HUMAN RIGHTS TREATIES

Other possibilities for formal measures to be taken against Iraq for breaches of the human rights treaties to which it is a party are very limited. Iraq has not accepted the individual complaints procedures under either the International

---

[222] *Chorzow Factory Case* (1928) PCIJ Ser. A, No. 17 at p. 47.

Covenant on Civil and Political Rights or the International Convention on the Elimination of All Forms of Racial Discrimination.

It has also not accepted the inter-state complaints procedure under Article 41 of the Covenant on Civil and Political Rights. The only available inter-state complaints procedure is that under the Racial Discrimination Convention. One or more states parties to that Convention could bring an inter-state complaint under Article 11 of that treaty, which is automatically applicable to all states parties. However, the procedure is weak, lengthy and cumbersome and has never yet been used. The content of the complaint would have to be restricted to alleged violations only of that Convention. Complaints are submitted to the treaty-monitoring body, the Committee on the Elimination of Racial Discrimination. The procedure can take up to nine months or more and at best only results in a set of recommendations which, if rejected by the offending state, are merely transmitted to the other states parties to the Convention.

Although the International Court of Justice may have jurisdiction over disputes concerning the application of human rights treaties, Iraq has not accepted the general jurisdiction of the Court under Article 36(2) of its Statute (and would be unlikely to do so for the purposes of adjudication of such a case) and has expressly excluded the Court's jurisdiction in respect of the Conventions dealing with racial discrimination and discrimination against women.

It has already been noted that violations during internal conflict of Common Article 3 of the Geneva Conventions do not amount to "grave breaches" of the Conventions and therefore do not engage the responsibility of other states to search for and to ensure that those responsible are brought to trial. A separate procedure to set up an enquiry into alleged violations is only available in international conflict as it must be exercised by a party to the conflict. The International Fact-Finding Commission, provided for in Protocol 1 and established in 1991, has a mandate to inquire into all allegations of violations of the Conventions and the Protocols at the request of a state party but can only do so in respect of states that have made the necessary declaration to accept its competence. Iraq is not a party to Protocol 1 and has not made such a declaration. That leaves only the general obligation on other states parties to ensure respect for the Conventions and to take necessary measures to suppress all acts contrary to them. It is not specified what these measures might be.

XII.3 ESTABLISHING INTERNATIONAL CRIMINAL JURISDICTION

Many of the acts for which Iraq is responsible would also constitute violations of the laws and customs of war or crimes against humanity. Such acts are considered to be crimes under international law for which individual perpetrators can be held responsible and prosecuted, tried and punished for their criminal acts.

At present no international tribunal exists which has general jurisdiction over individuals for crimes under international law. A proposal to establish such an international criminal court is presently under discussion in the General Assembly on the basis of a draft Statute prepared by the International Law Commission,[223] but there is no certainty as to when such a Court might be set up. In any event, although the Court would almost certainly have subject matter jurisdiction over many of the violations which have been committed in Iraq, it would probably be necessary for the Government of Iraq to agree to the jurisdiction of the Court before Iraqi officials could be tried before it. Although it is unlikely that the present Iraqi Government would accept the jurisdiction of such a court if it were to be established, the current draft Statute imposes no statutory limitation periods. Prosecution of Iraqi officials before such an international criminal court may, therefore, remain an option but only for some future date.

In the absence of a permanent criminal court, the Security Council has recently established two ad hoc international criminal tribunals in respect of certain crimes committed in the former Yugoslavia[224] and in Rwanda[225]. The setting up of these two tribunals in the past two years are evidence of the urgent need recognized by the international community to ensure that persons responsible for particularly serious crimes under international law are brought to justice, particularly when it is clear that there is no prospect of this happening in the state where the crimes occurred. It is open to the Security Council to establish an ad hoc international tribunal in respect of Iraq, although there is little enthusiasm among states for the creation of more ad hoc tribunals and it would be extremely difficult in practice to secure custody over Iraqi officials. The advantage of such a step is that there is no requirement of prior acceptance of

---

[223] The latest draft by the International Law Commission of a Statute for an international criminal court is contained in UN Doc. A/CN.4/L.491/Rev.2 (1994).

[224] Security Council Resolution 827 of 25 May 1993.

[225] Security Council Resolution 955 of 8 November 1994.

the Tribunal's competence by the state concerned as its authority derives from the Security Council resolution and not from a treaty.

The Statutes of the two ad hoc international tribunals already established, and the draft Statute for an international criminal court, provide useful guidance on the kinds of crimes which would be punishable, although it would be open to the Security Council to agree to a broader range of violations of international human rights and humanitarian law to be covered by the Statute of a tribunal in respect of Iraq if this were felt necessary. The draft Code of Crimes Against the Peace and Security of Mankind, which has been under consideration by the International Law Commission for many years, also provides useful guidance on the nature and scope of crimes which would carry individual criminal responsibility. As many of the violations committed in Iraq have been committed in the course of non-international armed conflict and some (such as systematic torture) outside of any conflict, it would be important for any tribunal to have a broad base of jurisdiction to cover all these illegal acts.

XII.3.1 VIOLATIONS OF THE LAWS AND CUSTOMS OF WAR

Any international tribunal established with jurisdiction over Iraq should include as separate bases of jurisdiction "violations of the laws or customs of war" and violations of Common Article 3 of the Geneva Conventions. The two concepts are not necessarily entirely co-extensive. Acts which do not clearly fall within the parameters of Common Article 3 may still amount to other violations of the laws and customs of war. Although there is been some doubt as to the precise scope of acts which may amount to "violations of the laws or customs of war", it appears that acts committed during internal armed conflict can fall within this heading. The commentary to Article 22 of the Draft Code of Crimes against the Peace and Security of Mankind states that "armed conflict" does extend to non-international conflicts covered by Common Article 3. The International Law Commission's draft Statute for an international criminal court refers to "serious violations of the laws and customs applicable in armed conflict" and focuses on the degree of gravity of the violations rather than whether they were committed in an international or non-international conflict.

Many of the acts which may amount to violations of the laws and customs of war in Iraq would also constitute crimes against humanity. Such crimes clearly do extend to a government's treatment of its own nationals in the course of internal armed conflict or even in the absence of any ongoing conflict. However, the two categories are not entirely coextensive so that it would still be important to ensure that breaches of the laws and customs of war and specifically of Common Article 3 were express bases of jurisdiction.

XII.3.2 CRIMES AGAINST HUMANITY

The concept of crimes against humanity is still developing. In many respects, it may overlap with the notion of war crimes although they have a wider scope and include acts committed by state forces in the course of internal armed conflict and may also be applicable in peace-time. Crimes against humanity should certainly be included as a separate and distinct basis of jurisdiction if any international tribunal were to be established in respect of Iraq.

Article 6(c) of the Charter of the International Military Tribunal at Nuremberg defined crimes against humanity as:
> murder, extermination, enslavement, deportation and other inhumane acts committed against civilian population before or during war, or persecutions on political, racial or religious grounds in execution of or in connection with any crime within the jurisdiction of the Tribunal whether or not in violation of the domestic law of the country where perpetrated.

General Assembly Resolution 95/I of 1946 affirmed the principles of international law recognized by the Nuremberg Charter and the Tribunal's judgment.

There is no single authoritative definition of crimes against humanity but subsequent developments suggest that the concept has been broadened since Nuremberg and now encompasses a wider range of crimes under international law and that these need not necessarily be linked to armed conflict. The Statutes of the international tribunals for the former Yugoslavia and Rwanda both include "crimes against humanity" as a separate and distinct basis of the Tribunals' jurisdiction. Their definitions cover a wide range of broadly defined acts: murder; extermination; enslavement; deportation; imprisonment; torture; rape; persecutions on political, racial and religious grounds; and other inhumane acts.

It is generally accepted that acts must be directed at a civilian population as part of a deliberate state policy in order to constitute crimes against humanity. Random acts against individuals would probably not fall within this concept unless they were part of a widespread or systematic pattern of violations. It is also not clear whether the required element of state policy can be established simply by reference to the scale of violations directed against a population or whether a policy based on political, racial or religious grounds must be demonstrated.[226] The Statute of the Tribunal on Rwanda states that the acts must be committed "as part of a widespread or systematic attack against any civilian population on national, political, ethnic, racial or religious grounds". The International Law Commission's commentary on its draft Statute for an International Criminal Court states that:

> ...the definition of crimes against humanity encompasses inhumane acts of a very serious character involving widespread or systematic violations aimed at the civilian population in whole or in part...The particular forms of unlawful act...are less crucial to the definition than the factors of scale and deliberate policy, as well as in their being targeted against the civilian population in whole or in part...The term "directed against any civilian population" should be taken to refer to acts committed as part of a widespread and systematic attack against a civilian population on national, political, ethnic, racial or religious grounds.[227]

The concept of crimes against humanity is no longer confined, as it was at Nuremberg, to acts committed in time of war. The Statutes of the Tribunals on the former Yugoslavia and Rwanda clearly cover acts committed during internal conflict and the concept may also be applicable in peacetime, provided the acts are of sufficient gravity and scale. The definition of crimes against humanity in the 1968 Convention on the Non-Applicability of Statutory Limitations to War Crimes and Crimes Against Humanity explicitly defines crimes against humanity as acts committed in time of war or peace. The International Convention dealing with the crime of apartheid states that it is a crime against humanity and the 1994 Inter-American Convention on the Forced Disappearance of Persons reaffirms that "the systematic practice of the forced disappearance of persons constitutes a crime against humanity".

Periods of statutory limitation probably cannot be applied to crimes against humanity or, at the very least, such periods must be of sufficient length commensurate with the extreme gravity of the crimes. The Convention on the Non-Applicability of Statutory Limitations allows no limitation periods for crimes against humanity. Neither of the international Tribunals on the former Yugoslavia and Rwanda nor the draft Statute for an international criminal court

---

[226] Some commentators argue that persecutions on political, racial or religious grounds were intended to be an alternative category of crimes against humanity in the Nuremberg Charter and that these grounds are not an essential characteristic of all such crimes. Recent definitions of crimes against humanity have not taken a consistent approach on this point, but in any event it appears that such grounds could be made out without difficulty in respect of acts committed against the Kurds in Iraq.

[227] UN Doc. A/CN.4/L.491/Rev.2/Add.1 at para. 14. The Statute of the Tribunal on the former Yugoslavia specifies only that the acts must be "directed against a civilian population" and does not state that they must be on political, racial, religious or other grounds.

envisage statutory limitation periods. The absence of applicable time limitations would preserve the possibility of bringing criminal prosecutions against Iraqi officials even if a considerable period were to elapse before circumstances permit such a course of action.

XII.3.3 CRIMINAL PROSECUTIONS BY OTHER STATES

Even in the absence of any international criminal court having jurisdiction in respect of Iraq, there may also currently exist the possibility for other states, at least on a permissive basis, to try those suspected of committing certain crimes in Iraq on the basis of universal jurisdiction. This envisages prosecution and trial by a state of anyone suspected of such crimes who is within its jurisdiction, regardless of where the offence was committed or the nationality of the suspect or the victims.

Some treaties dealing with international crimes, such as hostage-taking, apartheid, torture and grave breaches of humanitarian law, require state action in such cases - a state must either try suspects within its jurisdiction on a universal basis or extradite the suspect for trial elsewhere. Given the specificity of these treaty provisions, however, it would appear that crimes against humanity do not presently carry a general obligation on a state to try or extradite suspects found within its territory.

However, the principles underlying the development of the concept of crimes under international law and the increasingly common practice of requiring universal criminal jurisdiction in international instruments dealing with such crimes indicates that there may currently exist under general international law at least a permissive basis for the exercise of universal criminal jurisdiction in respect of crimes against humanity.[228] The draft Statute for an international criminal court imposes an obligation on states to try, transfer to the court or extradite to another state only where there are comparable treaty obligations (with the addition of genocide which is expressly incorporated into the obligatory regime).[229] However, in other cases, including crimes against humanity, the draft Statute does recognize the possibility of permissive jurisdiction by a state according to its own legal procedures if it has not accepted the jurisdiction of the court.

---

[228] See Rodley, n.133 above, at pp. 102-107.

[229] In its commentary on the draft Statute, the International Law Commission indicated that it had considered and decided against imposing an obligation to try, transfer to the court or extradite in respect of all crimes falling under its jurisdiction. It decided that this was particularly difficult in respect of crimes against humanity which are not the subject of a specific criminal law provision in many states.

Even so, the successful exercise of such jurisdiction is likely to be rare as it depends on i) the physical presence of Iraqi suspects in another state; ii) domestic legislation in that state which provides for universal jurisdiction over the alleged crimes; iii) the political will on the part of the state to pursue such prosecutions; and iv) the necessary means to do so in terms of gathering evidence and locating witnesses etc.

XIII. CONCLUSION
A UN PLAN OF ACTION FOR IRAQI KURDISTAN

"It is for the people to determine the destiny of the territory and not the territory the destiny of the people"[230]

The international community is at a cross-roads in terms of the future prospects for Iraqi Kurdistan. It cannot simply abdicate its responsibilities towards the Kurds but must address the consequences of the situation which has been brought about by the international intervention in 1991. By maintaining and protecting the special status of the area, the international community has allowed the Kurds to hold democratic elections and to develop, for the first time in their history, a functioning autonomous system of self-government. At the same time, the legal status of the area remains uncertain and confused. Iraq continues to assert its territorial integrity and its sovereignty over the area but has withdrawn its military and civilian control and is subjecting the area to punitive economic measures. The international community, through international aid and military protection, is assisting the Kurds to survive and to maintain their structures of self-government but refuses to accord them any political recognition, thus keeping them weak and insecure and ever more vulnerable to the shifting currents of international politics in which they currently play no part and have no voice.

In many respects the Kurds are at greater risk than ever before. They have openly defied the Iraqi Government which is already renowned for its brutality against them and has repeatedly demonstrated its determination to prevent them from exercising any real form of self-government. They are vulnerable to military attacks and incursions into their territory by neighbouring powers such as Turkey and Iran, openly taking advantage of the vacuum of security and authority in the area to pursue political and military objectives against their own Kurdish opposition forces. International protection, which holds the Iraqi Government at bay for the time being, has proved impotent to defend or guarantee the security of the area and could be removed at any time, regardless of the needs and wishes of the population it was set up to protect. The Iraqi Government continues to defy the UN at every turn and has given no indication that it takes any of its international legal obligations seriously, and certainly not its obligations to respect international human rights and humanitarian law.

---

[230] Opinion of Judge Dillard in the Western Sahara Case ICJ Reports 1975, p. 12 at p.122.

The present situation cannot be prolonged indefinitely. Emergency measures of protection to address the crisis that unfolded in 1991 are insufficient as a long-term solution. Formal legal measures that could be taken against Iraq for its violations of human rights and humanitarian law are unlikely to prove very effective and in any event the international community has not demonstrated any willingness to pursue these. Nor would they address the pressing issue of the political future of the Iraqi Kurds. A fresh and dynamic new perspective must be taken by the international community towards Iraqi Kurdistan that addresses the root causes of the situation, that tackles these complex issues as a coherent whole and that achieves durable and workable solutions.

It is imperative that the UN should step into this confused and highly insecure situation. The role of the UN should be to facilitate and advance a process of negotiation and settlement within which the Kurds themselves can decide their own future and which secures their physical protection and respect for human rights. The Kurds have never yet had any real opportunity to participate in negotiations about their future status in a context of freedom and safety. Certainly they must show that they are willing to participate in political negotiations in good faith and their wishes must be balanced with the competing interests and rights of others involved, but they must be allowed to voice their views and to participate in the process of negotiation. At the same time settlement of the future status of Iraqi Kurdistan cannot be pursued in a vacuum, divorced from the wider issues the international community must confront in respect of Iraq. It must form an integral part of the political debate and action on these wider issues, but equally must never be held hostage to them.

The UN should immediately move to designate Iraqi Kurdistan a territory under UN jurisdiction until a secure and durable political settlement is achieved. This would confer on Iraqi Kurdistan an internationally-recognized legal status which should be guaranteed by international protection of the area to be mandated and provided by the UN. It would provide a framework within which a negotiated settlement could be pursued without bringing about premature and permanent territorial changes or necessarily threatening Iraq's territorial integrity pending the outcome of negotiations. The aim should be to achieve a settlement that respects the wishes of the Kurds; guarantees their physical safety; protects their rights and enables them to develop their distinct identity as a people; and will be honoured and guaranteed by the present and future governments in Iraq as well as by the other regional powers and by the international community at large.

XIII.1 A NEGOTIATED SETTLEMENT

1. The settlement of the future status of Iraqi Kurdistan must be pursued under UN auspices with Iraqi Kurdistan designated and protected as territory under UN jurisdiction.
2. The Kurds must have the right to participate in the negotiations as full and equal partners.
3. The concerns of other countries in the region, particularly those with Kurdish populations, must be addressed.
4. The interests and needs of other minority groups living within Iraqi Kurdistan must be taken into account and their rights fully protected.
5. A form of autonomy must be taken as the starting point of negotiations. The settlement process should build on and draw lessons from the historical experience of attempts to secure autonomy.
6. Negotiations must address the long-standing contentious issues which have undermined past attempts at autonomy, including the delineation of the territory of Iraqi Kurdistan and the political and economic relationship of the area to the rest of Iraq.
7. The settlement must ensure the economic and social development of the area and the preservation and development of the identity and unique characteristics of the Kurdish people. International aid and assistance, including long term development and rehabilitation projects, should be provided under UN authority directly to Iraqi Kurdistan. As long as international sanctions against Iraq remain in place, Iraqi Kurdistan should be exempted from the sanctions regime as an area under UN jurisdiction.
8. The settlement should preserve and build on the democratic process and institutions already established in Iraqi Kurdistan. International assistance should be provided to strengthen democratic institutions and the rule of law.
9. The settlement must be backed by international guarantees and build in effective mechanisms for international supervision of its terms.
10. Clear objectives to be achieved by all parties should be established with a specific time frame to avoid any party prolonging the negotiations in their own interests. It could be implemented progressively, with the constituent components of UN authority and protection being gradually dismantled as objectives are met and successfully implemented.

XIII.2 INTERNATIONAL PROTECTION

1. International protection of the area must be maintained until it is clear that the Kurds are no longer at risk and that other guarantees are in place to secure

their protection in the long term.

2. International protection must be mandated and provided by the UN and not be dependent on the political will of a few countries nor require authorization by any one country.

3. Protection must be effective against Iraqi military activity and against military attacks and incursions into the area by other countries.

4. The Kurds themselves must undertake to respect security and measures should be taken to resolve and prevent internal conflicts, to control military activity by Kurdish political groups and to regulate the possession and use of weapons.

XIII.3 RESPECT FOR HUMAN RIGHTS

1. The settlement should include specific guarantees to ensure respect for human rights by all parties. 2. An on-site human rights monitoring operation should be put in place to supervise those guarantees and to take action in the event of breach.

3. Constitutional and other entrenched guarantees should be adopted to institutionalize human rights protection in the long term, both in terms of the future relationship of the Kurds with Iraq as well as within Iraqi Kurdistan itself.

4. The issue of past human rights violations must be addressed and the perpetrators brought to justice. There must be no impunity for those who violate human rights now or in the future. Commissions of Inquiry could assist in establishing the truth about past incidents.

5. International assistance and advice in the field of human rights should be provided by the UN to the Kurdish administration to assist with legislative reforms, the establishment of institutions to protect human rights, training of government officials, security forces, prison officials, lawyers and judges, human rights education and the development of the non-governmental sector.

ADDENDUM

TURKISH INCURSIONS IN NORTHERN IRAQ
March-July 1995

On the 20th of March 1995 up to 35.000 Turkish troops crossed the border into Northern Iraq, in one of the largest operations mounted by the Turkish Government in the history of the State. Turkey had been massing troops along its southern border for three weeks before that date. The expected offensive began on the eve of the Kurdish New Year. Turkey had in the past launched frequent forays into Northern Iraq as part of an understanding reached between Baghdad and Ankara that allows for a policy of 'hot pursuit'.

The joint US, British and French air force overflights of the UN protected area were suspended on Monday, the day of the incursion, with hopes that they could be resumed within a few days.

A statement on the Turkish Government's position stated the aims of the operation:

"The on-going power struggle between the two main groups in northern Iraq has led the PKK to establish itself firmly in the area. The recent spiral of terror in several areas of Turkey is linked to PKK camps in the area. ......"The Turkish armed forces, under the authority of the Turkish Government has launched the operation, the aim of the operation is to protect the lives of innocent people"[1]

Immediate reports from UNHCR representatives in the area on the day of the incursion expressed concern for the safety of the 4,500 Kurdish refugees from Turkey living in villages close to the border.[2] Two days later a UNHCR spokesman in Geneva said: "If these are armed PKK fighters, that is one thing. If they are unarmed civilian refugees, it is a very serious matter indeed" This statement followed from reports of Turkish Kurds being seized in the Zakho

---

[1] Government Statement, Subject: Military Operation in Northern Iraq, Permanent Mission of Turkey to the United Nations Office of the Press Counsellor, 20 March

[2] UNHCR Update on Northern Iraq, Public Information Section. 20.3.95

area and taken across the border into Turkey.³ Despite repeated denials by Turkey that any civilians were harmed in the operation, the Kurdish authorites and human rights monitors have documented serious violations of international humanitarian law and international human rights law by the invading troops against the mainly Kurdish civilians. Some 70 villages are claimed to have been destroyed and allegatiosn of the torture and killing of 7 shephards as well as the killing of a 5 year old girl by a cluster bomb are being investigated by human rights groups.

The United States Government position is reported as expressing "understanding for Turkey's need to act decisively" after receiving assurances from the Turkish Prime Minister that the military operation would be limited in duration.⁴

However, the French Presidency of the European Union, which two weeks ago agreed to form a customs union with Turkey, condemned the air and ground raids as a violation of international law.

The Iraqi Government blamed the United States for the Turkish incursion."

The Arab League has also condemned the military incursion as a violation of international law and called on the Turkish Governement not to escalate the situation further but to withdraw from Iraqi territory.

On April 26 the Council of Europe Parliamentary Assembly voted to suspend Turkish membership of the Assembly, because of its human rights policies and the invasion of Iraq.

The bulk of Turkish forces were withdrawn in early May 1995.

A further incursion into Northern Iraq by Turkish forces began on 13 July 1995. "Operation Dragon" was said to involve fewer than 3.000 troops.

---

³ "NATO in disarray over Turkish Strikes", The Guardian, March 22, 1995

⁴ Quoted in Reuters, Baghdad, March 23 1995